Schizophrenia: The positive perspective

Schizophrenia: The positive perspective counters a century-long tradition which has searched relentlessly for the critical deficits and dysfunctions in schizophrenic people. Peter Chadwick, who has himself suffered from the illness, shows that such people can demonstrate elevated creativity, empathy and social sensitivity and are by no means as irrational, misguided and unteachable as is commonly thought.

The author presents fascinating studies of some schizophrenia-prone people with whom he has worked. Using autobiography, biography and psychometric and experimental methods, he reveals areas of enhanced functioning in those vulnerable to the schizophrenia label, and argues for a much more positive picture of the schizophrenic mind. He raises important questions, such as whether schizophrenia should really be viewed as an illness that we want to eradicate, or does it instead actually endow its sufferers with valuable qualities we should be nurturing?

Schizophrenia: The positive perspective will be required reading for anyone working with or contemplating work with schizophrenic people, especially psychologists, psychiatrists, nurses and social workers.

Peter K. Chadwick lectures in psychology at Birkbeck College, the Open University and the City Literary Institute. His previous publications include *Borderline: A psychological study of paranoia and delusional thinking* (1992).

Schizophrenia: The positive perspective

In search of dignity for schizophrenic people

Peter K. Chadwick

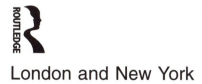

London and New York

First published 1997 by Routledge
11 New Fetter Lane, London EC4P 4EE

Simultaneously published in the USA and Canada
by Routledge
29 West 35th Street, New York, NY 10001

© 1997 Peter K. Chadwick

Typeset in Times Ten by Keystroke, Jacaranda Lodge, Wolverhampton
Printed and bound in Great Britain by TJ International Ltd,
Padstow, Cornwall

British Library Cataloguing in Publication Data
A catalogue record for this book is available from the British Library

Library of Congress Cataloguing in Publication Data
Chadwick, Peter K. (Peter Kenneth), 1946–
    Schizophrenia : the positive perspective : in search of dignity
for schizophrenic people / Peter K. Chadwick.
        p.   cm.
    Includes bibliographical references and index.
    1. Schizophrenia. 2. Gifted persons. 3. Schizophrenics.
4. Creative ability. I. Title.
RC514.C44 1997
616.89′82–dc21   96–40143
ISBN 0–415–14287–3 (hbk)
ISBN 0–415–14288–1 (pbk)

For Jill, Mimi and Robert

On the discrepancy between attitudes and behaviour in science

Letter from Thomas Huxley to Charles Kingsley:

> Sit down before fact like a little child, be prepared to give up every preconceived notion, follow humbly to wherever and to whatever abysses nature leads or you shall learn nothing.

Thomas Huxley's reply to an invitation from the London Dialectical Society to join them in an investigation of spiritualistic phenomena:

> I am no more interested in your offer than I would be to listen in to the chatter of old women and curates in a distant town.

(Rosalind Heywood (1959) *The Sixth Sense*,
London: Chatto and Windus)

Contents

Figures and tables

Preface

Most stereotypes and clichés are Kiplingian traps for fools. As anyone at the pen-and-ink end of the communications industry knows: if you can't live, you can't write. As anyone at the 'chalk face' of education can tell you: if you can't do, you can't teach. The same disdain is deserved for the age-old cliché: 'Whom the gods wish to destroy, they first make mad'. A saying more likely to spread prejudice against the seriously mentally ill it is difficult to imagine.

It is quite another thing, however, to claim that madness does not exist. Indeed it resists all efforts to politicise it away and remains one of the greatest and most intractable enigmas of our world. It is also an enigma that deserves recognition and study – and respect in itself as something other than merely a pale shadow of something else.

It is important in appreciating this challenge, however, that first we concede that the human body–mind has limits. There are certain acts: the James Bulger and Dunblane killings; the Holocaust; the Boston Strangler murders that are, for example, so horrific that somehow one cannot *feel the feeling* that we intuit is appropriate to them. They are 'beyond the outer limits of feeling'. Language too can fail not only mystics but even the most gifted of writers – Oscar Wilde, to take but one example, was speechless on the event of his mother's death (*de Profundis*, p. 186 in Hart-Davis 1989). But sanity too has its boundaries, the transgression of which is recognised in all cultures (Murphy 1976; World Health Organisation 1973, 1979). This book is about the exploration of that transition zone where sanity can grade as easily into insanity as into supersanity. This is a book, however, about the *positive* characteristics of people at that boundary and, to be more specific, is centrally about those who actually suffer, or are prone to suffer, that collection of illnesses loosely known as 'schizophrenia'.

Rather than concentrating on those aspects of the psychology and physiology of schizophrenic people that reveal *deficits* (e.g. Weinberger *et al.* 1986; Cutting and Murphy 1988; Morice 1990; Braun *et al.* 1991; Saykin *et al.* 1991; Baltaxe and Simmons 1995; Wada *et al.* 1995; Morice and Delahunty 1996), this work attempts to turn the coin over and seek what has become known as the 'schizophrenic credit' (Claridge 1985, pp. 149–53). In the context of this endeavour it is legitimate to ask, for example, whether schizophrenic or schizophrenia-prone people, known as schizotypals or schizotypal personalities (Raine *et al.* 1995), have areas of *enhanced* functioning compared to 'standard-minded' people and whether it is possible to construe the schizotypal and schizophrenic syndromes in more positive ways than hitherto has been the case. We may also ask: is it possible that the psychosis-prone mind can actually access states of mental clarity and profundity (the 'value-sensing experiences' of Donaldson (1993, chapter 14)) inaccessible to people of the middle ground? Hence may such people at times indeed be 'supersane' or 'superrational' (Lenz 1979, 1983) rather than 'insane'? Related to this, another question that clearly needs answering is: does the predisposition to schizophrenia sometimes convey such advantages in *empathy* and *creativity* that the label 'superphrenic' (Karlsson 1972; Rosenhan and Seligman 1984, p. 490) becomes at times more appropriate than 'schizophrenic'? All of these questions and their answers are clearly of the utmost importance to the characterisation of people who are vulnerable to insanity in terms of our attempts to create both adequate theory and also fair and adequate evaluation, treatment and rehabilitation. Given that most such people now live openly in the community, they are also important to the development of appropriate community attitudes to 'people of the fringe' which in recent years have become quite negative as a result of highly publicised cases of violent behaviour by discharged patients.

Alas, even the briefest perusal of the current literature on schizophrenia will immediately reveal to the uninitiated that this collection of problems is viewed by practitioners almost exclusively in terms of dysfunction and disorder. A positive or charitable phrase or sentence rarely meets the eye – a state of affairs that in many subtle ways must severely colour the perceptions of mental health workers, of all categories (particularly their perceptions of *the dignity of their clients*) when they deal professionally with people of this kind.

People with serious mental illness are now more likely to be viewed by professionals as consumers of mental health services rather than as patients on the passive receiving end of the work and ministrations of 'experts'. Hence their views and needs are increasingly seen to be essential to the treatment process (Coursey *et al.* 1995; Lazare *et al.* 1972, 1975; Lord *et al.* 1987). Clearly a profession which focuses so heavily on the dysfunctions and limitations of schizoid, schizotypal and schizophrenic people can hardly be producing research findings which give an accurate and adequate description of the various client groups and this is a serious impediment to interaction with service users at an individual level (see particularly Chapter 13 here). Deficit-obsessed research can only produce theories and attitudes which are disrespectful of clients and are also likely to induce behaviour in clinicians such that service users are not properly listened to, not believed, not fairly assessed, are likely treated as inadequate and are also not *expected* to be able to become independent and competent individuals in managing life's tasks (see for example the patient report in Coursey *et al.* 1995, p. 294 on this).

It is the purpose of this book, as it was of my previous texts (Chadwick 1992, 1995a), to attempt to redress this extraordinary imbalance – an imbalance that because it obtains in a literature which is written with academic correctness, distance and scholarship, poses as 'objective', when in fact it may well be nothing of the kind.

The organisation of this work broadly follows that of *Borderline* (Chadwick 1992) in having a more phenomenological first part and a more empirical scientific second section which is then followed by a detailed discussion of the implications of the research for therapy and a conclusion. Colleagues have generally welcomed this mix of the more artistic with the more scientific (e.g. Onyett 1992), something which is rarely, if ever, done in single works in psychopathology (incredibly a recent literature-search by one of my students, Richard Williams, of the number of journal articles in the field of paranoia over the past five years which report *both* descriptive case studies *and* experimental investigations produced a resounding *zero*).

One of my critical aspirations, however, in this work is to imbricate these two sections together as the lack of interrelationship between the analogous two parts in *Borderline* has been the subject of criticism (John 1992).

After (I hope) a clarifying preamble in Chapter 1 concerning the style in which this research has been conducted, Chapter 2 deals with 'The schizophrenic credit so far', basically reviewing the very scattered and dispersed research literature that already exists on this topic and attempts to integrate it such that it acts as a platform on which the rest of the book can stand. The following chapters present four mini-biographies of individuals prone to schizophrenia. In these personal histories I will attempt to bring the individuals concerned 'alive' to the reader by departing from the relatively dry academic prose usually considered appropriate to learned works. These chapters will be an exercise in *combining* reason and emotion so that the reader does in a sense 'hear' the music of the experiences despite the text itself not being over-emotive or effusive.

One of the four mini-biographies (Chapters 3–5) gives a third perspective on the pre-psychotic and psychotic experiences I suffered myself in the late 1970s. The first two perspectives are given in Chadwick 1992 and 1993b. Some further information relevant to diagnosis and therapy is also given in Chapter 13. This third perspective was promised in Chadwick

1993b (p. 244) and attempts to answer questions raised by the previous efforts.

The unambiguously scientific sections (Chapters 2, 10 and 11) deal chiefly with the topic of empathy and with the cognitive styles of schizotypal and schizophrenic people and the relevance of these to such phenomena as suggestibility, belief in the paranormal, creativity, social sensitivity and spiritual experience.

The knowledge gained from previous research, from the phenomenological and empirical arms of the enquiry, and that from my own experience are then gathered together to inform the two chapters on implications for therapy (12 and 13) before the related strands of the book are utilised to provide an overview in Chapter 14.

As colleagues familiar with my work will know, I have a distinct love–hate relationship with psychoanalytic and psychodynamic theorising and treatment. My personal experience of such therapy (in 1967–8) was generally beneficial but I have also found there to be many drawbacks to these forms of intervention (see Chapters 8 and 13). Although I appear at times to be very negatively disposed to this group of schools in these pages this is not to be taken to imply by any means that I believe the general approach to be worthless. However, it is clear that considerable changes and developments need to be made before the endeavour realises its original promise (e.g. Spence 1987).

Previous studies of enhanced functioning in people prone to psychopathology have focused heavily on very outstanding (but usually (if not always) *deceased*) individuals and most saliently on those loosely known as 'geniuses' (e.g. Juda 1949; Bett 1952; Lidz 1964; Joseph 1964; Jamison 1993). In the present investigation this line of approach is not shunned (see particularly Chapter 2) but in the biographical sections I choose to present three living individuals I have come to know well with, as yet, no public record of creative achievement but whose quieter creativity, none the less, has been of great functional value to themselves and to the many people with whom they have daily contact. These individuals may indeed be indicative of a great number of unsung but outstanding 'ordinary people' whom researchers in this vein simply never seek out, perhaps because they assume that research of this kind will have more impact if it deals with generally recognised people of distinction. (There is perhaps also a certain allure to geniuses and a certain prestige to be had in researching them, whereas 'ordinary people' are surely . . . well . . . just ordinary?) The issue is important since schizophrenic tendencies are now (if not always (Warner 1995)) usually clustered in people in the lower social classes (Faris and Dunham 1939; Hollingshead and Redlich 1958; Saugstad 1989), particularly in large cities, whereas serious manic-depressive inclinations are to be found more in the higher professional classes (Jamison 1993). This statistical evidence leads easily to the automatic inference that a person (such as Desmond presented in Chapter 6) with tendencies to schizophrenia and who is of the lower social class is there because he or she has no talent and that therefore schizophrenic tendencies confer no advantages. It is possible, however, when one focuses more closely on living people in this category, and at the individual level, to find that the real picture is not quite as simple as this.

I would, to conclude, like to express my thanks to the many colleagues who have given of their time during the evolution of this work. Gordon Claridge and Janie Brod of Oxford University; David Nias of St Bartholomew's Hospital, University of London; Julian Leff and David Hemsley of the Institute of Psychiatry, University of London; and John Wilding of Royal Holloway College, University of London, have been especially supportive. Their encouragement is acknowledged with pleasure. My friends and students have also been an immeasurable source of comfort and sustenance for me particularly during the researching of a project such as this which, though deeply needed, has received so little attention, time and recognition from the vast bulk of mainstream investigators.

Both Oscar Wilde and Nietzsche realised that one cannot ever write a book entirely out of one's own head. The general style and content (notably Chapters 6, 7 and 9) reflect the many discussions and exchanges that have taken place in a group with my very closest companions that we refer to as 'The Borderliners'. The theme of this book has been the central overarching ideology of this set in the many years since its inception. The gathering's members apart from myself: Desmond Marshall; Ivo Wiesner; Simon Blair; Geoff Garfield; Jane Howe and Jonathan Smith have contributed in so many diverse and subtle ways to the validation and content of my ideas that this book inevitably reflects their presence and air but in ways that, alas, cannot be explicitly specified. I thank them all.

The manuscript was typed by my indefatigable friend and confidante Sylvia Greenwood, who actually first met me when I was in the middle of the psychotic episode discussed in Chapters 3–5 and Appendix I and indeed typed the (now lost) manuscript referred to and outlined in the latter. As the only friend who knew me when I was actively psychotic, it is a pleasure to see her relief and gladness at sensing my madness subsequently transform into creativity.

Finally, my wife Jill Chadwick deserves the greatest credit. Jill and I met in the day centre at Charing Cross Hospital in 1979 when she herself was there suffering from a mild bout of depression. She it was who saw through my pathetic bedraggled state and medication-induced torpor to the true human being beneath. She has been beside me ever since I embarked on this often seemingly thankless task of trying to reproduce her attitude to me in the minds of doctors, social workers and psychologists when they face the patients with whom daily they work.

Peter Chadwick
Norfolk
Summer 1996

Chapter 1

Introduction

THE SCHIZOPHRENIC CREDIT

It is well known to workers who have a great deal of daily contact with people diagnosed as 'schizophrenic' that these patients have capacities as well as deficits. (It is, of course, usually nurses and residential social workers who have this contact but, sadly, not psychiatrists and research psychologists.) These capacities, collectively known as 'the schizophrenic credit' (Claridge 1985), are urgently in need of study but the capacities that these people display are often not amenable to the standardised methods of classical science (for exceptions to this (Chapter 2) see La Russo 1978; Keefe and Magaro 1980; Claridge 1988). When observers say, as they do, that such people have 'uncanny sensitivity', 'frightening empathy', and so on we are talking in the realm of vague impressions and intuitions that are very difficult (if not impossible) to operationalise.

In this text I am attempting to grasp hold of these intangibles in a way that hopefully conveys to the reader the essence of the schizophrenic credit. This is relevant also to those of classical positivistic orientation (e.g. Frith 1979, 1992; Crow 1980, 1988) because we do need to know, for example, what the functions are of the undoubted genetic predisposing factors for this family of illnesses (Gottesman and Shields 1982) that have enabled these genes to survive for so long (Heston and Denney 1968; Karlsson 1972; Jarvik and Deckard 1977). This is vitally important, given that we may, in the foreseeable future, be actually able to neutralise the effects of these genes. What, if anything, will we sacrifice if we do this? This we have to know, at least in outline, and we need this knowledge quite soon, as research in the partial genetic mediation of schizophrenic illness, although fraught with considerable difficulties, is none the less gathering momentum (see Sherrington *et al.* 1988; Kennedy *et al.* 1988; Gottesman 1991).

Objective analytical science has many difficulties with this task, which is why I am including a great deal of subjective material in this text. Science as we know it, for example, can say little about the meaning of the schizophrenic experience. The science of schizophrenia and borderline states echoes the characterisation of a church via an analysis of its bricks. The experience and its referent are simply ignored. Psychoanalytic treatises (e.g. Freud 1911, 1915; Kernberg 1975; Meissner 1978) are also not very helpful here as these writers prefer a somewhat aggressive rather than a sympathetic form of truth. The borderline patient or the psychotic is forever seen as 'escaping', 'running away from reality', or in some way making self-disqualifying intrapsychic *mistakes* of various kinds which give their experience little moment or external reference other than as clinical and research roughage for psychodynamic interpretation and speculation. (This of course says a little about the general attitude that psychoanalytic practitioners have to the seriously mentally ill.)

Research by psychiatrists (e.g. Kessel 1989) which purports to demonstrate how creatively ineffective are people in this family of illnesses produces nothing more than tautologies since one usually only *defines* a person as 'schizophrenic' or 'psychotic' when their renderings have lost all communal sense. To think 'laterally' for a moment, I would claim that we need therefore to search for the schizophrenic credit slightly *away* from the nucleus of maximum derangement as the latter may in fact be not the kernel but a *distortion* of the true schizophrenic psychic armoury only evident under peculiar conditions – such as severe life stress. (Mania may similarly be a distortion *in extremis* of a mood facilitative of creativity, e.g. Byron's 'wonderful glow' that occurred when he took up his pen.)

To look at 'the schizophrenias' in this way of course has considerable implications for the nature of our preventative and rehabilitative efforts. It may be that within the sordid quagmire of disease there are genuine flowers to be preserved. These we will totally miss if we focus on disease and on disease as the true and inevitable efflorescence of the evolving schizophrenic mental structure.

In this book I am therefore *not* regarding 'schizophrenia' as a pejorative term in any sense; it only becomes so, I would suggest, in the form of 'schizophrenic illness' – but that I am presenting as a rather different phenomenon. The purpose of my enquiry then is to explore the 'purple' territory *near* to outright madness in its many aspects to seek out not primarily the 'tangled intrapsychic dynamics' that can be involved or the 'aberrant genetic endowments', the 'errors in cognitive processing' and the like but real manifestation of the benevolent, the positive and the uncanny – often buried beneath the rubble of apparent pathology.

We are therefore adventuring into territory here which has not been greatly explored in the sense of there being a search for its intrinsic validity – although it is territory whose existence as a fact of experience we well know and do not doubt. To put a name on this zone between clear daylight sanity and the dark night of madness is difficult; many have been tried: borderline and schizotypal states; the Borderline, the Psychoid; the twilight zone ... really the name is not important. But in this sector where the schizophrenic credit manifests itself lies also great spiritual sensitivity coexisting with the darkest fears of fantasy. Here Fate can be a real living presence and the adventurer may come into direct, even terrible, contact with The Divine. This is why Zaehner (1957) speaks of it as 'knocking on the back door of Heaven'.

The schizophrenic credit has a number of dimensions: affective, cognitive, interpersonal and spiritual. The experiential state itself, however, gives one the sense of accessing 'the elsewhere'. To others the schizophrenic may not be 'in touch', yet on the inside may feel all too present. Whether this purple world well away from the middle magnitudes of everyday life is merely an illusion of madness, a fairyland of the gullible, a waking nightmare or whether it gives us a glimpse into the deep structure of reality, the reader in the end will have to judge for themselves. My belief (though dangerous) is essentially the latter, but I admit that this glimpse can easily be veiled by the psychological tricks that we can, at times, unknowingly play on ourselves in our search for *something* beyond the customary and the prosaic. The recognition of these tricks and distortions (e.g. Benassi *et al.* 1979; Marks and Kamman 1980; French 1992; Sutherland 1992a) is an important task which we have to face if we are to see Niels Bohr's 'Deep Truth' (1958) with any measure of clarity (in this context see particularly Chapter 6, pp. 70–1 and Chapter 9, pp. 107–11).

SYNCHRONICITY AND THE UNCANNY

In the Borderline territory there are many strange phenomena. Jung and Pauli (1955), for example, spoke of a concept outside our usual causal interpretation of the world: Synchronicity. This I will focus on, in different ways, many times in this book. It is essentially the co-occurrence of two events in time which are related not in terms of cause and effect but via *meaning*. Jung conceived the seeds of this idea during an analytic session when

> a young woman I was treating had, at a critical moment, a dream in which she was given a golden scarab. While she was telling me this dream I sat with my back to the closed window. Suddenly I heard a noise behind me, like a gentle tapping. I turned round and saw a flying insect knocking against the window pane from outside. I opened the window and caught the creature in the air as it flew in. It was the nearest analogy to a golden scarab that one finds in our latitudes, a scarabaeid beetle, the common rose-chafter (*Cetonia aurata*), which contrary to its usual habits had evidently felt an urge to get into a dark room at this particular moment. I must admit that nothing like it ever happened to me before or since, and that the dream of the patient has remained unique in my experience.

(Jung 1955/1985, p. 31)

The materialistic interpretation of the universe usually regards thinking of this kind as irrational or as childish and naïve, even psychotic (Fenichel 1946, pp. 300–1). Magical thinking was regarded as primitive by both Freud and Piaget (e.g. Freud 1979, pp. 200–2; Piaget 1958). It does not embed at all easily into the fabric of knowledge and thought we have come to develop and respect since the times of Socrates and Plato and particularly since the Enlightenment, with the immense strides in theoretical physics made by Newton (see Cranston 1965). Jung's insight is more reminiscent of the attitude of the poet and the mystic but poetic thought has had to struggle to find its validity ever since Socrates began the critical tradition. 'He who sits with Socrates ruins tragedy,' it was said (Snell 1953). Mystical thought has similarly faced severe criticism (e.g. the GAP report on mysticism 1976).

Jung himself never clearly came to grips with his concept of Synchronicity. Indeed, Pauli once remarked that he was not at all sure that Jung understood his own discovery or had a clear picture of what he wanted to say (Laurikainen 1988) but that he knew it was somehow important and needed to be put forward as a challenge to the established order.

One of my purposes and aims in these pages is to say as clearly as I can what Jung was trying to state and wanted to reveal but was unable to in his lifetime. In his writings (e.g. Jung 1955/1985) it is evident that the necessary thoughts were continually slipping away or trickling through his psychic fingers. Indeed, in this realm handholds are hard to find and the concepts at times barely graspable (see Progoff 1973). But still we must try – and I am sure that this is what Jung himself would have wanted.

My interest in this concept arose from independently discovering, or to put it more honestly, stumbling across, similar experiences and concepts to those of Jung in a mystical-psychotic experience I had myself in the summer of 1979. An outline of this has previously been published (Chadwick 1992, especially Chapters 4 and 5). On subsequently reading Jung (which as an experimental psychologist in the 1970s I had previously been loath to do), it was obvious to me that we had encountered the same realm but reported our findings merely in different language.

The uniform reaction of people close to me who have read my own report is that more material of this nature needs to be discussed in order to put the case I raised in that book across more definitively.

In understanding the 'Synchronistic realm', or what I call 'The Borderline', one is crossing discontinuities and the static approach of physics, i.e.

$$2A + 3B = C$$

becomes less appropriate. Instead one is required to redescribe the phenomena in a kinematic, developmental way, i.e.

If A (or B), then C, *then* D

(See also Chadwick 1978b on this.)

We are also speaking of a realm where the psychological and the physical are not independent or fully differentiated (Jung 1963, p. 416); hence, in describing the physical, the psychological must be imbricated into our renderings. This is developmental psychophysics, not mathematics. The access to the zone of the synchronistic requires a certain attitude of mind and this is the product of development; of IF–THEN sequences. This is how synchronicity differs from serendipity as clinical depression differs from ordinary sadness and as schizophrenic illness differs from super-stitiousness. This attitude and experiential state has to be reached over time *developmentally*, not simulated by changes in local brain chemistry, hence the accounts herein have a strong biographical orientation.

The quality of the experience in the synchronistic domain or at the Borderline critically depends not on such traits as intelligence or degree of extraversion but on the nature or degree of one's spiritual development. Indeed, a very rational orientation may bias the experience to the negative (Pauli in Laurikainen 1988), as will one of aggressiveness or hate. We will see more on this later (see particularly Chapter 7).

A ROMANTIC PSYCHOLOGY

It has long been appreciated that the techniques of extant science, the 'classical' way, which reveal schizophrenic *deficits* in profusion are rather blunt when it comes to the task of probing this experiential sphere as well. Shallis (1983) suggests the need, here, for a subjective science or for the 'descriptive science' of Schumacher (1977). Whether indeed science as we currently understand it is appropriate is another question. I am con-sidering this journey to be an adventure in 'romantic psychology' which will use the techniques of science, as we know it, when fitting. There are certain differences between the neo-classical approach that we are so used to in psychology and the ways of romantic psychology which I will briefly outline to the reader so that he or she can see what I am trying to do and the manner in which I am going about it. Then my departures from the classical manner will make more sense rather than being a continual source of disgruntlement and cause of complaint.

The classical approach has always been more concerned with the typical than it has with the extreme, the exception or the bizarre (Wilde 1882/1991; Harris 1991; Short 1994). Romantic writers such as Blake and Poe would, however, plough deeply into the extraordinary for their nourishment and inspiration and this I try to do in this account. There is also, in the romantic approach, a valuing of *expression* rather than sober calculation, a fascination with *realness* rather than cool orderliness and a willingness, as in the work of Goya and Victor Hugo, to portray the abnormal in a positive light rather than to categorise it as a departure from a more highly valued standard (Harris 1991, p. 11). There is a valuing of the non-rational, of the spiritual, of introspection and introverted self-examination rather than the decorum of rational materialistic worldliness.

An additional and very central difference between classical and romantic approaches is the sharp distinction the former traditionally makes between process and product, life and work. The personalities of classical thinkers are seen as irrelevant to the assessment of their creations (Popper 1959; Harris 1991). In romantic psychology and romantic writing generally this line, in contrast, is blurred. The romantic places the person at the centre of his or her creation (Wilde 1887/1991). This will be very evident but unavoidable in what follows. I reveal more of my own mind, emotions and experiences in these pages than psychologists previously have done in explicating their theories – and would indeed recommend other researchers to do the same. Psychology will surely not suffer from exercises like this. It is more likely to *gain* in warmth, realness and immediacy. As Oscar Wilde said, the advantage of the emotions is that they lead us astray, but let us *be* 'led astray', because in so doing we may discover the territory where the light of classical rationality has never clearly shone.

Although there are clear similarities between the romantic psychological approach adopted in this book and romanticism itself as pioneered by such giants as Rousseau, Baudelaire and Turner (see Vaughan 1994), there are also differences. The people portrayed in the present work (Chapters 3–8) regard themselves as Borderliners rather than as Outsiders (the romantics' preference). We also do not all have their aversion to town life, luxury and human civilisation (see Harris 1991, pp. 8–10) nor necessarily their thirst for 'everything pure'. Finally, our mysticism (except in the case of Desmond (Chapter 6)) is not necessarily of the form of Nature mysticism, as was commonly the case with romantic painters and writers. It would therefore be wrong to regard the approach as chained by a particular creed – and, as Cézanne always warned, it would also be wrong for it to be so.

The phenomenological sections of the book will, I hope, demonstrate the purchase of romantic realness to the reader as I deal with sanity, the productive middle ground of the Borderline and the hell of insanity. These chapters will hopefully also give the reader a first-hand acquaintance with the reasons I have had to abandon the cool rational decorum of the neo-classical air in order to open up this province of thought and experience for study.

Before embarking, however, on these biographical adventures, it is essential for us to see where research stands at the present time on this issue of the schizophrenic credit. It would be quite wrong to state that this perspective has been perennially ignored. By contrast, researchers and practitioners have long been aware of it (Jung's work tended to be charitable in this respect) but the dreadful toll of schizophrenic illness has slanted investigations towards prevention and cure (Newton 1988, 1992) rather than towards finding and assessing this 'other side of madness'. As I stated in the Preface we are now approaching a time where illness sufferers are seen as service users and 'customers' and indeed as the *employers* of their therapists rather than as dependants and 'know-nothings'. As we enter this new era of community involvement and care (e.g. Orford 1992; Meredith 1993), it is time to reassess our attitudes to psychosis-prone people and to start seeing them as total human beings with dignity and with capacities of choice and discernment rather than as malfunctioning organic entities to be plied with 'pills and bus passes'. In Chapter 2 I therefore assess the yield of research so far into this more positive conceptualisation of the psychosis-vulnerable person. We will see that this is a pristine field of considerable promise and as yet unrealised potential.

The schizophrenic credit so far
Empirical findings and conceptual issues

Elizabeth Mintz, a clinical psychologist in New York, and some of her fellow therapists once began experimenting with extra-sensory perception at the hospital where they worked. To contribute to their experimentation, on one occasion Dr Mintz decided to send one of her colleagues a psychic message while taking a break from her ward duties. So she sat in her office and tried to send the name 'Johnny Walker' (meaning the whisky) to him, since he was known for his temperance concerning such beverages. She was focusing on the name when one of the hospital's schizophrenic patients came running down the hall. He was extremely agitated, and kept complaining that he was being called Johnny Walker!

(L. Scott Rogo 1990, *Beyond Reality*, p. 73)

Anecdotes such as the above, although they are hardly convincing to scientists, none the less jolt and jog every researcher who has a lot of daily contact with schizophrenic patients over the years. Sometimes one really wonders whether or not this loosely connected family of illnesses involves processes which are maybe quite beyond that which current science could possibly explain. Perhaps only a more advanced system of knowledge will truly be able to encompass all the phenomena that come to our attention. But stressing the magical and mysterious sides of schizophrenia, for example via conducting ESP experiments, can produce problems for recovering patients (Greyson 1977, p. 198; Chadwick 1992, p. 136), possibly because it makes sufferers feel that they are permeable to forces beyond their control. Many patients may refuse to be tested for this reason and one of Greyson's subjects found the *negative* outcome of his experiment therapeutic. Strange phenomena such as that reported by Rogo do occur, and as we will see in Chapters 6 to 8 they can be productively utilised by less disturbed people – but this is much less the case in people who have actually been through an outright psychotic episode, where 'paranormalising' their illness, except in minor ways, is not usually helpful.

Recognising the presence of the uncanny in schizophrenia, however, does have the valuable effect of inducing humility in the researchers who study it. We are faced here with phenomena that tax our intellectual, empathic and affective powers to the limit and it is possible that some aspects of these conditions will forever elude our explanatory grasp. Of course we hope not and to talk of schizophrenic symptoms as 'quint-essentially ununderstandable' (Jaspers 1963) is alienating for sufferers (and their families) who actually benefit from feeling that the illness *is* understandable and on a continuum with normal functioning (Kingdon and Turkington 1994, pp. 21–2).

In this chapter I will present evidence and arguments to the effect that vulnerability to schizophrenia has advantages for the individual – and for humanity – and not merely disadvantages. My coverage is intended to be representative and to be a fair assessment of the state of the art in this endeavour but it cannot be exhaustive. Psychology as a realm or endeavour suffers from the difficulty that all investigators seem to present 'short blanket' views of their respective fields. If one pushes the conceptual blanket down to cover neurological and biochemical factors underlying the human psyche, social and spiritual issues are neglected. If one pulls it up to embrace these factors one finds oneself neglecting neurochemistry, neuropsychology and genetic factors. Research into 'schizophrenia' as a concept and a condition or group of conditions suffers in like manner. Medically trained personnel generally accept that the concept has validity and probe this group of illnesses largely at the level of brain mechanisms and genetic predisposition (e.g. Gottesman and Shields 1972; Crow 1980; Haracz 1982; Davis *et al.* 1991; Gottesman 1991). However, many psychologically trained researchers involve themselves with cognitive and phenomenological processes and with the social and political consequences of the schizophrenia 'label'. Some indeed have even raised doubts as to whether this entity has any validity or usefulness whatever (Szasz 1976; Bentall *et al.* 1988; Bentall 1990b; Boyle 1990, 1992, 1994, 1996).

My own identity is that of a phenomenological psychologist and writer (an 'artist-experimenter' (Chadwick 1996b)); I am not a scientist, although my formal training has been in science. It is possible, however, that, like everyone else, I too will present a 'short blanket' view here but my intention is to do otherwise.

To begin with: it seems reasonable to confront processes traditionally regarded as more psychologically 'peripheral' and then to move to more central and to conceptually higher issues as we proceed. Though the evidence and arguments for normality and credit discussed in the following pages are as stated, it is sad to reveal that even where credits are found they are usually reframed verbally by authors into deficits, said to imply deficits or said to be credits of no or negative value. Like Freud (see Kline 1981, p. 118) at the hands of his many 'assassinographers', schizophrenic people are almost always depicted as somehow 'wrong'; they do not achieve even chance success. But really in signal detection terms what we are often dealing with here are differences in criterion placement of one kind or another. And whatever placement is chosen, there are bound to be not only costs but benefits. It is high time that traditional researchers in this field removed their blinkers and became cognisant of this fact.

Clearly this chapter could easily be expanded into a volume in itself so the credit characteristics I discuss will, in one chapter, have to feature far more briefly than ideally is required in order to do them full justice. The reader should, however, be able to obtain both the flavour of the research and an idea of the main topic areas of investigation into the schizophrenic credit from this admittedly rather skeletal overview.

PERCEPTUAL AND ATTENTIONAL FACTORS

While the sensory quality of perceptual experience may be more vivid and intense in schizophrenia (Cooper *et al.* 1976), the formation of iconic (very short-lasting) images appears to function normally in schizophrenia (Knight *et al.* 1978). It also does not seem that schizophrenic people are significantly deficient in perceptual organisation of visual stimuli (Rief 1991). Although it is common to attribute perceptual dysfunction to such patients because they frequently suffer from visual, but more commonly auditory, hallucinations, it should be said in mitigation that hallucinations themselves are far from rare in people conventionally regarded as perfectly sane (Sidgewick 1894; West 1948; Posey and Losch 1983; Romme and Escher 1993).

Research has long attributed to schizophrenic people an attentional filter dysfunction causing the person to be experientially 'overloaded' with stimuli (McGhie and Chapman 1961). It should be noted that this insight actually came from a patient, not from the researchers (see also McGhie 1966 and Venables 1963 on this filter problem). Subsequent research, however, found a similar distractibility and 'allusive' attentional style in highly creative normal volunteers (Dykes and McGhie 1976). One might imagine that intrusion from the unattended channel could well on occasion be functional, not only for the enrichment of creative ideation but also for quite mundane reasons. To take an example from everyday life: Alana J., reported in Chadwick 1992 (Chapter 6), once detected, as we sat down to a meal at her flat and were both busy eating, that the oven was *still on* because of the very slightly audible spitting sounds being given off by the oven pan. This 'intrusion on the unattended channel' as it turned out actually prevented a fire as the pan had become ungraspably hot.

Difficulties that patients have in inhibiting attention to 'irrelevant' stimuli are currently a major focus of research interest as they indicate limitations in so-called 'cognitive inhibition' (Beech, Baylis *et al.* 1989; Beech, Powell *et al.* 1989; Laplante *et al.* 1992; Williams 1996). However, failures to inhibit processing of previously irrelevant stimuli can have beneficial effects when criteria are changed and to-be-neglected stimuli now need attention and recognition. This has been shown in sequences of Stroop task colour naming (Beech and Claridge 1987) and in latent learning (Garety and Hemsley 1994, p. 37; Baruch *et al.* 1988). In the former, the Stroop task (Stroop 1935), the participant has to name *the colour of the ink* in which a conflicting colour word is written (e.g. 'blue' written in *green* ink). Clearly one has to inhibit attention to the word itself to perform this task satisfactorily. However, if this inhibition is weak and the to-be-neglected word (here 'blue') becomes itself the colour of the ink *on the next trial*, one's naming of that ink colour is likely to be enhanced. This has been found to be so (Claridge 1988, pp. 193–5), although the effect is clearer for schizotypal normal participants than for recovering schizophrenic people (who do none the less 'outperform' control subjects).

In the second research paradigm mentioned above, that of latent learning, pre-exposure to a stimulus that has no consequences usually retards learning when that stimulus subsequently is paired with a second stimulus. Clearly, if the inhibition of this prior (disruptive) learning is weak, learning of new associations will be enhanced and this was indeed found to be so in acute patients – but not in chronic medicated patients or normal subjects (Baruch *et al.* 1988).

Although it is customary to point to deficits in facial perception and recognition of facial expression in schizophrenic patients (e.g. Braun *et al.* 1991), other work with such patients of paranoid rather than chronic schizophrenic disposition reveals that detection of *deception* via facial non-verbal cues can actually be enhanced (La Russo 1978). Clearly the likely detail-consciousness of paranoid patients compared to controls and to non-paranoid and chronic patients may be an advantage here.

BIAS RATHER THAN DEFICIT?

Since criteria for performance vary with situations and the latter are always in flux, it may be better to speak of *biases* in schizophrenic information processing rather than *deficits* (Bentall 1994). For example, someone who is a chronic externaliser of *blame* will be well placed to spot it when genuine injustice or unfairness is operating – and perhaps better placed than a more even-handed person. Indeed, a depressive might well blame *themselves* in circumstances where real neglect and injustice are operating.

Over the past thirty years biases in human reasoning have become a focus for intense research (e.g. Chapman and Chapman 1959; Wason and Johnson-Laird 1972; Kahneman *et al.* 1982). It appears that many of these biases are shared by mentally disordered patients who may only show them to an exaggerated degree (and indeed sometimes not at all (Bentall and Young 1996)). Hence it is unfair to regard patients as possessing reasoning *deficits* when normal people perform only moderately better (if at all) on tasks designed to assess reasoning efficiency (see Garety and Hemsley 1994,

Chapter 2, pp. 18–31). Biases such as selective attention to confirmatory information; the proneness to jump (the patients sometimes accurately) to conclusions (Garety *et al.* 1991); the relative processing of frequency data at the expense of probability data; the preferential processing of the most *available* data and the tendency to have judgement swayed excessively by merely small (rather than large) numbers of instances or events are characteristic of both delusion-prone and normal subjects (see Kahneman *et al.* 1982 and Chapters 6 and 9 here). This, however, is encouraging as it suggests that the mental processes of patients exist on a continuum with those of normal people and hence their minds are not under the influence of (to others) totally alien and 'ununderstandable' mental machinations. It is also clear that, while patients may have areas of severe irrationality in the area of their delusional preoccupations, other sectors of their psyches may be quite healthy and can be usefully worked with and strengthened by therapists to make inroads on the central problems (Molden 1964; Kingdon and Turkington 1994; Fowler *et al.* 1995; P.D.J. Chadwick *et al.* 1996).

CREATIVITY AND THE CONCEPT OF 'CREATIVE ILLNESS'

Folklore contains many references to the affinity of creativity with madness, and research on both sides of the Atlantic in the twentieth century has, despite much controversy, generally continued to sustain this belief (Barron 1972; Woody and Claridge 1977; Eysenck 1983; Andreasen 1987; Jamison 1989, 1993, 1995). Keefe and Magaro (1980) presented an actual experimental demonstration of creative performance in diagnosed deluded schizophrenic patients and found that non-paranoids were superior to paranoid patients and to controls on a 'Uses' test of divergent thinking. Here the participants were requested to imagine as many categorically different uses as they could for *a brick* and their offered responses were scored for the subjective strikingness of their productions. Since the scoring was subjective, the authors should really have assessed the reliability of their judgements but no reliability coefficient of their so-called 'graded measure' was reported. This, alas, remains a limitation of the study. The experiment may also have underestimated the creativity of paranoids – who Magaro himself has found to be very narrowly focused thinkers (1981) – since the Uses test requires very open-ended 'divergent' thinking rather than productivity along one singular theme. In their delusions paranoid patients can sometimes demonstrate the latter to a remarkable degree.

Although indisputably creative thinkers such as James Joyce, Ruskin and Ludwig Wittgenstein have often been 'accused' of possessing a schizophrenia-prone disposition (e.g. Claridge *et al.* 1990; Baker 1994; Post 1994, p. 30), and indeed Joyce's daughter Lucia did suffer from the illness, the creativity of actual schizophrenic patients and of schizotypal sane individuals is hotly disputed by other American researchers: Albert Rothenberg (1990) and Kay Redfield Jamison (1993). This is an issue also addressed in this book (Chapters 11 and 12), but here it will suffice to point out the limitations in the latter American research.

Rothenberg's thesis (Rothenberg 1990) rests on a large amount of anecdotal, biographical and interview material collected over many years and (valuably) enriched by access to the verbal reflections on their creative processes of actual living Nobel Laureates. A major empirical pillar of this edifice, however, is formed by Rothenberg's experimental work on word association (1973a, b, 1983), where Nobel Laureates are pitched directly against schizophrenic patients. The latter prove to be critically deficient in their capacity to produce so-called 'Janusian' responses – responses which are *reversals* of the probe words in the task. This facility for reversal has been argued by Rothenberg (1990, pp. 14–25) to be particularly enabling of creative work of quality in real-life tasks. For example, he cites the British sculptor Henry Moore as saying, 'To know one thing, you must know the opposite . . . just as much, else you don't know that one thing. So that, quite often, one does the opposite as an expression of the positive' (Rothenberg 1990, p. 19).

The arguments on this issue (which are extensive) are enlightening and convincing – indeed it is surprising that Rothenberg does not cite Oscar Wilde in this particular part of his argument (citing him (p. 104) only on the issue of homosexuality and creativity), as Wilde's predilections for contradiction, paradox and reversal (e.g. 'She who hesitates is won') were central characteristics, perhaps *the* central characteristics of his humour and of his cognitive skills repertoire (see Ellmann 1988). It is difficult, however, to decide whether or not the testing of recovering patients against Nobel Laureates is a fair way to assess the latent creative potential of a mind prone to schizophrenia. The complications produced by various side effects of medication (such as sluggishness, distraction by movement disorder, and apathy) combined with the after-effects on the operations within a person's semantic networks of the psychotic episode itself, to say nothing of the likely differences in test motivation, IQ and education between the Nobel Laureates and the patients, make any conclusions drawn from these studies highly suspect. Indeed the testing of intelligent schizotypals would surely have been a better strategy.

Rothenberg surely is right to stress the importance of *health* in out-standing creative production, as Storr (1972, 1990) and Kessel (1989) have done, but while outright psychosis is inevitably crippling of flexible, clear yet disciplined cognition this is not to say that psychoticism and schizotypy (as contrasted with psychosis and schizophrenic illness), as a constellation of temperamental neuropsychological and cognitive biases, are similarly devoid of facilitating effects (see Claridge 1985; Rawlings and Borge 1987; Rust *et al.* 1989; Eysenck 1995, Chapter 7).

Jamison (1993), in turn, cites (pp. 74, 107, 108) critical studies by Andreasen and Powers (1975) and Schuldberg (1990), where the investigators, while expecting to find relations between schizophrenia and creativity, actually produced results more favourable of a link with mood disorder. Earlier work by Schuldberg et al. (1988) suggests that the picture may not, however, be as straightforward as this. Generally they found that participants high on the Perceptual Aberration or Magical Ideation aspects of schizotypy did have elevated creativity test scores in comparison to a control sample matched for sex, age and vocabulary score. However, Schuldberg et al. (1988) are at pains to point out that the pattern of results on close inspection is complex and that *different* aspects of schizotypy, interacting also with 'Impulsive Non-conformity', tend to correlate with different facets of creativity. (This multidimensionality to the two constructs was also emphasised by Richards (1981).) Although this 1988 investigation did not find a significant correlation between schizotypy components and divergent thinking scores on a Uses test, the Schuldberg *et al.* study did confirm that creativity scores were meaningfully related to a combination of schizotypy components and a measure of non-conformity. This is a set of directions for future research that will be pursued in Chapters 11 and 12.

In a later study by Poreh et al. (1993) it was also found that schizotypal participants obtained higher scores on the (non-verbal) Figural Fluency and Figural Originality scales of the Torrance Tests of Creative Thinking than did controls – although the two groups did not differ on the verbal creative thinking scales. Ear preference in a dichotic listening task was also related to creativity within the schizotypal group (but not within the control group), with schizotypes of *right* ear preference scoring significantly higher than their left ear preference counterparts on the Verbal Fluency Scale and relatively higher on the Verbal Originality Scale. The general finding, however, was of a left ear preference in schizotypes and an advantage in non-verbal creativity in schizotypes compared to controls.

Although the arguments and patterns of results are not straightforward, it seems reasonable to claim that schizophrenia-proneness is none the less in some respects, if not all, facilitative of creativity. It is also important to consider the possibility that a schizotypy/creativity correlation may occur, as we may presume it did in Ruskin and James Joyce, particularly in participants of high IQ. This also will be explored later (Chapters 11 and 12).

Jamison seems cynical of a link between schizophrenia and creativity in the body of her 1993 text but relents somewhat on this issue when discussing it in the (far more dangerous) context of potential genetic screening of people likely to come to suffer from manic-depression or schizophrenia (Jamison 1993, Chapter 7). There she writes (p. 252):

few studies have examined the possible evolutionary reasons for the survival of *any* of the genes responsible for psychopathology, although some writers have suggested that schizophrenia, while devastating to those who suffer from it, might confer certain intellectual and temperamental advantages on first degree relatives.

It is therefore somewhat unclear what Jamison's position on this issue really is and the text finishes leaving the reader in doubt about precisely what she is claiming. It may be that in the interests of caution she is admitting the possibility of such an association whilst finding no experimental evidence for it so far.

Other research on the mental health of world-famous men by Post (1994, 1996), deriving from his study of over 300 biographies over a ten-year period, leaves little doubt that many highly creative men, more so writers and artists than scientists, were highly disturbed (Post 1994, Table 1, p. 25). Jamison (1993) has tried to argue that such an association is to be accounted for particularly through the disturbances in mood of gifted people. However, it is doubtful that this is so. Apart from the considerable difficulty clinicians still have in distinguishing manic-depressive, manic, hypomanic and other mood disorders from schizophrenia,[1] a problem which Jamison greatly minimises (see Jamison 1993, pp. 59–60) and which is recognised to be in no way as clear-cut as she maintains (Ollerenshaw 1973; Kendell and Brockington 1980; Zigler and Glick 1988; Bentall 1990a, p. 30 and references therein; Eysenck 1995, Chapter 6), it is evident that many of the sample studied by Post were of paranoid, schizoid or schizotypal disposition (see Table 2.1 here, Felix Post, personal communication: 5 April 1995), although none suffered from outright schizophrenic psychosis (Post 1994, p. 30). Similarities in cognitive styles in creative individuals and schizophrenics have also been reported by Hasenfus and Magaro (1976), Keefe and Magaro (1980) and Prentky (1980).

The distinction between 'schizophrenia-proneness' and 'creativity' as independently measurable variables then to be correlated is a strategy which even in itself may be flawed. In many cases 'illness' is a phenomenon inextricably imbricated into the creative process such that a life plan of research, as occurred for both Freud and Jung (Ellenberger 1970/1994), may flow from a period of severe mental instability. The access to preconscious and unconscious processes that specifically schizoid and schizophrenic states may permit (Frith 1979) need not be destructive or totally destructive but an occasion for renewal, enlightenment and insight to a degree where many decades are needed later to actualise in a disciplined way the material thus released to consciousness.

Table 2.1 Individuals showing paranoid, schizoid or schizotypal traits in a sample of 291 world-famous men

Of 46 statesmen and national leaders
Parnell, Chiang Kai-shek, Stalin, Hitler

Of 45 scientists
Einstein, Babbage, Mendel

Of 50 scholars and thinkers
Wittgenstein, Mommsen, Santayana, Buber, Ellis (Havelock), Freud, Jung, Schopenhauer, Spengler, v. Treitschke, Kierkegaard, Newman (Cardinal), Ruskin, Toynbee (Arnold)

Of 52 composers
Ravel, Mahler, Stravinsky, Bruckner, Mussorgsky, Satie, Schumann

Of 48 visual artists
Ensor[1], Epstein, Kandinsky, Kokoschka, Menzel, Utrillo, Van Gogh[2]

Of 28 non-English novelists and playwrights
Hesse, Hugo, Strindberg[3]

Of 94 English language poets, novelists and playwrights
Auden, Chesterton, Clare, Davidson (John), Eliot (T.S.), Fitzgerald (Edward), Graves, Hopkins, Housman, Lindsay (Vachel), Lowell (John Russell), Pound[4], Robinson (Edward Arlington), Boucicault, Joyce[5], Maugham[6], O'Casey, O'Neill (Eugene), Shaw, Waugh, Williams (Tenessee), Yeats

Notes:
1 Labelled by some as schizophrenic but by Felix Post only as schizotypal.
2 Also one or two allegedly schizophrenic first-degree relatives.
3 Delusional jealousy and a sister hospitalised for paranoid psychosis.
4 Grandiose paranoid delusions but possibly only overvalued ideas.
5 Schizophrenic daughter, Jung also regarded *Ulysses* as an example of the schizophrenic mind (see Post 1994, p. 30).
6 Paranoid symptoms only in senile dementia.
Source: After Post 1995

MEANING-SEEKING

Related to this issue of creative illness is that of the effect of the crisis in confronting one with one's life in full perspective and maybe even giving clarity to one's purpose. Sufferers of delusion do seem to be preoccupied, at least at the time of the illness, with issues of meaning and purpose (Roberts 1991; Bentall 1994, p. 349) and it may be that psychosis can in a sense enhance a person's apprehension of their wider context and of their place in the cosmic scheme of things. This, however, seems to be a two-sided coin as the preoccupation with meaning can easily intensify and be engorged into the delusion-creating process (see next section). Hermann Lenz, of the University of Vienna, once told me, regarding my own concept of the 'meaning feeling' (Chadwick 1992, pp. 91–2) as an experience intervening between delusional mood or 'trema' (Conrad 1968) and actual psychosis, that many of his patients spontaneously had said that were they to re-experience this feeling of meaning associated with their thoughts they would again 'go mad' (Hermann Lenz, personal communication, 26 October 1987).

Clearly the apprehension of a wider and deeper meaning to life than consensually is usually considered appropriate is a hallmark of the mystical state, and connections between schizophrenic experience and mystical enlightenment have in recent years been studied in detail (Buckley and Galanter 1979; Lenz 1979, 1983; Wilber 1980, pp. 151–9; Buckley 1981; Lukoff 1985). As I found myself, psychosis – particularly in the early euphoric phase, if it obtains – can be at least the *beginning* of spiritual enlightenment. It may open doors to such experiences that the person can make productive use of later when they are well.

'SUCCESSFUL' DELUSIONS

Delusional reinterpretations of one's life and of one's place and function in the world can often conceal and protect against unbearable intrapsychic anguish. It is bizarre and in a way sad to admit that on occasion these reinterpretations can be so successful that the person is far happier and they consider their lives more purposeful even than the staff who are treating them (Roberts 1991, p. 25). Indeed, some people in this category may be so successful that they are never seen by a psychiatrist and never treated. Roberts cites the case of a vagrant in his research with a zero depression score on the shortened form of the Beck Depression Inventory (Beck and Beck 1972) and the highest scores in his sample on the tests he used to measure purpose and meaning in life (see Roberts 1991, p. 22) but who actually dines out of dustbins and 'controls the world' from a makeshift tent. Two patients studied by Roberts ironically felt (on gentle questioning) that *without* their beliefs, say, were their beliefs discovered to be false, they would 'go mad' or 'dangerously mentally insane'. It was clear that the currently deluded patients studied by Roberts (Roberts 1991, Figure 2, p. 24) had higher feelings of purpose in life and lower depression scores than those previously deluded (but now in remission). Roberts studied patients with chronic systematised delusions and it could well be that the 'success' of the delusions was a major factor in their chronicity. People such as myself (see Chapters 3 and 4), who created delusions which eventually produced a *worse* life scenario than the one we had in a sense 'left', are clearly more motivated to disengage ourselves from our delusional constructions. It is evident – as in career change and love affairs – that, without a palatable position to move to, delusions are hardly likely to be solidly dispensed with simply on the basis of logical refutation. As in life, and even science, something more than logic is required.

'RECOVERABILITY'

Rather pessimistic attitudes to the prognosis in schizophrenia do express themselves in the current literature (see, for example, the general melancholy on this issue in Tyrer and Stein (1993)). Much research, however, indicates that the life course of schizophrenia is very varied and is not a relentless unfolding of a disease process except perhaps in a few percent of cases. Indeed, to see the illness as relentless itself is counter-therapeutic and misguided (Ciompi and Muller 1976; Bleuler 1978; Barham and Hayward 1990; Coursey *et al.* 1995). It may well be that institutes or units that *only* chemically target symptoms are succeeding merely in turning an institutionalisation problem into a revolving-door problem. The possibility of schizophrenic illness being at times a creative illness also is relevant here as there are occasions when patients not only get well, they go on to become weller still with time (Silverman 1980). Harding *et al.* (1988), in a meta-analysis of European research on outcome, found that about 50 per cent of schizophrenic patients were classifiable as 'cured' or only slightly disabled.

The conception of schizophrenic illness as a potentially valuable experience was of course central to Laing's thesis (Laing 1967) but also informed the Soteria House therapeutic community (Mosher *et al.* 1975) and that of Fairweather Lodge (Fairweather *et al.* 1969). Capacities for independent living were markedly better for residents in these communities than those merely treated by drugs but the philosophy of the communities was indeed that the illness offered possibilities for growth and integration (see Mosher and Menn 1978).

The targeting of symptoms rather than disease entities has become fashionable also for cognitive-behavioural therapists in recent years following the publication of papers by Persons (1986), Bentall *et al.* (1988) and P.D.J. Chadwick and Lowe (1990). Both the questioning of the validity of the disease categories and the tractability of symptoms to psychological intervention demonstrated in these contributions have ushered in a new optimism and a change of approach to patients suffering from problems previously considered resistant to all forms of help other than medication – without, it seems, producing or exacerbating the revolving-door problem. A number of publications in the last ten years or so (e.g. Lowe and P.D.J. Chadwick (1990); Garety 1992, 1993; Garety *et al.* 1994; Fowler *et al.* 1995; P.D.J. Chadwick *et al.* 1996), the last focusing on a 'person' approach rather than a 'symptom' approach, offer the promise that cognitive-behavioural intervention with deluded patients can at least reduce conviction and preoccupation ratings and at times even produce delusion removal. The tackling of hallucinations along cognitive-behavioural lines also has shown promise (Haddock *et al.* 1993; P.D.J. Chadwick *et al.* 1996).

'EDUCABILITY'

If we regard individuals with mental illness as customers for available services, rather than as passive receivers of illness-correcting operations of various kinds, it makes sense to provide them with information about their condition so that they can make wiser choices. There seems every reason to believe that schizophrenic people are educable about their illness and that such programmes of psychoeducation do valuably improve compliance with medication (Powell *et al.* 1977; Kelly and Scott 1990) – something that psychiatric patients are no worse at than any other patients (Buchanan 1996). Patients who participate also show gains in quality of life, social functioning and in the extent of their social networks (Atkinson *et al.* 1996). Increased knowledge about schizophrenic illness is also not therapeutically damaging (MacPherson *et al.* 1996). Increased information about medication and symptom reduction was also found to result from such a programme by Goldman and Quinn (1988). Patient (and indeed family) motivation to become involved with such interventions is often not high – and suspicion of medical authorities may play a part here – but the accumulating evidence demonstrates that they are effective and worthwhile.

GENUINENESS OF FEARS

Overenthusiastic diagnosticians are well known to pathologise patients' utterances and to disbelieve their judgements, a process that can be catastrophically counter-therapeutic (Chadwick 1992, p. 134). Instances have been reported in the literature, however, where so-called 'delusional' beliefs have proved to be true or partly true (Sagan 1977, p. 181; Chadwick 1995a, pp. 15–16). Other research has involved the investigators indwelling in the patient's perspective and in this way reality bases have been discovered for some of the reported beliefs (Lemert 1962; Mayerhoff *et al.* 1991). I have argued that insufficient attention is usually give to the potential veracity of patients' statements and that 'delusions' do occur on occasion in clinical practice that might repay being checked in the community (Chadwick 1995a, pp. 85–6).

BLAMELESSNESS OF THE VICTIM

It has been fashionable in recent years to attribute schizophrenic illness to factors *internal* to the individual. If anything is in any sense 'wrong' it is taken to be within the patient or client. Currently findings are accumulating, however, that factors in the family, a problem proclaimed loudly by researchers in the 1950s and 1960s (e.g. Bateson *et al.* 1956; Laing and Estersen 1964) may indeed play a part in the onset and course of psychosis

(Leff and Vaughn 1981; Valone *et al.* 1984; Leff 1991; Kavanagh 1992; Bebbington and Kuipers 1994). The more recent findings, however, centre on the damaging effects of overprotectiveness, overinvolvement and criticism, and perhaps also guilt induction emanating from, and overtalk-ativeness in, other family members. Evidence also suggests (Turner and Wagenfeld 1967) that living in lower-class environments produces stresses which can lead to a schizophrenic decompensation. Such findings are important as they lessen the chances of community attitudes hardening into a tendency to 'blame the victim' (Ryan 1971) and make clear that schizophrenia is the responsibility of all of us, from individual to family to town to country, and not merely a malfunction in certain brain pathways to be put right by a 'quick fix'. The lesson also emerges that some people's illnesses may be symptoms of something wrong with the wider community rather than evidence of 'personal failings'.

SCHIZOPHRENIA AS 'BEYOND CURRENT SCIENCE'

Many schizophrenic patients give evidence of uncanny sensitivity and a perceptiveness that can border seemingly on the paranormal. Patients' frequent reports of thought transference and thought broadcasting have been taken by some investigators in the past to be worth considering as evidence of a genuine telepathic capacity, particularly in schizoid and schizophrenic patients (Lewis 1956; Ullman 1973). Rogo (1990) devotes several pages to the work of psychiatrist James McHarg and clinical psychologist Elizabeth Mintz on this issue (Rogo 1990, pp. 69–74).[2] The evidence is certainly suggestive if not demonstrative (see studies cited in Greyson 1977) but is a useful anchor on any attempts we might have to be self-congratulatory about our understanding of this group of illnesses. It may be that the possible lowering of the threshold of consciousness in schizophrenia, should it obtain, enables an openness to 'subtle energies', as Einstein used to call them, about which science currently knows nothing. This is an invitation to all to access their own capabilities for humility when faced with the problems of the schizophrenic conditions.

   As a final comment on this particular issue, to which, at least officially (if not privately) the ears and eyes of most clinical psychologists and psychiatrists are usually closed, it is worth briefly reporting the recent work of Russian psychologist Andrey Lee (Lee 1991, 1994).[3] Lee tested the clairvoyant capacities of twenty-five acutely psychotic patients in the first three days after admission and then again ten days later after psychotropic medication had been administered. Testing took place over three days each time, two to three times a day. Patients had to sort envelopes containing concealed red and blue cards into piles by colour and guess the identities of objects hidden in boxes. The experimenters were blind to the contents of the envelopes and boxes on all occasions. It was found that the overall success rate of patients on admission was 88 per cent but this dropped on the second testing to chance level after medication had been taken – although the patients were in psychiatric terms much improved by the drugs (details on two patients are given in Lee 1994 and on the procedures used in Lee 1991, 1994). This research is clearly of interest and worthy of replication attempts. If this phenomenon is repeatedly confirmed, the implications obviously are considerable.

JETTISONING THE SCHIZOPHRENIA STIGMA

As stated at the outset of this chapter, there are some researchers (Szasz 1976; Boyle 1990, 1992, 1994, 1996) who would probably claim that one way to enhance the dignity of schizophrenic people is to dispense totally with the stigmatising schizophrenia label since this 'illness entity' serves no useful function for the client groups (although it does for medicine itself). Having suffered from what was diagnosed as a 'schizoaffective illness' in 1979, it is to me absurd, however, to argue as does Szasz, that all deluded patients lack is 'the confidence of their convictions'. There was no doubt that I was *suffering* to a degree far beyond anything I previously had ever known (something that Szasz neglects) and, it seemed to me, that I was suffering from *something* (see Chapter 4 also on this issue)!

There seems little doubt, however, that 'schizophrenia' is not a unitary disorder and may cover several illnesses that have been conflated because they all share similar, though far from identical, symptomatology. Bleuler's original (1911/1955) comment on the 'loose associations' of his schizophrenic patients rings very true, particularly in the cases of language-disordered and deluded clients, but even this symptom is not common to all people so diagnosed. Frith (1992) argues for a deficit in metarepresentation to cover a wide range of presenting schizophrenic conditions – making insight and management of one's own thinking difficult or impossible. But this is more convincing for the nuclear or Type 2 schizophrenic patients, very quiet and withdrawn, and characterised as suffering from deficiencies and deficits (Crow 1980) than for 'peripheral' or Type 1 patients who suffer from excesses and publicly observable bizarre behaviour such as delusional talk, grimaces and odd mannerisms and word salad speech.[4] The latter appear to have an ability to reflect on events and their own thoughts, although sometimes these reflections can exacerbate the condition (see Chadwick 1993b, p. 248).

The different subdivisions of schizophrenia traditionally presented do not, as diagnoses are intended, act as a reliable guide to treatment. Symptoms guide treatment much better (Johnstone *et al.* 1988). While the term 'schizophrenia' is still respectable in medical circles as a family resemblance concept, or, like 'beauty', as a transcendent concept which differs greatly in its expression at a particular level or in specific contexts (there is little common in the beauty of a daffodil and the beauty of a woman in analytical terms), it does seem to me that eventually the label will disintegrate and new illness labels will emerge more closely tied to genetic, physiological, biochemical and psychological/phenomenological evidence. The distinction between 'Positive' or Type 1 patients and 'Negative' or Type 2 is an early step in this direction and the four-factor model of Lenzenwegger and Dworkin (1996) a more recent move along the same lines.

However, a focus exclusively on symptoms, despite its current attractions, may prove to have its dangers. The symptoms of 'schizophrenia' are by no means the entire problem, so targeting them still leaves the issues of work and social skills, the community's attitude to discharged patients and the development of everyday coping and self-care skills (see Shepherd 1995) totally untouched. Similarly, the removal of the schizophrenia label will not make suffering go away. Indeed, it is well known that patients sometimes are even grateful for the diagnosis as it organises their perception of their life's history and removes their feelings that they are a morally 'bad' person. At the moment the phrase 'the schizophrenias' frequently is used to cover this assembly of illnesses until more precise terms are available and justified. In this book the positive qualities of sufferers are sought largely from those of 'positive symptom' disposition, whether they be recovering patients (Chapter 12) or schizophreniform individuals (Chapters 3 to 8) (although see Chadwick 1995a, pp. 101–5 on the positive connotations of 'withdrawal'). The British view of schizotypy, first suggested as a concept by Rado (1953) and Meehl (1962), owes a great deal to the work of Gordon Claridge (1985, 1988, 1990; Claridge and Beech 1995) and refers largely to the positive symptom constellation (as in the STA scale of Claridge and Broks 1984 and Jackson and Claridge 1991). It is also subject to the assumption that high scorers on STA schizotypy genuinely *do have* a predisposition to positive symptom schizophrenia. The latter is thus conceived as a systemic disease (like hypertension) (Claridge 1988, 1990) which reflects a genetic predisposition (see Roberts and Claridge 1991), turning into 'illness' as a function of such factors as life style, environmental stresses and level of coping ability. In the same way hypertension can pass into stroke and cardiac problems as a function of the life experiences and lifestyles of genetically vulnerable individuals. The great similarity in the factor structures of schizotypy and schizophrenia (Vollema and van den Bosch 1995) gives support to this view. Recent overviews of the status of the schizotypy concept are given in Tyrer and Stein (1993) and Raine *et al.* (1995).

While I am not suggesting, in this basically more charitable book, that talented schizophrenic people *always* be regarded as 'superphrenic' (Karlsson 1972), there seems little doubt that current research is excessively blinkered in its focus on deficit and disorder and that a more benign survey of these conditions will greatly repay the expense of its execution. One can indeed be too portentous about schizophrenic illness. It is true that this group of conditions can *kill* people – but of course so do mountains kill climbers. However if, as a climber, one is forever thinking of this fact (e.g. 'this peak has claimed three lives this year' or 'there's been a death on this mountain every year for the last four years'), one's capacities and confidence are greatly undermined. One has to have an attitude and 'Self talk' that breeds realistic resolve and which strengthens will. Forever harping on disasters, dangers, deficits and dysfunctions does *not* encourage the strength needed to overcome the problems that present themselves.

Chapter 3

A journey beyond the Self

What the public criticises in you, cultivate. It is you.

(Jean Cocteau, 1889–1963)

Traumatic experiences seem to prompt the sufferer eventually to construct an *account* of that experience, and to make attributions about their own illness, if that is what was involved (Brewin 1988; Molvaer *et al.* 1992). In the last ten years psychologists have also come to realise that accounts do show 'perspectivity' (Harré *et al.* 1985), that is: it is pretty well impossible to represent complex series of events and experiences from a singular viewpoint. Multiple accounts therefore are needed to do justice to the phenomena (Spence 1987).

In previous publications I have written about my own psychosis (in 1979) in a developmental autobiographical manner to present basically a longitudinal microprocess study (see also Strauss (1988, p. 328) on the necessity of this in research on delusion). The first perspective showed its onset partly after the collapse of a mystical state (Chadwick 1992, Chapter 4) and the second showed how it had a certain inevitability about it, given the terrible damage that was done to my feelings of self-worth at home (1946–1964) and by a small but extremely snide network of slanderers at school (1963–4). (See also Silverstone (1991) on the importance of low self-esteem in a wide range of psychiatric conditions.)

In this third account I will deal largely with aspects of my own experiences including those *prior* to psychosis but which are very critical to the understanding of the latter. They have not previously been revealed or at least not discussed very explicitly before, but particularly show a benign and colourful side to 'the psychotic mind'. This account, like the others, stands on its own two feet, however, as a compact narrative on the approach to my experience of insanity and the immediate aftermath and can be read without the reader having any prior knowledge of the previous publications.

Ever since Jean Jacques Rousseau (1712–78) and the publication of his novel *Emile* (1762), people have been mindful of the issue of what Man

Figure 3.1 The changing face of sanity and madness. The sequence shows (from left to right) the author in 1973, then in 1979, just two months before the onset of psychosis, and finally in 1984, well recovered.

would be like were he or she not subject to the sometimes degrading and restricting effects of western life and of socialisation in general. Rousseau's alternative and ideal picture was of 'The Noble Savage': Man in his pure pristine state, at one with nature, innocent yet creative, the subject of his own powers, uncontaminated by the cramping and distortional influences of so-called 'civilised' life (see John Berger (1980) also on this).

My own life's mission, since 1967 (at 20) and certainly since 1972 (at 25), was certainly related to Rousseau's early vision. I hungered to know what was 'back of' the social conditioning, the shared biases of my peers, and other forms of learning I had been exposed to as a youngster and also what the rest of the 'keyboard' of my mind had to offer.

Up to the age of 25 I had been a very sex-role stereotyped white (and sexist) urban male. As an example of this: in 1966 I had even won the Lancashire *weightlifting* title at Chester in the January of that year and very nearly lifted the British Universities title in the following March (I was only beaten on the very last lift of the competition). I had been into boxing, soccer and athletics and in those days a typical night out for me had meant large quantities of beer and several games of darts – a game for which I had some talent. My subject at that time at university was geology, so in between life on the streets and nights on the town in major British cities I found myself climbing mountains in North Wales and Glencoe by day and sleeping in youth hostels by night.

Yet, somehow, all was not right. In early 1967 a girl I held very dear ended our relationship saying (wrongly), 'Your life is all sex and violence . . . you only want me for sex' and so on. Later that year I reflected on the *simplistic* nature of my macho personality (in the sense of persona), where all tenderness, sensitivity and indeed all vulnerability were things to 'laugh away' (or drink away).

In 1967 and 1968, even as a student of rock mechanics at Imperial College, my interest in psychology – which had begun when I was a history A-level pupil at school in 1963 – was mounting and by 1972 had actually overtaken my love for geology – in which by then I had B.Sc., M.Sc. and Ph.D. degrees. Geology, at least in those days, had been a subject where a traditional male (what we would now call 'Old Man' as opposed to 'New Man') could happily behave as a traditional male. But I was going for something else, a journey to the Self, and in my quest I felt that psychology had the answers. I began, indeed even at Imperial, where I had therapy with Peter Storey, to look back on my past with disgust. I thought I had been a complete fool to have 'bought' traditional masculine attitudes and traditional working-class and lower middle-class ways of being. I felt I had been the victim all my life of a massive 'brainwashing' operation – which I guess in a way was true.

In 1973 I returned from a Royal Society research fellowship in geology that I had held in Uppsala, Sweden, and moved to Bristol, where I decisively made the career switch to psychology. Because of my background and previous reading I was generously allowed by John Brown and Ivor Pleydell-Pearce to do the psychology degree at the university there in about eighteen months and, aflush with vitality and enthusiasm from at last finding my true track, I was delighted to graduate with a clear First in 1975, while still only 28 and was off, as if after the briefest pause, on another research career, this time in psychology.

With my defection to the social sciences from the earth and physical sciences I sensed that the plaster of my 1960s macho mask was dropping away. I was *out* of my partly self-imposed prison and vowed with a vengeance to try and recapture my 'real organismic self' that, from the age of 5 or 6 onwards, had been so denied and distorted by the gentleness-hating and coarse machismo values of so many people around me – those of my own father and mother (and particularly enemies at school) included. I'm sure Rogers would have approved.

Alas, West Country 'real men' and 'decent women' didn't. They didn't approve at all. Following this disengagement from my rather 'industrially minded' past I was now no longer 'in denial' and was floundering in a psychic sea of newly experienced impulses of all kinds. But I was fast discovering not a Rousseauean innocent within but a true sybarite – perhaps not surprising given the rather rough life I had deserted. Fast occurring was a level of sensuality that a stoic would have regarded as salacious. To me it was disorienting but rejuvenating – and even my basic facial appearance began to change into a distinctively more feminine form. Now the rugged self-denial of Northern European Pure Man with his 'fundamentalist masculinity' was not for me – and nor any more was his drunkenness.

The public bars of pubs I shunned in favour of French-style cafés and brasseries; graphs and images from the Science and Natural History museums were replaced on my walls by photographs from the Moulin Rouge and the *Folies Bergère*. The colours of my life were changing from pale blue and grey to lilac, pink and purple. The temperature was rising: wine replaced beer; satin-sheeted beds replaced sleeping bags; smokey hard-to-find cellar dives full of 'green carnation corruption' (where silk dresses and black chiffon did not discriminate the sexes) replaced my adventures in green forests and mountains. Rousseau the nature-lover would not have approved though Beardsley and Wilde would have loved it. But as Oscar's mother always said, 'Respectability is for tradespeople, we are above respectability.' I would scorn stoic and callous values and create instead, with an Italian spirit, out of *decadence*!

I was besotted by beauty and glamour, by the lure of luxurious materials, fragrances and sights. I wallowed in exquisite glamour photography – my camera now being a close friend. On regular trips to Soho and to the wine bars and hotels of the London sexual underground, I talked for hours with gays and with stunning transsexuals there about the hypocrisy of provincial values and life. Courtesans, retailing the needs and desires of their sub-urban clients, down in the big city for their relief, would reinforce my belief in the sham that was 'decent provincial Britain'. I saw the pathetic weakness of Victorian character, as clearly as it was revealed, for all of time, during and after Oscar's trials (see Ellmann 1988, Chapters 17 and 18, and Goodman 1988).

My enemies were puritans of any sex, shape or form; my friends were not 'man mountains' any more but flowers of every sex, shape or form, the sweeter their fragrance the better. Deduction I replaced with dance, line with colour, analysis with ecstasy.

My sympathies were obviously strongly away from the dominant culture and sex, which I regarded as hard-featured, spiteful and unimaginative; I lived for the minority group, the disadvantaged group, and the small state. But more than this: I lived for *beauty*. With a new curvature of face I role-played a black man, a denim soul-man, a woman, an androgyne. I 'severalised' the self and multiplied my roles and my masks.

The first appearance of the 'black' version of my male identity was in the course of supervising the undergraduate project in proxemics of a psychology honours year student (Bill O'Hara) at the University of Strathclyde in Glasgow in 1978. We were interested in the amount of personal space people would give to a black man as compared to a white man in a public setting. To control for sex, height, body build and facial appearance I played both roles, with slightly different and more colourful clothing – provided by other honours-year students – in the black role.[1] Meanwhile, my first role-playing of a woman had been in a counselling role-play exercise in class as an undergraduate at Bristol in 1974.

I had obviously decided with determination that I would break free of the violent restrictiveness of small-town codes of conduct and *be* all that I could be. To me, the theories of Freud and his followers were those of capitulating cowards who had narrowed personal potential. I was going for the outer limits of role diffusion and sexual abandon, beyond categories, language, beyond all arbitrary rules. Timid theories which merely legitimated established working- and middle-class norms (particularly in sex and gender) I had no time for. It was time to 'break out'!

THE PICTURES OF DORIAN GRAY

But, alas, my steamy pink and purple ways did not go unnoticed. Gossip was starting. One of my lady friends of the middle 1970s, Denise, a clean-living country girl (who refused, of course, to sleep between satin sheets), finally decided that my sybaritic transvestic lifestyle was 'vile and despicable' and said (pathetically) 'if other people don't do it it's abnormal'. When she thought she was pregnant by me she nearly died of fright (it was a false alarm).

Neighbours (so I heard and believed) took photographs of me in the street (to 'illustrate' their gossip) and fed back to some people I knew, Denise included, anything 'slurry' they could find out. Rubbish was left outside my door. I caught them peeping through the windows of my flat – whereupon, being spotted, they would beat a hasty retreat. Days of 'rational paranoia' were upon me.

I had fled the West Country to Liverpool in 1975, fled Liverpool (unwisely) to Glasgow in 1976 and then (inevitably) fled Glasgow to the anonymity of London in 1978, resigning a university lecturing post at Strathclyde in the process. In the meantime I was none the less producing publishable work but the pressure of scandal was mounting. I knew I wasn't made for the provinces. But then one has to consider that if one wants to walk down the street as I was to do in Kings Road and in Shepherds Bush in brown suede cuban heel boots, skin-tight jeans, a black satin shirt, curly brown Afro wig, wearing black eye-shadow, perfume and multicoloured bangles, all in the name of 'free personality expression' and 'Androgyne and Transvestite Liberation' one is going to find that there are 'problems with the neighbours' *anywhere* offstage or outside of Chelsea. I had come a long way from the masculine clone who had won the Lancashire weightlifting title of 1966, but there was still quite a bit further to go.

BORDERLINING

With 'the vitality that precedes knowledge' (Berger 1980; Ellmann 1988) I arrived in Earls Court in London in October 1978 ready to be veritably catapulted into the future. Having totally rejected the domestic virtues of my earlier years, my task was to create or discover a new but real identity and a new life, based more on empathy and beauty than on analysis and evidence, however iconoclastic it might be. But this task was accompanied by an eerie sense of destiny, of mission; a 'feeling of meaning' slowly began to encroach upon me.

Having been (so I overheard) photographed in the male role by West Country neighbours, I felt intensely *self-conscious* (and this overperception of oneself as a target can itself lead to paranoia (Fenigstein 1984)). It was as if I was, in the way they would talk about me, 'a known pervert' – rather than truly anonymous and free. Denise's barbed words 'vile and despicable' would also echo around my mind as would 'rotter', 'rat' and the like from my equally barbed days with my delicacy-hating mother in the 1960s (see Chadwick 1993b). The baggage of hate and rejection of all things feminine and sensuous that I had brought down to the metropolis from the provinces wasn't on my back, it was in my head and it weighed upon me like lead.

But dispensing with the last vestiges of a machismo self undoubtedly did leave an inner vacuum. With its demise I attempted to dispense with all imitating, modelling and identifying, usually considered so important in the creating of one's sense of identity and social identity or role (see for example James 1890, 1892; Mead 1934; Bandura 1962; Bandura and Walters 1963; Bandura *et al.* 1963a, b). I tried instead to *feel* what I was, using my own inner voice, Emerson's 'affirmations of the soul' (Fromm 1947), liberally enriched by the research literature on fundamental psychological processes. I would self-instantiate therefore *from within* (see also Steinem 1993 on another approach to this quest). Alas, this very asocial streak in my theorising, produced by years of immersion in psychoanalysis and cognitive psychology, would prove to be a serious and dangerous weakness.

UNDERGROUND

As a teenager I had found most of the models of 'Man' that I had incidentally been presented with disagreeable and off-putting. I had also tried to retain my childhood sense of wonder (as I do to this day) while all around me those of my age were gradually becoming more and more dry, cynical and sour by the year. The result of this was that the young adult 'macho mask', particularly of 1964–6, was only ever weakly in place and the possibility that I consciously would reject my gender role socialisation and indeed the whole of my socialisation *per se* (!) was always on the horizon. Because of my troubled upbringing I had therefore not really 'bonded with society'. In the London sexual underground I felt I would find honesty and directness and a freedom from the stereotypes, clichés and 'shared biases' that structured so much male role-playing above ground. I had come across so much 'scripted' behaviour, so much blatant 'reputation management' (Emler 1984; Stephenson 1988, p. 437) – particularly among bullies at school 'performing' for each other's praise – that I simply did not trust the consensually agreed values, norms and attitudes of above-ground culture any longer. The only way, if at all, that I could find the truth about my own nature, and perhaps about human nature, was to seek it not in countryside rambles but in the fringes, at the borderline, of intense inner-city social life. I saw no reason why I should not 'try *anything* legal' and basically live in such a way as to break the rules outrageously – as to me 'the rules' had become empty, vacuous and meaningless.

Not surprisingly, black people, women and homosexuals had always been derided, sometimes subtly, sometimes explicitly, by the men indigenous to the rough culture in which I had grown up. Yet to me all these categories of people symbolised rhythm, beauty, grace, style and a certain effervescent magic and buoyant 'music' that low-key Northern European Caucasian men simply did not possess. My own femininity of temperament had not surprisingly been mercilessly scorned and punished at school and the softness intrinsic to it had been something that my mother had, as she put it, 'tried to knock out of me' – so frightened by it had she been. All of these people's efforts to shape me in a Northwest of England Skinner box into 'one of the lads' and 'a Real Man' I now threw metaphorically completely into the dustbin. In the underground perhaps femininity and 'altruistic and sensuous music' would find favour?

Not surprisingly, my friends there were all radical people: gender mavericks such as camp gay men, radical lesbians, transsexuals (TSs), other transvestites (TVs) and their ilk. And yet even with *these* people, empathic and seekers of beauty though most of them were, I did not quite gel.

'You're the *least* likely guy to get into this kind of thing,' said one man; 'it's not you.'

'I can't believe you're mixing with people like us,' said another.

A friend of mine in the London sexual underground (Ron F) later said that the impression he got none the less was that people thought I was 'an undercover psychologist collecting material on the gay and TV/TS scene' and also once commented: 'you're not *really* one of us'.

This really was mortifying. Although I was trying to find an identity outside the usual categories, I still saw such people as my closest allies. This statement of Ron's made me feel an outsider among my nearest relatives. Not surprisingly I was thus flung into a social void which was to make me feel that I didn't belong, not only in this subculture or in this society but *even on this planet*. I was left, desperately puzzling the problem: 'Who am I?! *What* am I?!' But even worse, I was beginning to wonder whether any secure core sense of 'I-ness' was present in me *at all*. To add to my anguish: images in my mind's eye of sneering smirking schoolboys, irate women and snarling macho men also followed me like ghosts from a land I had deserted (see Kaney *et al.* 1992 on the recall bias for threatening information in paranoid patients).

THE ANGRY YOUNG MAN EMERGES

Now my route to retaining some sense of substantiality was via anger. Anger, which eventually was nearly to destroy me, was holding me together. I became obsessed not with psychological theory or experimentation but with a desperate attempt at self-justification. I was 'alright' I sensed, not 'vile and despicable' or 'a rotter', and I would prove it. I bitterly and angrily resented my lifetime of 'brainwashing' and gossip. I would *get back* at 'the bastards', the 'mind wreckers', the 'homophobic scumbags' (and so it went on) who had done all this to me (see Kaney and Bentall 1989, for this self-preserving attribution of blame externally). I was *continually* talking to myself subvocally ('pressure of *subvocal* speech'), heavily and intensely *rehearsing* potential verbal attacks and defences should any neighbour confront me. This later developed, however, into a vocal tic, a mild form of Gilles de la Tourette Syndrome (see Robertson 1989). Hypomanically I started to go for 'big fish' – I wanted to change the world to make it a better place for beauty and for femininity in general and for feminine men, like me, to live. Maybe then I could at last love and be loved for what I was.

My closest friend was another radical androgynous maverick of a man who called himself simply 'J'. I had no interest in people from 'the centre' who I felt to be, like schoolboys, basically Fascist in underlying orientation. The sight of people I had been the best of friends with fourteen years before – boxers, rugby players, 'big drinking' men, etc., would make me very inhibited; to me machismo and macho cynicism were the sources of 'all the world's problems'.

THE DAYS OF MULTIPLE SELVES

In the sexual underground my 'severalising of the self' nevertheless met with approval. I adopted identities that psychologically I empathised with, that 'felt right' and that physically I could 'carry off' in daily life in a convincing way – although it required much preparation. As (albeit only occasionally) a black I was 'Jules', as a woman 'Linda', as an androgyne 'John', and as a naturally scruffy male intellectual 'Peter' (the central self as I saw it). Again I *tried* to externalise these selves from within rather than plaster them on from without. But the gear was expensive and I was rapidly going overdrawn. Counselling work and occasional temp. and modelling work I did was failing to cover my bizarre and varied outgoings. I saved partly by not eating and, conveniently, my waistline shrank to a mere

27 inches and chest to 38, circumferences that suited 'everyone'. (This was 1978 and my muscle-clad frame of the mid-1960s was now completely gone.)

This fully conscious form of multiple personality none the less caused a lot of problems. 'Peter must be queer, he's got a black man up there,' thought a neighbour; 'Peter's got a lovely blonde girlfriend, I saw her going into his room,' said Jim, an American I knew, down the house payphone to his ladyfriend. 'Who's the guy with the Afro hair?' and so on. Little did these people know that all these individuals were *the same* person.

But life could get even *more* complicated than this. Ron F, in confusion and haste, inadvertently arranged for Peter, 'John' and 'Linda' to turn up all together *simultaneously* one Saturday night at a South London pub (The Duchy Arms in Sancroft Street) to meet a man we had both been corresponding with. If this wasn't bad enough a girl, Karen, I was friendly with as a woman took a great liking to my lavish wardrobe of women's clothes and promptly disappeared back up to Rochdale with most of it in her collection of suitcases. I managed to trace her address but had to go into court in Highgate in North London, saying I was 'a drag artist' in order to get a warrant for her arrest. (I was actually doing some work at the time as a transvestite model.) She promptly returned the gear by post and no charges were brought. (Here the Metropolitan police were very helpful and good-humoured.)

During this period I lived in no less than seven different locations in the space of a year, mainly in West, South and East London. I continually kept on the move, fearing that gossip, and 'the photographs' from the provinces days, would catch up with me. My life was also a mass of 'quick-change acts' which in fact were not quick at all.

Not surprisingly gossip, real gossip, not deluded paranoid thoughts, followed me. Generally London people were very accepting, and tolerant. 'Great stuff. Go for it Peter,' people who knew my quest would often say, even macho types, but my 'baggage' from the provinces as I called it was making mere straws feel back-breaking. I started to see my twenty-first or, maybe, even twenty-second-century lifestyle as a set of subroutines that 'would not run on the world computer'. The hard-featured would make no 'concessions to pinkness'. Society could make no sense of someone like me, the 'liberated person of the future', the 'basic generalised person' who could 'be and do anything' (or so I liked to think).

My efforts at protective self-justification started to accelerate at a time when I thought overimaginatively that slander was raging around me. I penned ten articles in the first six months of 1979, all sent to magazines and newspapers outlining a new altruistic and androgynous philosophy of life and being, to replace the macho cynicism and cruelty of the world of Men (and of my mother). The first was quite reasonable and was published immediately (Chadwick 1979a), accompanied by a glowing editorial. The second was noticeably weaker and more turgid and only appeared, to my surprise really, seven years later (Chadwick 1986). The rest remain unpublished. I was writing myself up to a level of abstractness that a magazine and newspaper market just could not take. Still I felt I *had* to create a rationale that would validate my personal existence beyond categories.

In May–July 1979 I therefore retreated (or 'soared') into the intricate theory creation which was to catapult me to the mystical 'Borderline' state of that summer and to eventual psychosis.

The Borderline 'process theory of person' (Chadwick 1979b, see Appendix I) was to be my justification in the face of rejection by the world. '*Now* do you understand and accept me?!' was my preconscious motto. (See Horney 1937 on the role of preconscious mottoes structuring social behaviour.) The manuscript, which was entitled 'Half man, half boat, the mind of the Borderline Normal' (see pp. 173–9) was, however, flawed (so I felt) by this quality of self-justification that motivated it and that was imbricated into it. On realising this, my mother-inspired perfectionism defeated me and I crumbled. I had no other justifications left to offer so I decided to acknowledge fully the supposedly 'negative' sides of my personality that had in turn motivated this social rejection of which I had been on the receiving end for so long.

Perhaps my battle could have been won had I been reared to hold a self-accepting and self-loving attitude whatever. Alas, my mother, Edith Burghall, always made clear from as early an age as I can remember with distinctness her very low opinion of me as a person and all attempts on my part to 'be good' were met by sarcasm, cynical remarks or snide insults. That was her characteristically paranoid way: good behaviour (particularly from her straying husband's lookalike son) was a mask to get round her and was never to be trusted, while bad behaviour was genuine and gave her gleeful licence for the savage character attacks which came so easily to her. 'I have very high standards!' was her arrogant self-deceiving reply, said with flaming saucer eyes, when I challenged her on this. With a sadistic ball-and-chain of such a kind on one's self-esteem it is difficult ever to feel positive about oneself in any fundamental sense. Indeed, one can see how self-righteous bullying parents of this breed (who often are also selfishly ambitious for their children) could induce profound damage in them in a variety of ways – from anorexia to paranoia, depending perhaps on genetic vulnerabilities.

It has to be said, however, that my mother's life in Manchester (she was born in 1902) had been basically one of sorrow and betrayal. In many ways she was indeed loving and supportive but her view of people was jaundiced and acridly cynical. It was impossible to 'be good' around Edie. She lived instead to 'make good' through me and to make me 'hard', mistrustful, free of all weaknesses, worldly-wise, ruthlessly realistic and successful. That seemed sadly to be her way to protect me from 'being hurt' as marriage and pre-war Manchester life had hurt her. And she did it by this strange mixture of warnings about the evil of people, sadistic brutality directed at my character (a typical high-minded Mancunian (and Victorian) strategy) and praise for achievement.

Edie was obviously a poor and troubled soul and her faith in people had been greatly undermined by my father's unfaithfulness and by the dismissive and arrogant attitude of the Chadwick family towards her. But my *brother's* love for her always remained undented. He saw through the acrid and insulting exterior to the warm but wounded heart within. Alas, I, the lesser man, came to feel only a bitterness and eventually a hatred for her and her obnoxious attacks that matched, and eventually even exceeded, what I thought (wrongly) was her hatred for me.[2]

My father – a victim all his adult life of her ambition and moral bullying – was out of the picture, having died early when I was only seven. (Both of them were typical Mancunian 'softness-haters' in any case – even arts subjects like history and poetry were despised in our home as being 'of no use'.)

The grammar school where I spent my adolescence was a cesspit of homophobia, a merciless gossipocracy of CIA-level efficiency and an institution where any original thought in class and social eccentricity outside class was exceedingly dangerous. Not a single person of charm emerged from the place – and certainly no poets.[3]

The result of all this was that the 'essential self' that I had sensed and tried to externalise (feminine, epicurean, hypersensitive, contemplative, erotic and fantasy-loving) I had been taught, by a million inputs into my neural networks over the years, to loathe as soft, 'poofy', 'dirty', weak, unrealistic and unworldly (politics and engineering were far more important than fashion photography and floral art). Retribution surely was deserved for living as I had and was imminent: 'Just as I have been taught to hate this Self I'm sure you do too.' My ensuing persecutory delusions were jogged into place by coincidentally overhearing gossipy conversation in the street (I took to be about me) and eventually even by things said on the radio (see Chadwick 1992, 1993b) that fitted my situation, coupled with the products of my own now deranged creativity. Sadly, the latter products had a tendency also to be confirmed by these events (see Chadwick 1993b) such that I felt that I had no privacy whatever – a reactivation of my experiences at school. Following readings of Milton's *Paradise Lost* and of a book entitled *The Devil in Art and Literature*, a delusion of possession by Satan defensively took hold in my mind, namely: 'It is not I who have all this anger and these "weaknesses" and sensuous and "perverted" feelings, it is Satan!' Also my obsession with the people who I supposed had photographed me in my West Country days generalised and congealed into an idea now of a much larger persecutory network of people: virtuous right-minded (and right-wing) bourgeois types I called 'The Organisation'

– who, thanks to confirmatory coincidences, I felt now were monitoring me and even deigning in their spiritually superior 'worldly wise' way to try to *cure* me at a distance of my sensuousness and sybaritic 'vile and despicable evil'. Their (fascist) motto was 'Change or die!'

The end result of these ('existentially true') delusions was, horrifically, that I threw myself under the wheels of a double-decker bus on New King's Road in Fulham, to thrust (the old king) Satan out of my mind by literally trying to have my brain crushed under the wheels (thus bringing Jesus the 'new king' into the world once again). I survived, though tragically my right hand was crushed, and I was taken by ambulance to Charing Cross Hospital. I was in despair at this survival – having sided, when mad, with the viewpoint of my antagonists – and hated this 'Devil-possessed thing' in proportion to the seething hatred I had seen in the faces and heard in the voices of the Victorians, the stoics and the self-righteous homophobes and transvestophobes I had been unlucky enough to have to interface with in my formative years.[4] The illness was put down to 'overactivity in dopamine pathways'.

It is clear from the above that the experience of being 'known', 'monitored', gossiped about and rejected for my own femininity and erotic, artistic inclinations produced a very rich source soil for persecutory delusions of all kinds. Really it was inevitable that rational paranoia would turn into irrational paranoia with someone who was so 'unEnglish' and who was 'breaking the common law' so flagrantly as I was.

The critical question none the less remains as to whether or not the lifestyle I created for myself was 'normal' or 'abnormal'. Peter Breggin in his 1991 book *Toxic Psychiatry* repeatedly argues that the medicated lifestyle, rather than being a better one is merely a socially less troublesome one. It could well be contended that my life of 'multiple selves' such as I have just described was indeed a twenty-second-century lifestyle, a program that would not run on 'the 1979 world computer'. The price I paid for my creative rebellion was slander and gossip-induced paranoia in which I merely made (imaginatively) an Everest, not out of a molehill but out of a Ben Nevis. Some would say that this hardly justifies the label 'Schizophrenia' in any pejorative sense. A further positive perspective on the whole affair which I articulated in the unpublished 'Borderline' manuscript is that this was indeed a psychological breakthrough to a deep structure *realm of potential* beneath 'decent suburban living', where I felt I could indeed do or be anything. Many men I knew in those days said to me that they would 'give anything' to live as I was living but that they were 'trapped by responsibilities'. In a more flexible world there might have been no gossip, no slander, no delusions and no suicide attempt. Who was 'in the wrong'? Myself or the times in which I then lived?

I came to refer to myself as a 'Borderliner' and still do – although this is not in the sense of the psychiatric term 'borderline' (see Tyrer and Stein 1993; DSM IV 1994). I mean by the term a person whose identity is in *process not content*. Such people of great fluidity and multiple aspects, which include actors, artists and writers, particularly playwrights and poets (see, for example, Thorpe (1926) on Keats), often find traditional categories aversive and restrictive and therefore live 'on the edge' (admittedly some psychiatrically termed borderliners can be like this). This was the way it was for me – and, as we have seen, the cost of being 'socially uncategorisable' in the end was outright madness. It is a sad reflection on western society that, rather than valuing the *range* a person can display in their being, one's very sanity, to some degree, depends upon the predictability and social acceptability of being 'a type'. Range, as in cyclothymics, is seen as a sign of pathology, which thus courts rejection and diagnosis, while *lack* of range is actually perceived as a virtue! (See also Jamison 1993, p. 127 and McGann 1968, p. 65 on this.) It is clear here that psychiatric and psychoanalytic theorising in this respect is subtly capitulating to the need, and demand, for what is called 'observer comfort' (Rosenhan and Seligman 1984/1995, p. 10).

REFLECTIONS AND CONSEQUENCES

Three perspectives on my 1979 psychosis have now been published; is it possible to identify core causal pathogenic influences from such a wealth of information? With this third perspective readers of the previous two will no doubt see the picture much more clearly. There is no doubt in my mind that the Rogerian hypothesis for mental disorder as caused by frustration and denial of the real organismic self is fully appropriate in my case even though conventional therapy of the Rogerian kind could never have 'cured' me. I was living and working initially as a very narrowly focused masculine convergent-thinking young man, and later scientist, of instrumental analytic attitude, whereas temperamentally I am undoubtedly a liberal receptive androgynous man, really a divergent thinking artist of empathic and *expressive* style. The whole of my personal battle in the 1970s was an implicit attempt to 'give birth' to that latter real self via a long and tortuous path. But the emergence was continually blocked at every turn, not only by circumstances, but by the horrific pejorative attitudes I had learned as a youngster and young man from my mother, from schoolboys and from scientists and sportsmen to anything 'feminine', vain, expressive or 'arty'. Topics central to me – empathy and beauty – were simply never discussed. When I said, in the field, to a group of geologists, 'I wonder what a poet would make of this (rock) exposure?' they all burst out laughing and walked off. Very often the general appreciation of beauty, and certainly this was so at school, was seen as akin to 'sissiness'. Hence I had learned to despise what I really was and was essentially a prisoner of the very neo-stoic values against which consciously I launched my tirades. Scratching at the ceiling of a cage I had partly built myself, the inner anguish of being caught in such an internal battle between automatic and effortful processes was utterly excruciating.

My journey to the Self, and indeed beyond, through 'deviance and perversion' was harmless and absolutely necessary. My mission could never have been lived out in the confines of the consulting room. It had to be lived out in *life*. In the end I guess it was all part – paradoxical though this sounds – of *being a man*. As a schoolboy in Manchester with no father I thought that being a man was merely being physically powerful, highly sexed and sexist. It was a child's idea of manhood. Now my stormy days of cross-race and cross-gender transition are over and I am a peaceful feminine man of placid lifestyle who loves his wife, his friends and his work unthinkingly. It was a journey in the style of Dante to a new state of being right through a hole in the middle of Hell itself. But somehow I knew inside back in 1967 that it did indeed have to be faced, whatever the cost, or I would never know *who I really was*. I had obviously been born, as many people are, at the wrong time into the wrong place – it was my attempt, I guess, to get myself an authentic life.

In the next two chapters I will briefly chart my experiences when I was under the care of professional mental health authorities after admission to Charing Cross Hospital in London in September 1979. The critical purpose of presenting this information is to facilitate the treatment process for recovering psychotic patients and to help future workers to avoid some of the pitfalls that occurred in the handling of my case.

Chapter 4

Hospital life while psychotic

For he who lives more lives than one
More deaths than one must die.
(Oscar Wilde, *The Ballad of Reading Gaol*)

The main purpose of this chapter, although it should certainly be of interest to the layperson and student, is really to help medical and mental health professionals to empathise with and understand the experiences of acutely psychotic patients who come, usually suddenly and unexpectedly, into their care. Here I will continue my autobiographical narrative but will also comment on how professionals *reacted to* and *dealt with* my behaviour on admission (which was in fact at first to an orthopaedic unit). In the previous chapter the narrative was largely intrapsychic; it was a story concocted within a single mind. Here that story was, to a degree, shared with others. What did they make of it? And what did they do? In what follows I will discuss the kinds of events that eased and those that worsened my condition, of which there were several. Perhaps the information that can be gleaned from my own case will be helpful in facilitating the management of psychotic clients in the future, if only in modest ways.

First I will discuss the transfer or generalisation of my delusions into the context of the hospital setting, how some events disconfirmed them, but others exacerbated them. Then I will deal with the immediate effects of medication and subsequently with ward and day hospital management of my condition after the medication brought me back to a sane state of mind.

Following the accounts of previous researchers and writers such as Goffman (1961/1991), Rosenhan (1973), Sutherland (1976, 1992b) Baruch and Treacher (1978), Breggin (1991), and Pilgrim and Treacher (1992), it has become somewhat fashionable to have a rather jaundiced view of how insane people are reacted to and treated by medical and mental health authorities. It will be of interest to most readers, I am sure, to see whether this general theme can be sustained in what follows.

The interfacing of a psychotic person with the normal and sane is a jarring and disturbing one for both parties. Once delusions are in place and systematised, no two sets of people have a bigger gulf between them. Be they black and white, French and English, male and female, heterosexual and homosexual, the gulf separating them pales literally into insignificance when compared to that between the sane and the floridly insane.

For months I had largely kept my outrageous thoughts to myself – except for brief opening of windows on to them with J and Ron F. But the glimpses I revealed to them did not really capture how kaleidoscopic and bizarre they truly were. Once in hospital, however, I was asked to *account* for myself. After all, one doesn't throw oneself under the wheels of a double-decker bus every day of the week. This was a violent and outlandish incident. After the immediate physical treatment to my hand in casualty, people wanted *explanations*. And this was particularly so after I initially refused to have the hand operated on.

Alas, when one is beyond the Borderline into the dark and eerie territory of madness, the picture as one perceives it is not quite as simple as this. In a paranoid deluded state one literally *trusts no one*. I was told by the ambulancemen that I was being taken to Charing Cross, but being unfamiliar in those days with Fulham (to where I had recently moved) and ignorant of the relocation of Charing Cross Hospital *to* Fulham in 1973 I could not understand how the ambulance had traversed the distance so quickly (a distance which is in fact quite short) between New Kings Road, where my suicide attempt took place, and the hospital – which I assumed must be near Charing Cross Station, some considerable way away from Fulham. Also, my ward window looked out over what seemed to be an expanse of green gardens (in fact a large cemetery). What on earth were green fields doing near Charing Cross Station located, so I thought, in the heart of London's West End? This could not *really*, I thought, be Charing Cross Hospital *at all*! It was a set-up, a simulation of a hospital! An Organisation trick! So everyone must be a *member* of the Organisation! My torment was continuing but now I was literally right there *among* them, in their hands and at their mercy! One can see here how this novel contact with a new district and with new people thus adds new dimensions, very quickly, to the sufferer's thoughts – and in ways that no sane person would in any sense easily anticipate.[1]

When a young dark-haired doctor came in to my side ward in the orthopaedic unit to ask me why I had attempted suicide I replied boldly, trying to sound as sane and as measured in my delivery as possible:

> I sincerely believe that there is an organisation of people out to discredit and humiliate me and to induce me to kill myself. I know that this sounds like the content of a paranoid schizophrenic delusion but nevertheless I claim it to be true.

On hearing this he made some hurried notes, then quickly walked out, followed by a nurse.

This to me, however, was all rather weird and unnecessary. Why should he ask me this when he was a member of the Organisation? He already *knew* (surely) why I had done what I did! Why pose as totally ignorant of my motives? All of these people must be *actors* really trying hard to play the parts of doctors and nurses, keeping up a pretence, keeping me in agonised suspense and uncertainty, *until, in their cold clinical way, I really was eliminated.* The double reality of the past two or three months over the summer of 1979 was being maintained – at one stratum events occurred which seemed quite innocent and innocuous, but on another level they had a portentous and sinister meaning directed at me, all in the service of driving me to self-destruction. It was like a Euripidean dual-plane Greek tragedy: the gods above, at one level of meaning, everyday life below, at another, transferred to the latter half of the twentieth century.

I thought nevertheless that the 'acting' of the doctors and nurses was really quite good. They 'pretended' care and concern very well, although underneath it all I 'knew' they hated me, like my mother, the slanderers at school, the neighbours in the West Country, etc., etc., and, like them, wanted me *dead.* They were just menacingly biding their time before in some way 'pouncing' once again. I scrutinised their faces, especially their eyes, with the intensity of a laser every time they interreacted with me for give-away signs that they were not in fact genuine, not who they pretended to be. The almost ferocious way in which I paid attention to the minutiae of faces may have been the reason why one nurse said to the others as they entered my side ward to dress my damaged right hand: 'Don't come in here if you're not good looking!' I took it to be the Organisation's way of mocking me for my transvestic overvaluation of beauty, particularly female beauty. It was just another sting, one of the thousands of mental bites and stings I had received relentlessly since about the middle of June.

Predictably I decided to *test* the medical staff who attended me, in an innocent-sounding way, with questions (inserted into general conversation) about anatomy and physiology, nursing practice and brain function (not all of which I knew the answers to!) but to 'catch them out', to rip through their actors' masks and 'show them up' as imposters. One nurse, alas, didn't know what the difference was between systolic and diastolic blood pressure. She stammered, made an excuse, rushed out and then ten minutes later came back to me in a more composed state with the answer. I only saw her again weeks later, by which time I was well. I assumed the Organisation had sacked her, maybe even killed her, for 'a bad performance'. Another nurse was also 'in trouble' with another question but excused herself by saying to me that she 'hadn't done much on the brain yet'.

It will be obvious to the reader from the above that when dealing with a newly admitted deluded patient the terms on which you think the interaction is taking place are *not* anything *like* the terms as seen from the patient's perspective. It is not simply a matter of there being likely suspiciousness, misinterpretation and misunderstanding, the patient is literally living and behaving *in a different world* from you. The 'plane of meaning' that you are tuned into is markedly oblique to theirs.

None the less, the number of behaviours of the medical staff that I could assimilate to my extant delusion, constructed as it was from every experience of cruelty and sadism I had ever suffered and which sprawled like a massive magnetic net ready to attract or 'fit' virtually *anything* to it, was, remarkably, not impressive. The staff really were caring, concerned, efficient and well informed.

I initially refused to have my right hand, my writing hand, operated on, taking its near obliteration as a fitting punishment for writing, as I now felt I had been doing for years, under the inspiration of Satan. In reaction to this a parade of nurses and doctors marched one at a time into my room one evening at about ten-minute intervals to try to persuade me to agree to having the operation. Since I didn't any longer trust 'anyone', they were all unsuccessful. Eventually, however, a *paraprofessional* did the trick. A short *black* woman, a ward domestic of about 50, who I sensed affinity with immediately, persuaded me with a non-stop monologue of several minutes which I felt came 'straight from the heart'. This woman obviously wasn't a member of the Organisation, she really meant it. The Organisation, so I fantasised, were of ordinary decency but beneath it all secretly galvanised by sexual virtuousness and an 'intellect only' attitude (with all the cold-ness and sadism that these deep down imply). This woman was a 'heart' and 'from the gut' person. I believed and trusted her, and agreed to the operation – which in fact was very urgent as four of the five fingers were abominably badly damaged. (At one point doctors apparently did think that I would lose the hand.)

My talk to the medical staff about my supposed Devil possession not surprisingly reached another valuable paraprofessional, the hospital chaplain, who, to his credit, promptly paid me a visit. On being introduced to him I said, in a suitably deep and menacing voice as he took his seat by my bed: 'You know I'm *The Devil* don't you?' He reeled slightly to his left but quickly gathered his composure and quietly and calmly replied, putting his hand on my forehead as he did so: 'Now just relax. Relax and put your faith in God. Be at peace. Bask in God's love.'

Amazingly this really *did* relax me and made me feel noticeably better. This was most peculiar! What on earth were the Organisation sending *a chaplain* to me for?! Were these people *real*? Were they *actually* who they seemed to be? This was most extraordinary. The bouncy black domestic and the loving chaplain could not co-exist with personnel from the Organisation. The generalisation of the delusions into the hospital environment, a phenomenon which seems to be quite typical with deluded patients, was beginning to be undermined. Note that the events that did this were not the interventions of key mental health professionals, or even 'clever' cognitive events – but events of great care, passion and tenderness.

Alas, two sets of events were to reinforce the delusion to a degree where anti-psychotic medication eventually became the only avenue that the medical authorities decided they could take with me. These events were, however, totally beyond the hospital's control.

I was walking around my small side ward soon after admission (all of the events above took place in the course of three or four days). I glanced out of the window, lazily looking at the clouds on what was a very sunny September day, when the sight that met my eyes pierced viciously through my brain as if lightning had struck me frontally. There in the clouds before me, *needing no effort whatever* to 'read the shapes in' to an ambiguous cloud mass, were the *profiles* in white of my dog Penny, on the left, and of John Yates, who was my Fulham housemate, on the right. Of course it sounds utterly silly. Although any lecturer in perception psychology (and I had been one myself) will tell you how easy it is to see patterns in clouds, coal fires and ink blots (and indeed in the Moon and Mars!), particularly if one is very visually imaginative (e.g. Gregory 1970; Sekuler and Blake 1985), these two 'profiles' went far beyond any semblance to an 'ambiguity' form of illusion (e.g. Gregory 1987, pp. 339–40) (in this case cloud/face). There in the clouds, as if painted by Constable, in diaphanous white on a uniform blue background, *were* the profiles of Penny and John!

Now I 'knew' that somehow the magic, the synchronicity, the torment by the uncanny, was continuing. I inferred (wildly) that the Organisation must have engineered these devastatingly lifelike profiles with some kind of laser or 'heat ray' located on the roof of the building I was now in. How else could *clouds* be moulded or sculpted into such perfect gossamer configurations? As the reader can see, if one accepted my exotic and fantastic premises, the conclusion would be perfectly rational.

A few minutes later I went back to the window, worried that perhaps the sight, because of its *un*ambiguity, had been some kind of misperception. The profiles were still discernible but now sheared and dispersed somewhat. No. There had been no illusion or hallucination.

I mentioned the event to a nurse who quickly dismissed it. Alas, this perfectly understandable offhand dismissal, far from making me feel better, made me feel totally bewildered. If she was a member of the Organisation she would *know* that this prank was being played – why dismiss it so breezily?

But then a second assault of the uncanny began – and this one would resist all dismissal. Lying there in my hospital bed, in a state of anguish, frustration and doubt, I noticed one afternoon that taps and clicks, coming from the walls and ceilings, some single, some double, were perfectly synchronised with the termination of my ongoing thoughts. To Spiritualists of course, single and double rappings have long been regarded as a means of spirit communication, but, dedicated monomaniacally only to the scientific literature as I was in those days, I had no knowledge even of this fairly common belief. To me it was a totally novel and unexpected phenomenon.

In the same way that hallucinated voices occur in states of great doubt and uncertainty and give a kind of (usually malign) guidance (Jaynes 1976; Boyle 1990, p. 199), so these rappings gave answers and certainty that I longed for so much. In a way they eased my tension and my panic but in a manner that proved, alas, to be deeply terrible. They were not initially very loud but through mentally and subvocally 'talking' to them and asking them questions I quickly discovered that one tap or click meant 'Yes' and two meant 'No'. (This apparently is indeed their usual code.) Now my mind was not coding external reality, external reality was coding my mind! The catch was, however, that the thoughts they guided me through always led eventually to sequences such as:

'I am a good soul really?'
'Tap, tap.'
'Then I am evil?'
'Tap.'
'Girlfriends are dead because of me?'
'Tap.'
'Surely there's a way out?'
'Tap, tap.'
'So I must kill myself?'
'Tap.'
'Can I be saved?'
'Tap, tap.'
'Suicide then is the only way?'
'Tap.'
'I must do it *now*?'
'Tap.'
'Right *now*?'
'Tap.'

My side ward was no longer a ward but a torture chamber. The membrane between internal and external which I had conceptually diffused in my theoretical article on the Borderline: 'Half man, half boat' earlier in the summer was now *definitely broken*. Internal and external were one. Nothing that anyone did or said could possibly override the 'messages' from the rappings. If a psychosocial intervention had ever been possible, if far-fetched, in its appropriateness now it was utterly useless. If a cognitive therapist had then come in to bombard me with reason I would either have been abusive, become violent or had a heart attack. Now I knew that the Organisation had indeed decided to pounce again and this new avenue of approach was how they'd agreed to do it.

I tried to break the windows to the side ward to cast myself down from the seventh floor. The windows would neither break nor open. The nurses hurried me into bed. Later they tried to put my right arm, bent at the elbow, into a suspended sling. As the sling swung around towards my face the linen moulded itself into the unmistakable form of the Madonna. My blood-oozing right fist and forearm were right up inside Her. I screamed as I have never screamed before or since. They removed the sling.

Not surprisingly, I assumed that the rappings came from speakers hidden in the walls and ceilings. The Madonna figure had presumably been produced by pre-set creases in the linen used for the sling. The knowledge about my thoughts might come from 'electrodes' or perhaps from a simulation of my neural networks (at 'Organisation headquarters') fed with stored knowledge of my past gleaned from all the ('betraying and slanderous') people I had known. (Here we can see how cotton-thread thin I had come to think my bonds with the rest of the human race were. I assumed really that *everyone* had betrayed me.)

That night I lay on my back in bed staring at a rather moist but dark ceiling. The twinklings from the moisture, which looked like stars, I took to be the souls of people who had died because of me (an interpretation other psychotic patients have reported to me). They were all up there, looking down on me. I was now heaving with Tourette Syndrome coprolalia, offensive utterances were rising within my body but, with teeth gritted, I stifled every one of them – Satan was not going to 'get out'. (That this illness involved an aspect of Gilles de la Tourette Syndrome, which is often attributed by sufferers to Satanic possession, was not, alas, diagnosed for over *two years* (see Chapter 13).) It is impossible for any sane person even to begin to imagine how I felt. It is also obvious to anyone with a shred of common sense that I was *ill*. Any characterisation of my behaviour as merely 'bizarre', such that an 'illness' attribution would then be an act of social control (to empower the medical profession), is clearly utterly absurd. No, my only source of real consolation came from something a girlfriend – (I presumed now dead) – had told me some fourteen or so years before – that one must *never* despair of the love of God.

With eerie taps going on all around the room, 'souls of the dead' viewing me with scorn and contempt from above and my body almost retching and twitching with odious impulses that seemingly came from nowhere, I lay there ('trapped and possessed'), in a crucible of the sadistic Organisation, repeating in desperation over and over again 'I will not despair! . . . I will not despair! . . . I will not despair!' Incredibly, sleep eventually overcame me.[2]

The next day the rappings began again and yet again suicide was demanded. Indeed the taps even reinforced the thought that the longer I delayed the act the more people died (again a thought other sufferers have reported). I *raced* out of the ward and down to the foot of the stairs to get out of the building and throw myself under a lorry. But the door opening on to the outside wouldn't open. I was back in my bed maybe for half an hour when another sequence began. Now, unbeknown to the staff, 'the drive to suicide' was upon me. I raced past the nurses' station yet again (seemingly unnoticed), down the stairs and tried to plunge down the stairwell. But it was too small and narrow – a wise design by the architects. There was nothing for it but to plunge headlong at high speed down a long flight of about thirty stairs. Which after a deep breath I did. 'Alas' my body somersaulted in mid-air, I landed at high speed on my buttocks, slightly scratched my right toe and then slithered and bounced down the last few steps of the flight on my rear, otherwise unharmed. I was phenomenally lucky to escape a broken spine or a fractured skull. After this I 'knew' that suicide bids were useless. Somehow, despite my four frenzied attempts to taste of death, I wasn't really 'meant' to die.

Taken back to my side-ward by the nurses, who by now had detected my absence, the taps and clicks began to reinforce such thoughts as 'This is Hell, I am in torment for ever'. Not surprisingly, I eventually broke down screaming and, when a number of doctors and nurses rushed into my room, asked for 'voluntary anaesthesia' (I meant euthanasia).

'Do you want to *die*?' said a nurse severely in a deep voice, approaching me with a syringe. I nodded. Obviously this was at last the final curtain. But in fact I was injected with anti-psychotic drugs (major tranquillisers) and, to my surprise, woke up in Banstead Hospital, a young Indian male nurse gazing down on me with a wry smile. He encouraged me to wake up and told me where I was. As he walked away from my bed on my awakening I said, or rather wailed after him: 'Is there any *hope*?' (I meant of saving my soul), to which he replied, turning back to me as he did so, but in a tone of confident, almost sinister self-satisfaction: 'We *always* succeed.'

This cryptic comment (like all the others) did me no good at all. I took it to mean that the Organisation 'always succeeded' in totally destroying who-ever they chose. Not at all what *he* meant. I arose from my bed expecting the worst. But my time in Banstead Hospital (now closed) was to prove very brief. I did not like the time-worn and antiquated state of the ward and buildings, the dated furniture, the absence of knives with which to eat, the (to me rather sinister) uncommunicative 'smouldering' quality of the other patients (Organisation stooges I thought) and the decrepit toilets. There was nothing to do, no one to talk to and nowhere to go – only to smoulder in dreadful thoughts. It is true that surroundings such as those do not help anyone. I asked (amazingly) if I could go back to Charing Cross and when a bed was vacant and my operation scheduled I was transferred. The drugs had reduced me to a near trance-like state, my delusions vaguely present but muted. I remember Banstead as if through a gauze-covered lens.

Back in Charing Cross and feeling a lot better for that, I was prepared for surgery, and fell asleep quickly under the pre-med. The next thing I remember was awakening to see my right hand down at my side feeling good and in comfortable bandages. Then I suddenly realised – and anti-psychiatrists should take note of this – that my delusions, in all their complexity and emotional force, and my horrific coprolalia and rappings had *totally vanished*!

Whether there had been a change of medication I don't know (I think there had) but I felt as sane as anyone, quite refreshed in mind, and despite the gauntlet of knives I had just run, I wanted to go home immediately. As if by magic, the psychosis was finished – it was as though an unbearable and excruciating horror film had suddenly, in a flash, been revealed as 'only a dream'.[3]

Chapter 5

Hospital life when sane

One does not love a place less for having suffered in it.

(Jane Austen, *Persuasion*)

After readmission to Charing Cross Hospital on 18 September 1979 I had essentially turned the corner in my careering headlong flight into oblivion and gently readjusted to everyday reality. In this chapter I will therefore outline the incidents and strategies that were so critical in my (quite rapid) revival and recuperation in hospital (and shortly afterwards) as these may act as useful guides for workers in this field. (In Charing Cross my treatment team (on Ward 3 West) was headed by three psychiatrists (but no psychologists): Steven Hirsch,[1] Geetha Oomen and Malcolm Weller.)

THE VALUE OF HOPE AND OF SPIRITUAL INTERVENTION

Given the spiritual and religious nature of my delusions, it was a great source of comfort to be able to regularly visit the chapel on the ground floor of the hospital. Visits from paraprofessionals such as the chaplain and from Reverend Richard Harries[2] – who, actually, I had seen on the night before the first suicide attempt (see Chadwick 1992, Chapter 4) – were also of tremendous value. They eased me out of seeing God as potentially vicious and punitive, a common attitude among psychotic people and an attitude that had been planted there by doorstep Jehovah's Witnesses some fourteen years before as well as by Old Testament readings at school. This dissolution of my image of 'the savage God' gave me much peace and (most important of all): hope. This was very critical to my recovery. Indeed, I would say that hope was as important as any pill (see Nunn 1996).

It was also useful for me to have my 'possession delusion' cognitively disentangled by talking with vicars. It really should have been obvious to me that anyone who *really was* possessed by Satan would hardly rush in a frenzy to kill themselves to save others from dying. He or she would be far more likely to relish or ignore the pain and destruction they thought they were causing. Also, with my new calmness of mind I saw the vain and sybaritic deeds that had caused me so much guilt as relatively trivial when measured against the scale of evil that some people had perpetrated. I came to realise that I was, after all, what Alan Watts (1978) would call 'an average sinner'.

Arguments from a religious framework to the effect that Satan does sometimes trick people into *thinking* they're possessed (e.g. Peck 1988), although obviously not scientific, certainly made sense of much of what I experienced and (despite their irrationality) were comforting. Repeated talk of the wonderful *forgiveness* power of God also helped to rekindle my inner sense of hope and self-worth which was to prove so crucial for the future. It is interesting that, despite the quite incredible power of the medication to wipe out symptoms (for which I will always be grateful) the inner feelings of downheartedness and guilt were still there – but responded well to these admittedly 'non-scientific' methods. Panscientists should be mindful of this.

My own religiosity, limited though it was, also came to my assistance. Some two years later, there was a recurrence of the rappings, much louder this time, shortly after I had been discharged from an aftercare hostel and was living in the community in a basement flat with my future wife Jill. Jill could also hear them (as had others before) and was understandably very frightened. I decided to attack them not with a feeling of anger and not with reason (which by now I knew was useless) but by reading the New Testament. Somehow I completely trusted this act to defeat what I truly felt was a manifestation of evil. I sensed that no cognitive intervention had the slightest hope against it. Indeed, soon after I started reading, the taps began to lose their synchronisation with the termination of my thoughts. It was as if a machine was starting to malfunction. I sensed an uncanny quality of fear and desperation in the air. By the time I had read some three or four pages any sounds I heard were quite random. Essentially they had gone. I think this event, more than any other, made me realise how utterly stupid I had been to allow my life to be dominated by positivism and empiricism in the 1970s – as if the latter was some kind of moral high ground (Radford 1993) and a sure-fire guide to Truth to be contrasted with 'worthless armchair speculation' (such as that often attributed to Hegel). Repeated readings of Dostoevsky's wonderful *Notes from Underground* confirmed this impression of the naïve, almost schoolboyish arrogance of an exclusively scientific orientation. I now realised that I had faced the territory of madness in 1979 knowing virtually *nothing* of any value. It was time to 'wake up'. The alternative to empirical psychology was not armchair speculation at all but intrepid questing, rather like a romantic and rather like a 'field psychologist', into every crag and ridge of real life and experience – *if necessary with an abyss beside one*. I knew that the subject of psychology would not thrive if everyone sat (as I felt they did) in a safe hollow.

THE VALUE OF WARD AND DAY HOSPITAL CARE

Daily periods at the day hospital at Charing Cross were a great relief in the autumn of 1979 and infinitely more helpful than 'stewing in my own juice' on the wards, friendly and caring though the ward personnel undoubtedly were. The only way I tolerated the boredom of ward life (other than meal-times), before access to the day hospital was allowed, was by incessant exercise of my right hand with a much beloved slab of silicone putty. I was quite mortified when this little item was taken away from me (for use by another patient) when the maximum regainable function of the hand had been achieved. The fact that one can become so devoted to a slab of putty in these circumstances shows how stressful and uneventful ward life really is. Because of this it is of no surprise to me that Hirsch *et al.* (1979) and Knights *et al.* (1980) found brief stays of a week or two to be no less useful than standard stays of six or so weeks. Dick *et al.* (1985) are also positive about the value of day hospitals and comment, after a controlled study, on their high patient satisfaction and greater opportunities for patient–staff contact (Paykel and Marshall 1991). (See also Sutherland (1992b) on the stressful boredom of life on the wards.)

One of the great advantages of the day hospital and its activities was the *structure* to the day, which was otherwise only punctuated by much-longed-for meals. Also the chance for sustained talk and conversation was some relief from the state of continually attending to drug side-effects. Fragile or psychotic patients may be inclined to make a great deal out of short cryptic remarks from nurses – *indeed such remarks are best left unsaid* – but in sustained day hospital talk most ambiguities can be resolved. One also has a chance at last to make real contact with other human beings after the claustrophobic, closed-in, isolated and narcissistic months of private psychotic thought.

Contact with people while on the wards was in contrast fairly limited except during ward-round chats. Although the nurses, sister and matron were friendly, caring and supportive, the surgery on my hand brilliant, the physiotherapeutic advice excellent, the surroundings modern and the beds comfortable, there was inevitably what seemed like aeons of time during the day when one had simply to be left to one's own devices. Other patients were not very communicative (largely because of the medication) and as I did not smoke I could not interrupt the flow of time with cigarettes, as many other patients did. Without my beloved (and as it turned out exceedingly useful) putty-squeezing exercises I really do not know what I would have done – as one was always sternly reproved for lying on one's bed (watching television was unbearable because of drug side-effects). Added to this I had terrible constipation from the medication – something not to be made light of – and eventually had to have an enema. During the ensuing evacuation I eagerly and fervently kissed the hand of the nurse who gave it to me, so blissful was the relief from the week-long torment of this enormous impacted stool which had staunchly resisted all milder methods. At the time it was actually difficult for me to decide which was the greater agony, the psychotic episode or the constipation. A lower drug dosage (and of course this was in the days of typical neuroleptics) would surely have been just as psychologically effective (see Johnson 1988) and might not have produced such distressing spin-offs. Unlike a GP, who may quite easily suffer from influenza or arthritis and need his or her own pills, psychiatrists, even as part of their training, do not have to take their own medication. During research in which normal volunteers, medical students and physicians have indeed taken low doses of haloperidol (Kendler 1976; Belmaker and Wald 1977; Anderson *et al.* 1981) the effects have been distressing and not necessarily ephemeral – with akathisia lasting up to fourteen days after oral ingestion of 5 mg (Anderson *et al.* 1981, 1996). Research of this kind is controversial (King *et al.* 1995; Anderson *et al.* 1996) and not without risk but I believe in principle is valuable for dissolving the barrier between patients and staff as well as for alerting staff, at least to some degree (Anderson *et al.* 1996), to how unpleasant the side-effects really are.

With akathisia there is never *any* peace from this insistent urge to *move*, be it rock backwards and forwards in a chair, shuffle around the wards, kneel and huddle in a chair or go for a walk. It is like a tinnitus of the body; there is *never* a moment of inner silence. Indeed, going for walks, from the ward to the day hospital and back, from the ward to the chapel and back or out briefly along the Thames when J visited were the nearest I could get to a state of physical equanimity when this side-effect was at its height (for more on this problem see Sachdev 1995). But I remember one day staring into a mirror on Ward 3 West at Charing Cross. My eyeballs were bulging, my skin was greasy and grainy, my hair like rats' tails, I was stiffened and troubled by constipation and simultaneously racked by akithisia – worsened perhaps by the fact that I was apparently anaemic at the time.[3] I looked like everybody's image of a mental patient – but it was entirely a medication effect. Reflecting on the pathetic sight that met my eyes I thought to myself, 'Now I know that the days of the old mind *really are* dead. I, as I was, am really and truly *finished*. I start again, this time from the bottom, not with all my mother's self-sacrificial help but I make my *own* life, my own Self, and do it *my* way this time.' This was perhaps something that I'd always cryptically wanted. That day on the wards, for all the bad things I may say about the side-effects of medication, was nonetheless a final breaking of the umbilical cord with my mother and with the past and was a truly new beginning. 'Rebirthing' may not be a scientifically respectable therapy, but I can certainly understand that it *could* have tremendously powerful effects for some people at the right time.

The umbilical cord with the hospital was severed gradually by frequent walks out in Fulham with J (non-trivially this also helped me to readjust to *traffic* and the noisy life of the city), visits back to Rigault Road, where I was living, to see my labrador dog Penny and John Yates (who was kindly looking after her) and through chats with visitors. The siting of the hospital right in the middle of the city was very helpful in preventing feelings of alienation from the community. I also made a number of friends in the day hospital and one on the wards – Elaine Gallagher. Because of my damaged hand Elaine would always peel my (constipation-preventing) orange for me at meal times because at first I could not. We had many long talks and many chuckles and are friends to this day.

GENERAL IMPRESSION

On reflection, as a genuine patient not a pseudopatient faking illness (as was the case, for example, in reports by Goldman 1970; Weitz 1972; Rosenhan 1973; and Reynolds and Farberow 1976), I simply cannot adopt a complaining stance about the way I was treated in hospital. I came out in an infinitely better state than when I went in! I was listened to seriously and attentively; my requests, e.g. to move from modecate injections to pimozide or haloperidol tablets; to have a day's leave to sort out financial problems (despite recent suicide attempts);[4] to be moved from Banstead to Charing Cross; to be put on an 'anti-constipation diet', were all complied with quickly and treated with respect. Doctors did not look straight over or through me, they treated me like a substantial human being and were very sympathetic, especially concerning the *terrible* feelings of humiliation I had about my delusions. Nurses did not generally adopt a controlling, domineering attitude but were usually sensitive, responsive and human. Even ward domestics played a significant role in my recovery (see also Durlak 1979 and Hattie *et al.* 1984 on the great value of paraprofessional help). The medical, surgical and psychiatric treatment that I received was as good, it seemed to me, as the degree of development of the respective disciplines at that time would permit.

The only really substantive criticisms that I feel can be levelled at my treatment team are that first: they too, at times, showed evidence of the same bias, to seek *confirmation* of their ideas, that I too had had when ill and that had landed me as a patient right in their lap! Second: the community's attitude to psychiatric patients as inferior beings would also *just occasionally* show itself or 'leak out' in unguarded or ambiguous circumstances – although this was *exceptional* rather than usual. More on these complaints in the later chapter on therapy (Chapter 13).

I was discharged from in-patient treatment on 30 October 1979 on 6 mg of pimozide to be taken at night and 50 mg of disipal to be taken three times daily. This medication was later changed to chlorpromazine. My case notes of the day strangely describe me as having improved 'extremely slowly' but this was not the subjective experience. The staff apparently felt 'that although he was doing well, there was a possibility that he was withholding information from us'. This latter remark was correct. I was extremely unhappy about going back to live in Fulham and was grateful eventually to obtain, via my social worker, a place in a hostel. The case notes concluded with, 'a few days prior to discharge Peter was doing extremely well . . . all laboratory investigations were normal'.

My diagnosis was changed from 'acute schizophrenic episode' on admission to 'atypical hypomania' to 'mild chronic hypomania' (at worst schizoaffective illness). My social worker's report to the hostel that I moved to terminated with:

> I feel, though Peter intellectually realises his difficulties and problems, he has not been able to accept them or work them through. He, at this stage, is very changeable and needs a firm handling. I hope in a supportive therapeutic setting Peter will be able to work through his feelings, relationships etc., and learn to be a more confident, independent person.

Amen to that.

REFLECTIONS

The 'drug removal' of my delusions was a remarkable testament to the likelihood that, although disordered thinking may encroach on a person over years, even decades (and presumably involves the operation over time of the whole brain), it can none the less eventuate in malfunction in a relatively restricted array of 'final common pathways' which can be chemically targeted. It has none the less to be said that for this drug removal to be maintained over years, spiritual, psychosocial and cognitive-behavioural methods were required – otherwise medication dosage would have needed to have been extremely high.

At an experiential level the low dose of maintenance medication on which to this day I rely (2.5 mg haloperidol nocte) has had its greatest impact on reducing both felt anger and on pressured subvocal speech. There was no noticeable *short-term* effect of either the episode or the medication on subsequent IQ, sex drive, self-esteem, guilt or social extraversion–introversion. Again in the short term, degree of *socialisation* if not *sociability* was somewhat improved, as was anxiety – but over the long term body weight has rocketed while on medication from 130 lb. (about 9 stones) in September 1979 to 224 lb. (16 stones) in the summer of 1996 – not something women readers will take lightly (see Stanton 1995). Attentional control also considerably and rapidly improved on anti-psychotic drugs. I personally doubt that any of these changes would have happened anyway except perhaps for the enhanced degree of socialisation with age (see adult age trends (cross-sectional) in EPQ P scores in Eysenck and Eysenck 1975, Figure 2, p. 19).

Long-term changes that medication may well have facilitated, particularly via improved attention and socialisation and decreased anger, are increased self-esteem, improved conversational skills, decreased impulsiveness and self-preoccupied egocentricity and also greater life steadiness via decreased distractibility and decreased novelty seeking. Some inevitable confounding by ageing effects will be involved here but such trends were not at all in evidence during the baseline ten years prior to the episode and treatment.

These medication-induced or facilitated changes do need to be seen in a total life context. The psychodynamically informed reader may argue that my Rogerian meta-perspective (pp. 36–7) is not all there is to this crisis and I think they would be right. To a certain extent it is true that the emotional and physical abuse I took when young has necessitated, with the aid of medication, the construction of an alternative, a second personality – something that many abused children do. Indeed, some create *many* personalities, as in my own conscious way I did too, to reach towards health and enable them to live in the world given what has happened to them (e.g. Thigpen and Cleckley 1954, 1957; Schreiber 1975; Jeans 1976; Ross 1989). But despite my many and varied attempts to kill it, the pre-psychotic 'First Mind' in all its diversity cannot *really* be annihilated. It lives on as a masked, almost buried pattern of complex synaptic connections in the neural networks of my brain – available perhaps but not accessible. The more direct and obvious manifestations of it are hidden behind a state-changing inner cloud of haloperidol medication. The only difference between me and someone who suffers from true Multiple Personality Disorder is that I am, and have always been, fully aware of what I am doing.

The experience which comes with time, and age, does change the weightings of connections in a human brain. No network gestalt is ever really frozen. The First Mind is now somewhat 'dissolved' or diffused but the stored material is still there in long-term memory. But what *can* be changed is the *use* I make of it and the way I interpret it. In this way the First and the Second Mind have something valuable to say to each other.

A kind of (more positive) conceptual integration is none the less possible. Basically, this Second Mind, though partly the result of abuse, is much closer to what I *felt* I was and *wanted* to be anyway. Even in 1977 I sensed that *something*, perhaps an arousal disorder or something at least partly organic, was wrong. I sensed that deep down was *a perfectly normal and healthy personality* but that my mind, raging as it was with bitterness, was at the time like two blocks, one slightly rotated relative to the other. I felt that *if something* could rotate the upper block *just a little* it would be flush with the lower, and all would be OK. I tried consciously to rotate that upper block for years *using only intrapsychic psychology* such as cognition and psychoanalysis. But I failed. Now, in 1996, the blocks are indeed flush.

The then very different hidden or latent healthy personality which I first sensed within even in 1967 and which I strove for – via the many roles that I played – has emerged. But it emerged only with the aid of medication to dampen my angst (at 'unfair treatment') and with the aid of calming, validating and supportive community influences in their many facets. In this alternative bio-psycho-social-spiritual model there was only a slight disorder or 'potential illness' (reflected perhaps in my 'angry young man' and distractible novelty-seeking behaviour) in an otherwise sound mind and person. In this co-existing alternative model, in which a prior but *productive* vulnerability developed unluckily (via rejection and slander) into illness, I do find peace and a kind of integration both experientially and theoretically.

POINTERS TO THE FUTURE

The experiences of neurotic and psychotic patients are worth studying. Allowing patients indeed to research their condition as I have would, I think, be a sound move towards regarding mental health care as a round-table *team* effort in which, rather as in the brain (Allport 1983), the components of that team who have the most relevant information and most appropriate skills temporarily become the focus. This is a true process view. In mental health and mental illness *no one* is 'The Expert'.

The distinction first made by Bertrand Russell between inside knowledge, 'Knowledge by acquaintance', and that obtained by distant objective study, 'Knowledge by description', urgently needs to be dissolved. Researchers who have themselves been ill and thus have both types of knowledge (see also Sutherland 1976; Toates 1990; and Jamison 1996) are essentially 'peer-professionals'. It would surely be extremely valuable for the mental health field if *more* research of this kind was done. Perhaps the admission requirements for access to research degrees could be relaxed for ex-patients to facilitate their entrance. For example, they might be required to have at most an Extra-Mural Psychology Diploma or two or three Open University psychology course credits to their name (a biological one included) rather than a full Upper Second or First Class honours degree. Their own experience, I would propose, should be respected as making up to some extent for the formal knowledge they lack. Also access to other patients for research should be encouraged and facilitated rather than denied (see Chadwick 1993a). Such peer-professionals would clearly and in many ways be valuable links between professional and parapro-fessional spheres. I would suggest that the more people of this ilk we have the better.

Appendix to Chapter 5

Some hints and advice for recovering patients who would like to research their own condition

Man needs difficulties, they are necessary for health.

(Carl Jung)

It is recognised that there needs to be more of an attempt to involve service users themselves in research (Rogers *et al.* 1993, p. 12). This short section is therefore aimed at people recovering from all manner of illnesses, be they mental disorders, neurological problems, general medical problems or whatever. I sincerely hope that some of you reading this will indeed take up my challenge to pursue research in this vein; your inside knowledge, I assure you, will be greatly valued by the professions (see for example Bentall 1992; Claridge 1993; Pilling 1995). Your task will be difficult, perhaps *very* difficult; indeed, I should warn you of this, but it will not by any means be fruitless. In these few pages I will outline some of the problems you could well face in your task, and I'll try and give you some guidelines about how to get started. If you are forewarned you may well be forearmed! You will have to tailor and amend what I say below, however, to fit your own particular scenario.

Poverty

With the exception of cases involving compensation for injury, it is often the case that illness brings about poverty and unemployment (the converse is also true, e.g. Brown and Harris 1978; Newton 1988). This means that you will probably start out with a massive disadvantage. Your finances will be low and you'll probably also feel pretty dejected. In 1980, for example, while I was living in an aftercare hostel, we were only eligible for two or three pounds a week pocket money as our board and food was taken care of. On some days I literally had difficulty finding the few pence required to buy the newspapers which had the job advertisements I was looking for in them. Buying books or collating a typed and photocopied curriculum vitae was usually quite out of the question. The few pounds needed to put together such a multiple-copy document as the latter (and post it!) was far more than I could put my hands on at the time. I would imagine that you are likely to be in a similar predicament. It is vital therefore that you ask your local authority via your social worker if there is *any* way that they can assist you and that you find which library in your borough or area specialises in the kind of books you need. Help with travelling, postage and book-reserving fees could well come your way. Read *everything* you can get your hands on. If you do aspire to a research qualification (it will probably have to be an M.Sc.), your most likely starting point will be either an Open University degree (and the OU has a fund to help the unemployed) or an extra-mural diploma (concessions are always given for the unemployed or the low-waged). You will also need to be knowledgeable about all the potential and relevant registered charities that might help you. Don't omit to write to companies (e.g. drug or medical equipment companies) for support, but show them that you have made an effort to know your subject and that you have an inkling, however slight, about what you can contribute. If you are in residential care, the local authority may still help you. In my case my rent was reduced to help me make daily visits to London University library and to purchase writing paper and stamps in order to write to professionals in the field I was studying.

Contacting professionals

If a research degree is out of your reach, you may well find that profession-als in your geographical and/or research area would be keen to collaborate with you. Sufferers of various conditions (even autism) have published 'inside story' reports (e.g. Williams 1992) in learned journals or books helped and backed by staff at local hospitals, day centres or research insti-tutes (e.g. Wigoder 1987; Jolliffe *et al.* 1992; Blaska 1995). There are also numerous 'first person accounts' published in the journal *Schizophrenia Bulletin*; in the newsletters of the SANE charity and in the magazine *Open Mind*. The important thing is that you don't just sit there in lonely isolation in your bedsitter, flat or house. *Write* to the local hospital department or the local psychology department, whatever is appropriate, and tell them that you *exist*. Let them know that you want to become knowledgeable about your illness and that you might be able also to contribute to the profession's knowledge of it were you to be given the chance to do so. The jaws of good research scientists are always dripping with saliva at the chance of a new lead; it is highly unlikely that they will ignore you. If they *do* then you know it is a poor or complacent department; go elsewhere, *but don't give up*. You are bound to eventually reach a listening ear.

The peer network

Don't try and do what you do entirely out of your own head. Contact *other* sufferers and share your experiences. This basically amounts to 'fieldwork' but it's therapeutic for all concerned. You may find, and this is certainly the case with most sufferers of mental illness, that they are far more open with you than they are with the doctors and nurses, etc. There is no status gap when they talk to you and they feel relaxed in the knowledge that you *really do* understand and sympathise with how they feel and what they are saying. Forming self-help groups is useful here (e.g. Orford 1992). Whatever you do, however, *don't*, I repeat *don't*, start advising other sufferers to take this or that medication or to change their medication or give it up. Medically qualified professionals may not know what the drugs *feel* like but they are infinitely more sophisticated than you are on their behavioural effects. They have treated hundreds, even thousands of patients with various combinations of this and that drug and although they don't usually have insider acquaintance of drug consequences this immense observational knowledge that they have deserves your respect. They will also know of such things as drug combination and withdrawal effects and the (sometimes dangerous) results of taking drugs with certain foodstuffs – of which you could well be *totally* ignorant.

You will probably find that other sufferers are eager to help you. At the beginning of my research, which eventually led to a second Ph.D., I said to a number of friends in London who had suffered delusional thinking, 'Look, I've done years of psychology, I'm going to *research* what's happened to us and find out what causes it. I'll help you out and tell you all about what I find if you'll be a guinea pig in the project. How about it?' Nobody refused. Once again London people said, 'Go for it Peter.' This is very likely to be what you will find too – but it will only be so if you work with mutual respect and are *fair* and empathic in your dealings with them.

Don't get tunnel vision

Researching your own condition is fascinating, but maybe it can be even a little too fascinating. The great danger here is that you will become sophisticated in only a very narrow area which is relevant to you (stress itself can narrow your vision). Don't for goodness sake let this happen. Read widely and become informed about the general field which includes your illness. You will find that material in areas well removed from your topic none the less is very relevant to it – and digesting it also makes a refreshing change from continually pondering one issue.

Motivation and Empowerment

Where there's a will there's a way. So, as Nietzsche said, 'if you have a "why" to live for you will make do with almost any "how"'. If you really believe in what you're doing, feel sure that you have something to offer and you also *enjoy* the field that your illness has 'landed' you into, you have a very good chance of ending up in print and being asked to communicate your work in the relevant field. If you don't feel that you're tremendously bright you may not have to worry that much. It will amaze you what years of immersion in a topic of great personal relevance will do to your powers of memory, thought and communication. Indeed, the research will change you as a person to a degree that could surprise you – and could be a useful alternative to just 'feeling ill' but powerless to do anything about it. Research into your own condition definitely empowers you and can give you a multitude of coping techniques.

Prejudice

You are bound at times to come up against prejudice – and arrogance. Particularly if you've been *mentally* ill you are bound to come across people who think your mental disorder disqualifies you a priori from having *anything* useful or meaningful of your own to say about anything. Some people (not many) have reacted to me in that way over the years, usually psychodynamic psychotherapists. In one case (not in print), from a 'distinguished psychotherapist', the remarks were so offensive and insulting that they would undoubtedly have counted as libel had they been published. It is extremely important that you still keep going after interfacing in one way or another with people of that kind. There is no theoretical reason whatever why your illness should automatically induce areas of severe psychic blindness in you when contemplating and reflecting on what has happened to you or indeed on anything else. Whatever you do, do not be brought to a standstill by prejudice and arrogance. Fight it. If you have something to say, go ahead, keep working, keep thinking and say it.

Get a little help from your friends

Even counting the support of other sufferers, social workers, research men and women, you will find it extra hard going without the help and faith of other friends and family. In my case my wife and pals have stood by me through thick and thin, the research *could not* have been done without them. Don't try to be a Robinson Crusoe character; there is no reason why the community should not get involved in what you are doing. (Families, for example, could seek empowerment by *themselves* researching family processes – as could anorexics and bulimia sufferers.) It is after all, in essence, research from the community anyway. Let it explicitly be that in character.

Don't be all negative

It is very easy in a research project on illness and disorder to focus exclusively on malfunction, suffering, deficit and pain (Gergen 1990). In the schizophrenia research field, many professionals have succumbed to this cyclopean approach. Don't let it happen to you. Many people have turned their illness around and put it to their own advantage – and to the advantage of others. This is after all what you are doing anyway. Damage and disorder is also not always totally dysfunctional. To speak of damage: the terrible injury to my hand in 1979 (but thanks also to the surgery) has actually made it a *better* instrument for writing than a normal hand. The reason for this is that my pen sits snugly in a curved indentation in the bone in the second finger of my right hand and so I can write for unlimited time – even fifteen-hour stretches – without *any* of the pain in the phalanges that people normally suffer (for example during exams).

To speak of disorder: sickle-cell anaemia, for example, confers relative immunity to certain types of malarial infections and indeed it has been argued that such functional genetic mutations may be more common than we realise and genuinely *necessary* to the gene pool as a protective survival device (Suzuki and Knudtson 1990; Jamison 1993).

Speaking generally: it is also true that various 'pathological' conditions such as paranoia, manic-depression and depression do have their functions. Paranoia may motivate avoidance and withdrawal – and hence aid survival (Jarvik and Deckard 1977); manic depression can facilitate creativity and achievement, particularly in artists and writers (Storr 1972, 1987; Jamison 1993); and depression in one person may stimulate altruistic and supportive co-operative behaviour in others, as Charles Darwin suggested, as well as being a time for critical reflection about the feasibility of one's current life goals and a time for renewal of resources.

Oliver Sacks (1986) describes a man ('Witty Ticcy Ray') who was a keen drummer but, like me, had Tourette Syndrome partly in the form of a movement tic (this is its more usual manifestation). To cope with his problem while on stage he would creatively embed his involuntary tic movements into his routine(!) thereby producing some brilliantly novel sequences (Sacks 1986, p. 92). The beauty of spirit of learning-disabled children; the empathy of some neurosis sufferers (as Jung knew); the islets of ability in some autistics (Davison and Neale 1994, pp. 477–9); the poetry of speech of patients with Wernicke's aphasia; the entrepreneurial skills of some psychopaths and the extraordinary fiction and art of individuals with sexual paraphilias and 'off-centre' sexuality (e.g. the work of Aubrey Beardsley, Patrick Robinson and Marcelo Benfield) all testify to the fact that survival and evolution are not simplistic processes in which only flawless 'James Bond'-style characters are highly functional. Physical, neurotic and psychotic conditions can have their uses and can even confer advantages, depending on the magnitude of the difficulties and on the situations encountered. Do not ever allow yourself to lose sight of this.

Good luck!

If you decide to get yourself involved in a quest of this kind you are likely to need quite a bit of luck on your side. In my case I was commissioned out of the blue to write an article on perception for Marshall Cavendish Partworks back in 1981 (Chadwick 1981) just as I was looking around for some way to pay my first-year part-time Ph.D. fees at Bedford College. The payment for the article pretty well paid the fees! Then I managed to get a couple of part-time teaching jobs (itself a therapeutic move, Bell *et al.* 1996) and the flywheel of my life at last began to accelerate. (These could be considered to be 'fresh start events', which are known to be highly therapeutic (Brown 1991).) Most of the money for my research on schizophrenia and borderline states has come out of my own pocket (all the (pretty penniless) scientific research councils of the early and mid-1980s – who were struggling themselves – refused to help; something that may happen to you as well) but support from elsewhere did come along when I really needed it – mainly from industrial and literary bodies. Somehow one gets the job done, as it *must* be done. Sometimes even the uncanny gives us a little help along the way. May Lady Luck be with you!

The Aftermath

A final comment: If you do eventually reach the printed page or the radio interviewer's microphone with your story and with your interpretations this is not, alas, by any means the end of the matter. There will be an aftermath and you must be forewarned about it and ready for it. Western society stigmatises the mentally ill and also the neurologically damaged – but it is not particularly well disposed to illness of any kind really. It will take some nerve to write up your condition and there are going to be some negative consequences. There are quite a few people I have known (but not known well) who (even if contacted) I none the less have never heard from again after they read the first account of my illness in *Borderline* (Chadwick 1992), in which the sinister spiritual aspect of the crisis is stressed very strongly. Others (again not many) disappeared from my circle of contacts after my second publication (Chadwick 1993b) emerged, possibly because the description of the *acute* phase of my illness was so graphic and this is known to increase stigma (Penn *et al.* 1994). I also heard a student say to another laughingly, 'I told her I've got a lecturer who's Satan!' Others, of a psychodynamic psychotherapeutic persuasion, have sometimes put scornful, contemptuous and obnoxious interpretations on my case. There is also the danger of course that some colleagues, if you've been mentally ill, will see you as 'unreliable' or as a 'bad risk' to cite. All these things are unavoidable and have to be faced and lived down.

Generally, however, the chances are that most people will look, as they usually do anyway, on the bright side and will be constructive and positive about you and what you have done. It is important, however, not to be complacent or too sure, even though it is true that you do know your condition from the inside. In the end research is a team effort; we are all in a side playing not against each other but against a powerful opponent – the gestalt of ignorance, prejudice and fear. Sometimes we even score 'own goals', but hopefully the *real* aftermath of what you do will be knowledge, understanding and care. I guess on the grand scale of things these have to be considered as prior to one's own petty fears. Let us hope then that peer professional research will increase and hopefully contribute over the years to the 'higher good' of the helping professions: that of the *prevention* of illness and the related enhancement of *health*.

Chapter 6

Desmond
Comedian mystic[1]

There up and spoke a brisk little somebody, critic
and whippersnapper in a rage, to set things right.
(Robert Browning, *Balaustion's Adventure*)

INTRODUCTORY SKETCH

Desmond, when I first met him, was an adult student of mine on an uncon-
ventional course I was running at the so-called 'Working Men's College' in
North London in 1985. The course was unusual: it was called 'Supernormal
Psychology'(!) and was basically an antidote, rather as this book is, to
the emphasis on the abnormal in psychology (see also Maslow 1968, 1971,
1973 on this). The first time I remember him speaking up in class was in a
lecture I gave on some aspects of humour. Rather contrary to the spirit of
the course I argued that, according to some views, comedians should be
neurotic (and perhaps underneath it all, angry), both statements with which
he heartily concurred. Perhaps it also was something about the way he
spoke and the spontaneity of his agreement but he had a penetrating effect.
I did not know at the time that he had been a professional comedian himself
spotted in *The Melody Maker* at the same time as the Rolling Stones and
Bob Dylan(!). But none the less I felt: 'This is a man who knows himself.'

Desmond became a lively contributor to class discussions but when
eventually I moved the lecture topics deep into the areas of mysticism and
the occult he left. But it was not because of lack of interest – it was obvious
to me during a chat we had at one of the coffee breaks that I could teach
him nothing in these areas.

Desmond is a small man, drawn in the face, only about 5' 4" tall and
with a rather frail bird-like frame. Although physically he is a diminutive
figure, there is a strange quality about him which makes him seem as if he
is occupying more space than tangibly is the case. This in fact is slightly
unnerving; indeed, irrational though it sounds, there are times when
Desmond seems to 'fill' the room he is in. I have 'seen' this at the Royal
Festival Hall, where we now meet regularly – and of course that is some
space! It is not at all clear to me why this is so. He projects a curious blend

Figure 6.1 Desmond Marshall
Source: Carol Quinn

of vitality and sadness. At times he has a rather portentous stillness about him (even when walking), yet his eyes may be darting everywhere. When seated he holds his head very slightly raised, so his (rather prominent) nose is ever so fractionally upturned. He also seems to have a quality of 'waiting' or 'readiness' about him – as if *something* involving him is surely soon to 'happen'. This is also rather disturbing, as if a kind of 'field' emanates from him, into the future (see below and also p. 69).

Des provides us with a running commentary on his thoughts in a book he was trying to write a few years ago entitled *The Leper Man Walks*. The section below focuses on his stream of consciousness as he treks through the streets and alleyways:

He went out into the street knowing his alienation would envelop him like a protective cloud. He felt numb inside, each step was an effort, as his feet touched the sloping uneven ground of the paved stones.

The streets were cold and grey. Looking at some of the faces of the people some looked as if they were in Hell. With their haggard grief-stricken expressions and vacant eyes they wandered the dirty litter filled roads.

He was an outsider looking in. He felt he never belonged to any particular group of people but mixed with them all. . . . A leper who walks the streets of an urban town.

The streets made him uneasy. People seemed to stare at him as he walked. Mostly men – and more so big men. They seemed wary of him somehow. He had to avoid staring back. The streets were filled with tension, and aggression wasn't far away. One man who happened to stare at him too long got a mouthful as he walked by – but he just walked on without turning round.

The streets were important to him. He needed time to get rid of the pent-up feelings inside him. The long walks used to relax him enough so that he could sleep at night. The nights were times of nostalgia of past memories. Memories he wasn't sure belonged to him – like times when he used to wait at the institution gate of the home he was in, waiting for his mother to visit him. Waiting, waiting, waiting, the long drawn-out space of endless time. And now his life seemed to be one long wait – waiting, waiting. For what? Inside him he knew he had the answer, but dared not rake through too deeply the turbid depth of his knowing.

Here Desmond hopefully comes across. A sad and sensitive, at times tormented body and a harrowed soul thrown into the brutal wood of life. Periodically a refugee from reality yet noticing things that are usually only detected by the eyes of the deaf and the ears of the blind. He once told me something that John Lennon had said, namely: 'I am a violent man, that is why I talk about love.' This was a statement that resonated deeply in Des. As the reader will see, he too has had a life tinged with the violence of the Krays and the Richardsons – and perhaps that is partly why he too is a man of peace and of love. Yet, like me, Des also carries his past with him, some of it deeply buried, some of it more evident, and this past, as Kelly (1955) would expect, although not totally explaining him, is none the less what much of his present thinking has had to come to terms with.

Des is very 'fluent on self' to a degree that at times smacks of an obsessive self-preoccupation. This is a flaw. His background, as we will see, has cultivated his sense of humour, which he uses extravertedly to 'hold' audiences, however small. This slightly dominating quality none the less is expressed in ways for which his friends do not chide him (although at times we should). Despite a rather lovelorn background, particularly when he was very young he is a very endearing man.

He speaks quickly, with a London accent, often with eyes enlarged and pressure to his (rather poetic) words as if he *must* say what he is saying and one *must* hear it and *fully* understand. Desmond indeed takes badly to being misunderstood and can even be mildly insulting (at least to me) when this happens. Perhaps he has been misunderstood just too much in his life and can barely tolerate any further instances. But it could be deeper than this. Jean Cocteau (1891–1963) once wrote that the worst tragedy for a poet is to be esteemed through being misunderstood!

Desmond is a chameleon. He simply cannot provide reliable answers on personality questionnaires and on meeting him one never quite knows how the day has found him. What gives him his stability, at a level deeper than that of his changeable persona, is, amongst other things, his commitment to *empathy and love* and the basically mystical knowledge he has amassed over the last thirty or so years. Via all these things he lives a life at the borderline but without any anti-psychotic drugs. He is a testament to the use of an adaptive strategy that makes no recourse to biochemistry.

BRIEF BIOGRAPHY

Born on 31 March 1941, in Suffolk, during the Second World War, Des spent his childhood, from the age of about 2 months through to 11 years, away from his mother in convalescent homes in the wooded country-side because of disabling eczema and asthma. In a way he never really recovered from this awful separation. He also suffered from pneumonia, diphtheria and a mastoid in the early 1940s and very nearly died on two occasions. Really he was brought up by nurses and sisters. His father was Jewish, his mother Church of England. She later converted to Judaism but Desmond rejected it. Desmond's physical disabilities were in many ways his salvation from very destructive influences. His father knew both the Kray twins and the Richardsons, who opposed the Krays, and worked for the Richardsons in a cut-price store in Brixton, South London. When Desmond emerged from convalescent home at 11, he was pitched through-out his teenage years into a world of anti-social people, street fighting and 'birds and booze'. He survived through his sense of humour. Though not at all identifying with them, he could make gang members laugh while playing the macho role well enough to get by. Fast reflexes (and a sharp tongue) settled many arguments one way or another.

Desmond's chronic eczema turned him into a revolving-door hospital patient but this at least reduced the amount of contact he had with criminals. The agony of eczema all over his body was also to make him eventually attempt to go *beyond* the body to the spiritual level of awareness. At first his method of dealing with it was to say 'I feel *nothing*'. But this was no use. Indeed, eczema (the Greek word literally means 'to boil') was to become not a leprous curse but Desmond's 'gift handicap'. He knew there was *plenty* of feeling there. As his younger brother said, without it he simply would not be the Desmond Marshall that we know. In fact, he could not *be* Desmond Marshall *at all*. He intuited, however, that he would have to change his life context radically if he was to throw off aggressive street-life values. But to do so too soon would make him unable to cope in the scenario in which he found himself (see also Bender 1976, p. 60 on this).

He didn't like working for his look-alike father. His strange pedantic ways were irritating and they had occasional violent disagreements. Indeed, Desmond once dropped him to his knees with a punch – but ironically gained his respect by doing so.

His relations with his very moody and extraordinarily neurotic mother were little better. In late 1963, at just 22, in the middle of this quagmire, he attempted suicide by overdose and was hovering in a blissful state between life and death for many long hours – happy that he was dying. But this event was to produce not his own extinction but the first of the many strange coincidences that were later to pepper his adult years. Seemingly deep in coma, he suddenly awoke, sat bolt upright in bed with eyes staring and shouted out, 'Who's dead? Who's *dead*? Who's *dead*?' His startled mother quickly replied 'No one!' Then he immediately slumped back into stupor. He was subsequently to learn, without surprise, that President Kennedy had been assassinated while he had lain there at death's door. After this suicide attempt, his reflective capabilities, which he claims had been there since he was 5, started to accelerate. He desperately wanted to know why he existed. After all, why was Kennedy dead and he alive? Had he somehow paranormally *sensed* Kennedy's death? It sounds ludicrous but perhaps he had. It was this train of unsettling events and their immediate impact that awoke Desmond's spiritual consciousness. Returning from the borderline between life and death had kindled a flame in him that no amount of bodily or psychic torment was ever to extinguish.

The effect of this spiritual flame on Desmond's life was relentless but gradual; not superficially apparent to others at first. Always a man who felt that he looked odd – but who had none the less always made people laugh – he worked as a popular professional comedian at Butlin's holiday camps and in clubs between 1970 and 1974 (and later from 1988 to 1990), with the stage name 'Dizzy Desey', but dropped the stage career as a serious endeavour largely through ill-health but also when he felt it was becoming too much of an egoistic experience. After his days in show business he became anonymous and worked as a luggage handler at Britannia Airways – and took advantage of cut-price flights around the world. But during time off, he took to reading *An Autobiography of a Yogi* by Paramahansa Yogananda. This was to be a transforming experience. It firmly set him on the spiritual path.

Over the years that followed he read with passion: Gurdjieff, Ouspensky, Sartre, Camus, Meisster Eckhart, Colin Wilson, the teachings of Sai Baba, the healer Edgar Cayce and those of St John of the Cross all being deeply influential.

But while such people have helped Desmond validate his spiritual self, he has also needed, as he puts it, to be 'grounded'. He has thankfully never lost touch with the down-to-earth and practical matters of life (something a mystic can very easily do), and this has been thanks to a completely unsung friend of his, a man called Fred Robinson, who sadly died in 1992. Fred was in the Black Watch regiment in the Second World War. He was an ardent Socialist and had a family of seven boys and two girls. He treated Des like one of his sons and always helped to return him to the here-and-now, the immediate, the present. Fred was a vital influence in Des's life in providing care, love, balance and a sense of belonging, a sense of rootedness. All of his family, Des included, somehow cannot believe he is no longer with them. Des himself is obviously still reeling from his loss as Fred in many ways gave him the family he never really had.

One of the cardinal features of Desmond is the way that he does indeed allow his feelings to buffet him; there is no room for stoicism and spartan denial of affect in his soul. So, unlike the vast majority of men, Desmond is one man who really *can* cry! He has cried for Fred as he has cried for everyone.

OF WHAT USE IS A MYSTIC?

Widely travelled and quite widely read, what has he to offer to life? Desmond, alas, is one of our many millions of unemployed. He exists on invalidity benefit, his legs and arms still racked with the agony of eczema to the extent that some nights he sleeps not at all. Officially Desmond 'has no job'. His extreme sensitivities sometimes hamper him. For Des doing is not *being*. To quote him: 'If I do without being I am dead.' The paradox is that he operates in the world and loves people and humanity through the state and act of being – but 'has no job'. Are people of this ilk of any *real* use to society in these days when marketability counts for so much, indeed for some counts for *all*?

Perhaps it could be said that Desmond is *vital* to the world? He is in a way a kind of 'street mystic' – rather than one who lives remotely in the hills or in the temple. Rather in the spirit of a community psychologist (Bender 1976; Orford 1992) his is a *seeking* rather than a *waiting* mode. Des is *present* in the world, *there* on Regent Street, in Camden Town, on Oxford Street. A 'café cosmopolite', he roves the sandwich bars of Drury Lane, High Holborn and Bloomsbury as if 'everywhere', talking, talking, talking. He breaks all the capitalist rules yet he brings people together, gives ministries at Quaker meetings, inspires, yet 'has no job'. Weaving tales across café tables he takes away the lofty, pious quality of mysticism, makes it relevant, and available to all. 'The only difference between Jesus and me and everybody else is that Jesus *knew* what he was.' He goes on: 'Other people do not. They don't see their own divinity! I am *consciously* aware of God. For most the presence of God is unconscious.'

But despite these portentous remarks, there is really no heavy quality to his talk. My wife even thinks of him as a 'comedian mystic', rather as was Oscar Wilde, using comedy to rip aside the pretence of forced erudition or fashionable ideas to plunge through to raw truth (e.g. short of cash in a café one day: 'Jesus didn't pay for the Last Supper').

'By their fruits shall you know them' was one of the teachings of Jesus. Des really in his own way could be seen as a cementer of the world. A deeply empathic man who lives at a level deeper and higher than the action movies, computer games, fashion shows, fast cars and Mediterranean holidays. He is a man who inhabits a realm which is the *real* foundation of life. The world of love, of meaning and compassion, of the absolute *essentials* without which ritzy glitzy life could not obtain at all.

THE UNCANNY

The thinking of this man is clearly far removed, both in form and in content, from anything that most academic researchers in the human sciences are familiar with – unless they happen to meet people of this kind as patients. It is known that although 68 per cent of British adults do believe in God (Cox and Cowling 1989), 67 per cent of psychiatrists do not (Neeleman and King 1993), and hence it is very difficult for professionals such as these to establish 'joint reference' (Freeman *et al*. 1982) with people like Desmond. It is doubtful that they could productively help him even were he to consult them and indeed it may be that such professionals in the field of psychopathology have counter-transference difficulties with those of Desmond's ilk and underestimate the health of religiously minded people (see Shams and Jackson 1993; Neeleman and Persaud 1995).

Although volatile, Desmond's scores on the psychometric measure of schizotypal personality, the STA (Jackson and Claridge 1991), oscillate over time (three testings over two years) in the upper half of the range reported in that validation study (his scores range from 20 to 24), given a mean for normal males of only 13.00, SD 7.43 (N = 97) (Jackson and Claridge 1991, p. 316). His most noticeable 'symptoms', to speak medically, are occasional ideas of reference; excessive social anxiety; 'odd' beliefs and magical thinking; unusual perceptual experiences and speech (perhaps) that a standard-minded diagnostician might easily regard also as odd. He has also suffered from inordinate paranoid ideation concerning people's reactions to his appearance. However, it has to be said here in his defence that he certainly does not look like a prototypical Englishman.

Believers in the paranormal, clairvoyance, 'sixth sense' and so on have many cognitive biases which sustain these beliefs (French 1992). However, it is recognised by researchers that believers in the paranormal *really do* score more highly on tests of telepathy than non-believers (Schmeidler and McConnell 1958; Palmer 1971). Hence a cynical attitude to such belief is not warranted by the evidence – and indeed in this light it is arguable whether such convictions should be regarded as symptomatic of pathology at all. (In this and related contexts Russell (1994) argues that the authors of the 1994 DSM IV manual which includes both 'spiritual disorder' and the schizotypal personality diagnostic criteria (as did its predecessors DSM III (1980) and DSM IIIR (1987), which include belief in the paranormal, might be validly accused of having 'overtight associations'.)

Researchers also recognise that actual belief in the paranormal (which is also high in incidence in schizophrenic people (Irwin 1993; Thalbourne 1994)) is very often initiated by real events which were genuinely strange and even uncanny (see references in French 1992, p. 295). It is worth dealing briefly with some of these events that have taken place in Desmond's life so that the reader can judge how *they* might adjust their ways of construing the world-inclusive-of-Self had these incidents happened to them. Three will suffice, I hope, to convey the flavour of what Desmond has had to deal with in order to come to the philosophy he has constructed and to the way of life he has chosen.

First: he was at a Quaker meeting at the Friends' Meeting House in Euston. A man by the name of Dougan was there, a pleasing man of child-like temperament. Des was not really very surprised when he looked across the room to see seven or eight children sitting around Dougan at his feet, looking up at him. But he was staggered when, in the blink of an eye, these children *disappeared*.

Being no angel, Desmond has always had a weakness for gambling. In his heart he took it lightly until he began to win, and win . . . and win. Over a period of several weeks, betting intensely but only in pennies, Des literally won hundreds of pounds day after day, week after week by *visualisation* of winning on the race, visualisation of moving to the counter and collecting the money. The names of the winning horses would stand out from the board to him. There was no doubt of the outcome. Every gambler's dream? Yes and no. For Des it became a nightmare. The quality of relentlessness is a quality we associate with processes that move from present to future. To experience relentlessness transmitted from what seemed to Desmond to be *the future to the present* turned out to be positively terrifying. Rather than going eagerly to the betting shop, Des eventually became afraid of the strange active/passive state he was in that seemed, fragile though it was, to permit this kind of thing to happen. He *had* to stop gambling for a long time. It was as if his intuitions of the future, if that's what they were, became a burden of immense weight. He sensed that they would crush him *if he did not stop*.

Finally, he was attending a 'Self Transformation' weekend workshop in 1984 to explore and benefit from childhood experiences. There were about thirty people in the hall being used for the weekend arranged for this particular exercise, in six groups of five. Desmond took his turn to be in the centre of his group with other members standing round him. The task of the central person was to face some critical question by making an emotive statement and simultaneously hitting the floor with hands and feet.

Desmond chose a time when he was distressed in the convalescent home as a child. He shouted out, 'I wanna go home!' whereupon the group members around him were instructed to answer back with 'You *can't* go home!' This dialogue continued back and forth:

'I wanna go home!'
'You *can't* go home!'
'I wanna go home!'
'You *can't* go home!'

until a hopefully cathartic crescendo of inner anguish was reached. At that moment Desmond heard an ear-splitting piercing *scream* from across the room, presumably from one of the other groups. It really shocked him, how that person must be suffering!

At the termination of his exercise Desmond was laid on his side next to someone else who had also been 'in the centre' in order to recuperate. As he lay there he asked the man, 'Who was that screaming over there? God it was terrible!' The man replied naturally . . . 'It was you'.

Clearly these incidents do not *demand* belief in extra-sensory powers or in an extra-dimensional reality. The first, of course, could have been a visual hallucination; the second the result of a misconception of chance (Tversky and Kahneman 1974) (such 'unlikely' sequences do occur by chance, as in random number generation); the third the result of a temporary displacement of the position of the self's viewpoint within the internal representation of the room Desmond was in, as has been suggested to account for ('bird's-eye view') out-of-the-body experiences (Blackmore 1982, 1987; Irwin 1986). The best we can say for them, and for the attribution (that he did make) that he may have paranormally sensed Kennedy's death (p. 66), is that his interpretations are permissible and suggestive rather than *required*.

The scientific model of reality and its logic of justification, however, are not without their own philosophical contradictions and vagaries (Weimer 1979; Gergen 1985), particularly in the collection and evaluation of evidence (Chadwick 1975a, b, 1976, 1977, 1982; Chadwick and Hughes 1981). It could be argued that there are indeed many permissible ways to construe the world and the Self (Bannister and Fransella 1971). To actually *diagnose* Desmond as 'personality disordered' and 'cognitively biased' in a direction approaching schizophrenic illness would in this instance be a misuse of power and the anti-psychiatrists' perspective would here be fair because he has orchestrated his experiences into a usable holistic view of reality and of life that for him is functional and does indeed allow him to cope (see also Jackson and Fulford (1996) for a similar view). For him 'in life' his model of the world has an *intrinsic validity* and at least an existential truth that is *more* useful and indeed coherent in accounting for his experiences than is the available scientific model of conventional psychology – which would count many of his daily impressions and intuitions as mere myths and illusions. Such a way of thinking would surely have anyone reaching for pills – thus circularly confirming a biobehavioural 'industry' that offers both 'the explanation' and 'the remedy' in its own terms for those who can find no alternative. In the interests of diversity we must ask: what then is Desmond's alternative?

HOW A MYSTIC AVOIDS MADNESS

We have seen that Des is far from ethereal but is clearly not a standard-minded Englishman either (if such a person exists). He is a nervous man, distractible, wary of strangers, a man of highs and lows, prone to overreacting. Perhaps many of his temperament and personality have indeed gone insane, particularly those who, like me, have sought mystical enlightenment (Greenberg *et al.* 1992). But Des has not. Desmond's stability not only hinges on his creation of a coherent philosophy but on the use of practical *techniques* when he is under various forms of stress. One pair of methods he repeatedly uses is that of *visualisation* and *affirmation* of benign images and phrases and positive consequences. For example, if he finds himself in a busy and slightly threatening environment, he shuns taking, say, a Valium tablet and instead visualises *rings of white light* surrounding him, protecting him as if a field of love is about him. If he finds his thoughts being steeped in vengeance and recriminations, he doesn't go further in to this state but changes the polarity of his experiences by stopping this flow and saying to himself repeatedly: 'No! I choose *love*' over and over until the calming and uplifting quality of the words transforms his feelings and intentions. When he feels himself overwhelmed by stimulation, again there is no reaching for medication. Instead he describes himself as voluntarily 'closing down', relaxing, focusing on some mundane, concrete everyday entity so as to become 'grounded'. (This latter process, which is obviously a protection against an attentional filter problem (see McGhie and Chapman 1961; McGhie 1966), has, however, taken him many years to cultivate.)

Des is also extremely wary of imagining cruel and horrific scenarios. He argues that such imaginings, if repeated, have a subtle way of structuring one's behaviour over long periods of time in such a way that they really do eventually come true! '*Beware* of what you imagine!' is one of his most urgent claims. Therapeutically, the beautiful solace and closeness to nature of Hampstead Heath and Regent's Park enable him to disengage from human horror and indwell in the unity of the natural world.

He is also exceedingly dismissive of comparing himself to others in an envious way. Such a process of 'upward comparison' we do know is damaging of self-esteem (Weber 1992, p. 54). His emphasis, however, is placed not on the esteem-enhancing converse process of *downward* comparison but rather on a more 'level' attitude of *acceptance* of others. One might argue that spiritually this is a healthier and more enlightened strategy.

Now these are actual specific mental procedures that Desmond does not merely talk about as theoretical abstractions but really does repeatedly and consciously instantiate. All of these strategies are *wilfully* and frequently entertained as ways of coping with stress and of creating a resilient *attitude* which is protective of mental health. It seems at the individual level that he finds these stabilising and restorative (Victor Frankl (1969) also suggests positive meaning-seeking approaches related to these).

Once a comedian, Des is now not only a mystic but also a prose-poet. Perhaps it is also in the 'internal sentences' that he both generates in such work and reiterates to himself that he finds strength. Here are some of these lines and couplets that act not only as spiritual philosophy but as informal spiritual-cognitive therapy. He writes:

Past is guilt, future is fear
  Freedom and love is *now*.

We weren't born to be manipulated through guilt.

Fear is the forgetting of love.

We are here to find out what we are
  And what we are not.

Out of the head
into the heart
  to rest.

Empathy and compassion for oneself
  is the same as for others.

It is evident that imbuing oneself with thinking of this kind, some of it more, some of it less original though it might be, is likely to be calming and clearing of the troubled psyche. It is for some people perhaps even *biologically* preferable to ingesting anti-psychotic drugs with their long-term dangers and side-effects – although such medication has recently been suggested as effective for schizotypals (Serban and Siegel 1984; Goldberg *et al.* 1986; Soloff *et al.* 1986). The only medication that Desmond actually uses is steroid cream for his eczema. Despite the tirade of impressions, impulses and affects that populate and pepper his day he avoids the attraction of a chemical soporific in order to strive to be what he organismically is. To be what he is, however, may make his self unmarketable, but perhaps he *should* in any case be unmarketable, as that is not his way and not congruent with his values and aims. Des is not of the marketplace and productivity, he is of the borderline and of being. Here is where the ground of being itself peeps to the surface as a rim around a basin of 'pleasure, pain, money and facts'. This rim is where Des belongs even though our crass society has little recognition and appreciation to offer him – and really no place to offer him within either its socialistic or capitalist structures. The success he has had in his own personal endeavour goes unrecognised as artists and poets are only recognised in the West if they are truly astounding. Des's solution then is to *weave* his life into the world not as an entity-in-place, making money and achieving fame, but as a catalytic personified thread or theme suffused through the body of what is reminding it of its terra firma and its fundamentals.

I will conclude this basically sympathetic presentation of Desmond as a productive if hidden schizotypal with a small offering he had published in the Quaker Friends' House Newsletter in 1991. This is one of the rare occasions when this 'man of the underground' has raised his head above the tree-tops to speak out in public. It is fitting therefore that it should be reproduced.

ONLY ONE TRUTH?
I come across many Christians who think theirs is the only true religion.

There are apparently about seventy religions in the world, and if one of those religions is the 'real' truth, all the other paths – sixty-nine of them – must be untrue. And yet possibly the real essence of each one, if it comes from the heart and has the fundamental principle of unconditional love, must also be the truth. How can we really know the absolute truth? Just being a part of matter distorts our perception, our sense of what the real truth is, and we feel separate in our pain, with all its fears, bias, hurts, resentments, anger. The separateness that we feel is the forgetting of who we really are: beings of light who just happen to be in matter, in the human form.

Neither Christianity nor any other religion can claim that it is the only true way. And do we really believe that it makes any difference to God whether we make the sign of the cross, pray towards Mecca three times a day, or wear a capel on our head? The only thing we can be sure of is unconditional love, the universal law, which we may have a glimpse of now and then, if we are aware of it at the time.

There is only one religion, the religion of love.
There is only one caste, the caste of humanity.
There is only one God, the ominipresent God.
There is only one language, the language of the heart.
(Sri Sai Baba)

What we need today is not a new society, not a new education, not a new religion, but individuals with purity of mind and hearts, to heal the deep wounds, conflicts and misconceptions of our country and our world. I don't see the Resurrection in the Christian sense, as being in a different dimension, but the Resurrection as a change in consciousness on this planet.

(Desmond Marshall, 1991)

AFTERWORD

Desmond Marshall eventually became a Quaker. He now lives in Brighton and runs self-esteem groups at the Quaker Friends' House and at the Centre for the Unemployed. He regards the acceptance and use of his schizotypal tendencies as having been positive moves towards helping him to be both at peace in his own body and to be a functional member of the community.

Chapter 7

Ivo

A butterfly among bulls[1]

If one does not understand a person, one tends to regard him as a fool.

(Carl Jung)

In pre-war Germany the Hitler regime, with its crass philistine ways, induced many spiritual people to leave the country as esoteric thinking was in no way congruent with tough Nazi 'philosophy'. It took decades after the war for the spiritual tradition to reassert itself in any measure. Ivo Wiesner, a young spiritual healer, who was born in north Germany in August 1960, was thrown therefore into a barren culture where his sensitivities found little endorsement. Unable to feel really at home in his own land, he came to England in the summer of 1991 to practise healing. Although there was no organised culture of this kind in Germany and no facilities there to develop spiritual awareness to any serious degree, he knew that there was a long tradition of spiritual interest in this country – represented particularly by the Spiritualists' Association of Great Britain (the SAGB) and also by the Society for Psychical Research in Kensington.

He is a professionally qualified healer himself but healing by the layperson in Germany is actually illegal unless one is a 'qualified alternative practitioner' and it is punished by severe fines there. This says something of course about the strictness of the Germanic attitude to esoteric practices, an attitude indeed which induced Ivo to leave. If they are allowed to exist at all, they must be harshly monitored, hence the bizarre arrest in Germany of the internationally known, and even scientifically tested, healer Matthew Manning (see tests by Brand *et al.* 1979).

Ivo tasted of the preternatural at an early age. In the mid-1960s his father died in a car accident. He was a gentle man, then still only in his thirties, and he died when Ivo was merely six. However, a few weeks after his death cognac glasses in their home were *cut in two* yet undisturbed, as if sliced by a fine laser. The upper halves of the glasses could be gently lifted from the lower and then put back in place. Glass vases were smashed or rather 'imploded' in the room they were in and photographs of his father even rapidly changed colour. Remarkably, both he and his mother, whose

Figure 7.1 Ivo Wiesner
Source: YAPH

flat was opposite the graveyard where the father was buried, could both see *balls of blue light* hovering and dancing around over the grave at night. A parapsychologist in Germany took a great interest in the Wiesner family phenomena and made a film which featured these details and a book was published shortly afterwards including and discussing the events. It transpired later, when the father is claimed to have 'come back' through mediums, that he was angry about his death, which he saw as premature and unnecessary.

Ivo was therefore left as an only child in 1966 and, as we have seen, quickly confronted with the uncanny. He was rather materially spoilt but he says that he was none the less basically unhappy until recent years. School was unenjoyable and he was a mediocre student although fairly talented in gymnastics and the martial arts.

When he was eight his own sensitivities started to become apparent – he started to hear a voice inside his own head. It was like a thought that would appear when he was in an empty state of mind, a clear line of words. The voice did not echo his thoughts or comment or argue about them with another voice, as is frequently the case in schizophrenic illness (e.g. DSM IV 1994, p. 275); it would talk as in ordinary conversation and actually tell him things that were not, as far as he knew, in his own mind. It was a man's voice and to Ivo's astonishment on occasion he uncannily *predicted* events. Ivo, very frightened, told no one about all this, not even his mother. Though he thought he was going mad, this small, thin, unhappy but extremely brave child saw no psychiatrists and had no treatment of any kind. He was never diagnosed as schizophrenic – although probably he would have been had he consulted medical authorities, as hallucinations for many clinicians are seen as a first-rank schizophrenic symptom (Schneider 1959). Instead he carried this experience around with him, in silence, unknown to anyone, for years.

One might imagine that Ivo could have been the victim of a cold, domineering or an overprotective, critical mother, sufficient perhaps to induce states like this. But not really. His mother has been a little over-emotional and possessive (more so, however, only in later years) but he was always brought up to have an independent mentality and a positive attitude to himself. Both of these things have been a great source of strength.

When he was ten he and his mother moved to Trier near Luxembourg, a totally different environment both physically and psychologically from that of his earlier years. But he still had few friends and the only subject he could relate to in school was music. The others meant nothing to him. Eventually he decided to study it at the College of Music in Cologne and became a professional musician for a few years. Then he moved on to train in alternative medicine and therapy and finally specialised in healing. This kind of training was able to give Ivo a meaningful framework which helped him to understand and cope with the eerie experiences he frequently had. He had realised that they belonged more to the realm of the mysterious than to that of pathology through involuntary out-of-the-body experiences he had had as a child. On several occasions he had tried in his bedroom to switch on a light while floating out of the body (interestingly *not* in 'bird's-eye view' fashion) but his finger had passed *through* the switch. He had been so frightened by this that the surprise would immediately 'fling' him back into the flesh. Clearly, by the time he was 20 Ivo's experiential life was totally discrepant with those of his unempathic contemporaries. What was *common* to him was quite *outrageous* to them! This has been a theme which has since remained pretty well unchanged.

IVO THE MAN

To most outsiders Ivo Wiesner is a totally inscrutable man. Here is someone who regularly 'hears voices', floats out of the body, 'travels' to parallel worlds (or so he claims), senses auras and has seen ghosts and psychokinetic events, indeed here is a man who seems to live in a five-dimensional (rather than our four-dimensional) world and yet betrays not a hint of it on casual acquaintance. Ivo has no need of LSD, or PCP, he has no interest in virtual-reality experiences, and he has no such interest because he can sample all of these things drug-free *in his own head*.

But Ivo is difficult to know. Physically he is fair, of medium height, a good-looking fellow always popular with the ladies. Soft-spoken and very serene, he seems to float as he walks and there is melody in his voice. His facial expression tends to be very still and, perhaps not surprisingly, he has a quality about him in which he always seems to be 'visiting' wherever he is. Just as Desmond seems to be 'waiting' and 'about to talk', Ivo seems to be 'paying a call on the world', popping in, looking the world up, as if not really of this world but temporarily *in* it. Were we all sitting in the restaurant in the Swiss Centre in London (as we have done) and Ivo were suddenly to glow white, or to disappear, it wouldn't (really) shock me that much. In a way I half expect it. How on earth can any human being convey such an impression? In a single chapter one can only begin to answer a question like this.

Ivo is a slim man, deceptively delicate, basically quiet. He is an empathic person who feels his way and never *pushes* himself. In conversation, whereas Desmond leads, Ivo is a counter-puncher, he orchestrates his flow in reaction. Though rarely raising his voice or getting angry, he holds his beliefs strongly and cannot be argued out of them as (he says) they are rooted in his own experience.

Although attractive to women, Ivo is what we English would call 'a man's man'. Among men he is at peace, his thinking, esoteric though it might be, is precise in its own terms. Under fire from men he is never in trouble, not seriously, and his mind, despite the strangeness of its contents, is obviously crystal clear. Among men one can see the German in him. Women are a different matter; the only vacancy in his life is that which will be filled by a deep nourishing relationship with a woman. But for the time being that is in the future.

Ivo's phantasmal qualities, however, are a fair reflection of the essence of the man. His spectral characteristics do indeed project the man as he really is. If one's whole life has been spent in a realm that standard-minded people only experience when they go to the cinema, somehow one has to come to terms with it in such a way as to retain one's dignity. It is hardly surprising that Ivo is slow to reveal himself. Positivistic science is no route to dignity for men like him; it is only likely to be so for people whose vision of reality has no need or experience of anything beyond the material. Ivo could never be of this ilk as materialism makes no sense to him and could never do so. The system is inadequate. How then *has* Ivo 'come to terms' with a life that would send most people into either a manic frenzy or a state of utter anguish? This has been no easy task.

In the pages that follow I am going deliberately to ignore Huxley's scientism, adopt an open-minded stance, and take Ivo at his word. This will be an empathic attempt to both understand and convey him in his own terms. Many psychotherapists may see Ivo's ideas as merely projections of phenomena that are totally intrapsychic but then again this may not be so. At our present stage of understanding, a prudent person would have to admit doubt. But whether or not Ivo (and I myself here) are 'projecting' to a dimension that 'really' is only psychological there is *no* doubt, as both of us have found, that these procedures and ideas do *work* as protective devices against the 'dark side' of nature, mind and perhaps cosmos. Even the very cynical reader then could productively regard this as an empirical practical chapter at least, and relegate it as *theory* to either the past or the future.

TAKING ONE'S HEALTH INTO ONE'S OWN HANDS

From an early life that would undoubtedly have led him to be pronounced as psychotic by the medical profession, Ivo has emerged now in good shape. Really he has done this, like Desmond, by taking his health into his own hands and searching for a positive and charitable rather than a cynical interpretation of his experiences.

Interestingly, Ivo has a very practical and sensible attitude to spirituality and to 'spirits'. For him spirituality does *not* any more mean talking with and being guided by people on 'the afterlife plane' as he calls it. This he has sampled, but now it means instead having a calm, creative, positive *attitude*. Having awareness of the subtler and finer vibrations of spirit energies, as for example in audioclairvoyance, does not for him by any means make a person spiritual. In his view there are many spiritualists who are not, in their hearts, spiritual at all and there are as many illusions to be had in communicating with this purported afterlife plane as there are in everyday life. It offers no guarantees. For Ivo dead people are only distinguished from us by the fact that they are *dead*. He does not regard them as wiser nor does he trust them as guides. To have a model of reality in which spirits are making one's life decisions for one (as some people have) is not Ivo's way; this kind of experience and practice he totally rejects. In this respect he is close to Desmond in taking personal responsibility for his own life.

Having realised, where many in the mediumistic subculture have not, that spirits, if they *do* exist, are no more capable of coming to correct conclusions than we are, Ivo has moved away from spiritualism and is highly critical of it. He has stepped out of that belief system. He interprets spirit activity instead as merely confirming one's *own* belief system! To his way of thinking 'they' merely amplify one's wish to be confirmed, they 'pick up' on people's thoughts and feed back to them what they secretly want. However, if a person is latently suicidal, some spirits will, alas, take them along that path too. This not surprisingly is the way he interprets my own experience of paranormal rappings when I was in Charing Cross Hospital (see Chapter 4).

The true spiritual path for Ivo is therefore not to spend one's life sitting around tables at seances but to become self-loving and loving towards every thought and being. This, along with discipline, in itself gives protection as, without the right attitude and without discipline, disaster, as I found, is bound to overcome a person with etheric sensitivities. Ivo is quick to point out that such sensitivities will not automatically enrich a person's life simply because they are there. One has to be *trained* to deal with them, train oneself to 'close down' lest they become overwhelming and be strong and sure of oneself in belief and motive. In complete contrast to the aggressive cynic, it is Ivo's philosophy that to be loving and sensitive is really the *only* safe state: *it is not a state to be afraid of.* And, in contrast to the ascetic, for him spiritual awareness includes awareness of the body, not flight from it.

SPIRITUAL LAWS

Like Desmond and also Deonne (see Chapter 8), Ivo senses the presence of actual spiritual laws. The spiritual realm is ordered, has harmony and a kind of predictability if one knows its ways. These are laws, for him, beyond the laws of physics, laws more powerful than physical laws, that he sees as being able to pattern our lives but that may reduce to physical laws in certain circumstances – rather in the manner that Einstein's equations can reduce to Newton's as certain terms approach zero.

Ivo's great wish therefore is for an understanding of these laws by a blending of esoteric knowledge with scientific knowledge. For this he argues that science has to realise that mystics are not all insane and mystics have to realise that scientists are not all cynical. Concessions are needed on both sides as deep prejudices divide the two – as, of course, does arrogance. It is his belief that integration will need awareness, open-mindedness and a *vision*, something positive, not bitter in-fighting and destructive criticisms – but that humanity is becoming ready for this integration. At a practical level, however, he does recognise that we will have to find that something *is* the case and *that* it works, then we can try to find *why* it works. This is the case in the understanding of both the physical and the spiritual. Practical techniques and advantages precede theoretical explanation.

THE SPIRITUAL ATTITUDE AS COGNITIVE THERAPY

The introduction above I hope gives the reader a taste of the flavour of Ivo's life and experiences and of his manner of coming to terms with the stream of his day-to-day awareness. My own access to realms such as Ivo speaks of is obviously pretty limited; I cannot travel with him to meet 'spirits on the afterlife plane' or try and press light switches while 'out of the body' to see what happens. I do not have to fight off seemingly alien voices in my own head by 'closing down' nor do I, unlike him, sense auras or physical mediumship capacities (e.g. psychokinesis) and the like. (Intriguingly he claimed to sense the latter in me minutes after we first met.)

Ivo lives in a land where I am merely on the shoreline, confronted with a cliff that for me is unclimbable. There is no doubt, however, that in terms of behavioural criteria Ivo is perfectly sane. Unlike many hallucinating schizophrenic people, his conversation is not odd, meandering or vague, he does not show quick topic or theme changes, he does not make 'plays on words' or pick up on double or triple meanings to what one says. He is neither paranoid, schizoid nor avoidant; on the contrary, he is a warm, affable, quite confident man, a man of charm and good humour, careful and measured in speech, clear, rational in all everyday matters, sober, responsive and extremely caring. If the overall clinical picture shows that Ivo is not schizophrenic, and not personality disordered, if he shows no 'cognitive slippage', 'word salad' speech or 'interpenetration of thoughts', then what on earth are we dealing with here? Is all this *real*? Do these juicy anecdotes of weird happenings and strange talents represent tangible real events and real energies? This is all most peculiar. Huxley would just walk away but that way one learns nothing, as, paradoxically, he himself well knew. No, I prefer that we go forward and *into* the deep and even dangerous mystery with which Ivo confronts us.

Let us go back for a moment to the analogy of the beach and the cliffs: I am on the beach, remember, looking up and, in effect, Ivo is at the top of the cliff from where he can see directly a vast countryside of rolling hills and dales but with some threatening features. In our time as friends he has called down to me on the beach and told me about lots of things that he has seen and all about where he's been. But I cannot see or experience what he can. The cliff is for me unclimbable; indeed, as you have heard, I am pretty lucky to have even reached the shoreline itself here in one piece, let alone be on the top of the cliff. Since I can't climb the cliff, since I can't see what he sees, I do the only thing I can do, I take what he says to me and use it to make a map. If I can't have first-hand knowledge of anything beyond the beach I can at least make a map with the help of better climbers than myself.

What Ivo is telling me and what his life really is concerned with is the search for coping with the preternatural via the discovery of spiritual laws, even if these at the moment are only empirical. Ivo is like a geologist or geographer of another dimension, searching for a practical understanding of alien, if wondrous, territory by experiencing and studying it so as to discover its regularities and its pattern. If he can do this, then he can actually sample and move around in this territory quite safely, and come back and forth to the beach any time he likes without injury. My job, since I've at least (just about) got on to this dry land through my own bizarre adventures, is to collate my experience with his so as to create as good a map as I can make in the circumstances. Then if anyone crash-lands on this island they can at least survive here, as long as they have it in their possession.

The map is really a form of cognitive self-help or self-therapy for dealing with alien territory of mental experience. Very few cognitive therapists, however, know much about this land. This is not the territory of depression or anxiety, this is the territory of dealing with experiences that at least seem to come from beyond space–time and from beyond the Self. This is something else.

Ivo tells me that there are more treacherous areas here than most people realise, and more than he first realised himself when he came here as a youngster. The territory can only be safely negotiated in certain ways. Here then we have to look at these ways and also discuss whether they have any general use as well. Maybe if one can get around in *this* territory one can get by under *any* circumstances!

HOW TO UNDERSTAND AND GET AROUND IN ANOTHER DIMENSION

What follows is essentially a collaborative effort between Ivo and me. I have been mapping the shoreline and the beach/cliff junction where outcrop begins, but Ivo is giving other directions about expanses further inland. From now on the analogy breaks down as we have to move from a visual to a largely verbal format but I hope none the less that the sense of exploration and uncertainty will remain.

We are really at the edge of where the geology and geography of sanity still applies. Here, as Casteneda warned, life can turn bad just as easily as good. It seems to depend on two things: one's degree of *spiritual development* and one's *current attitude*. A feeling of fear, or of doubt and profound self-doubt or even a purely rational-intellectual attitude will lead one sliding into quicksand very suddenly. One must *not* be afraid, and one's thoughts and feelings must be together in harmony, not characterised by the schizoid split so endemic among intellectuals.

There is much evil in this strange land that we are now within but it can evidently only exert itself or manifest itself *with the traveller's cryptic permission*. It will indeed use you as a channel to eventuate itself in reality if it can: the only way to block and fight it, as Desmond also has said, is to choose *Love*. Love somehow appears to be fundamental, a characteristic or quality of the deep structure of the reality here. We know not why. It seems that, by generating it, one simultaneously 'tunes in' to it, as if it were a feature of some Hegelian World Soul or Cosmic Mind to which the personal mind has access. Turn to hate and you will 'attract' the 'energies' of hate – which in one way or another will eventually destroy you. This seems usually to be so. If you point a gun at someone, someday, sometime in the future, *someone* will point a gun at you. This is the probability, but who it will be we cannot know – and maybe we are forbidden to know.

From this angle it appears also that all people's behaviour and attitudes have interactive mutual effects and rebound effects. What Desmond used to call a 'network of colliding ripples moving through time' is to Ivo 'The Law of Mutual Vibrations'. We ourselves make the world and all the people in it. It is we in interaction who subtly shaped Hitler, the James Bulger schoolboy killers, the Yorkshire Ripper, because in the realm of behaviour it is rarely the case that a genetic endowment is totally and utterly inevitable in its effects. Life is the result of mutual orchestrated influences. And as we influence each other, rather in the manner of the butterfly effect in chaos theory (see Gleick 1987, pp. 20–3), we all in turn shape the world around us every second, every millisecond. We do not merely adapt to it, we creatively or destructively change it ourselves in turn, as indeed do all organisms.

The emphasis in this 'territory of the mysterious' is not on *proving* things but on the cultivation of a sincere wish to help others, to be of service. The aggressive urge to dominate, control and standardise is irrelevant and even *dangerous*. Here one must approach phenomena with the same caution and peacefulness that one uses to approach feeding birds, lest the process or gift vanish. Phenomena usually regarded as 'schizophrenic symptoms' – the contents of delusions and hallucinations – must not be dismissed as merely pathological symptoms but accorded some truth or reality status, if only in an existential Laingian sense. Some such phenomena are merely mental, but others are profitably regarded as not so and hence may reveal the operation of 'higher' orchestrating forces and indeed other (unseen) forces but not necessarily representing the good. The most important strategy with *troubling* voices then is *not to listen to them*. Similarly it is actually therapeutic to regard weakening and terrifying coincidences as *tricks* intended to destroy via a force which makes use of one's own cryptic wishes for self-destruction. In these circumstances it is vital to 'close down' the feeling of fear as this will only exaggerate problems and permit further coincidences to follow. In a state of great anxiety, doubt and fear, parlour games such as tarot cards, pendulums and ouija boards are *most definitely to be avoided*. They are *exceedingly dangerous* and will only produce results (and there will be results) that worsen a negative state of mind. Even the occasional 'positive' result will be a trick or a confuser, it will lead nowhere and certainly not in a productive direction. Continued use of such 'pastimes' by the fragile and frightened can easily lead to a form of psychic and spiritual overwhelm. Their 'messages' must be *ignored* in such circumstances as just *worthless dross* sent only to capitalise on every weakness and self-doubt for the purpose of causing as much misery as possible. Although one need not be *completely* immune inside a church, the calm positive spiritual presence in such places is generally repulsive to forces that work in malign ways, so such havens are valuable (indeed vital) and hence well worth seeking.

Truth and real clarity come from calmness. The void of the Positive can even be visualised symbolically as *white light* which one can imagine surrounding one and indeed one can project it from oneself at critical moments out to others to bring peace, love and harmony. The very visualisation of this for Ivo has brought about a growth in strength which has kept negative 'energies' at bay. Through such visualisation (with affirmations) he has gained control of his own psychic sensitivities; they do not, as in some psychotics, control him. In this way he neutralises threats and attempts to create an inner sense of the positive to which others cannot help but respond or, as he says, 'resonate' to.

It would be wrong to say that he *causes* the positive in others in this way. Really he acts as a vehicle to facilitate the appearance of the positive as if from beyond. Some people, alas, can have the same power of enhancing the appearance of the negative. In this manner there have even been murders, a quite recent one in Tottenham comes to mind, where no one knew, even the murderer himself, *why* it was committed! It was not a caused effect; it was simply 'inevitable' because of the 'atmosphere' at a particular moment and place – as if the act was pulled out of the person by a kind of psychic field.

These 'psychic fields' Ivo well knows can also be created in the positive but they will not be so if people are continually opening 'cans of worms' in their own minds, as I used to do. This can only facilitate the apprehension of the negative. The focus on positive beliefs about oneself – affirmations – is a far more powerful strategy. Similarly, as Ivo has found as a healer, doubt and fear in a patient can *repel* the healing force and prevent its effectiveness. It does seem that people can unconsciously *prevent* themselves from ever experiencing the kind of realms we are dealing with here.

Away from this land of the uncanny, *reason and experiment* rule – as most scientific readers probably accept. But here reason has to be put to a new use: here events reflect the power of *love and coincidences*. Here in the world of the Borderline it is clear that one can slide one of two ways, to the Positive or Negative. These territories are very different.

THE NEGATIVE AND POSITIVE BORDERLINES

This is a brief exploration into the ultra-violet and infra-red of human experience. One realm, the negative, is typical of persecutory experiences in psychosis where the individual feels trapped at every turning by Fate. Many people confused and muddled by the Negative Borderline have sought solace in suicide, others have claimed to be victims of demons, of a hierarchy of gods or of super-powerful destructive forces. What people *attribute* such experiences to is variable. The Positive realm, however, is also seen as real by many spiritual and religious people. It operates over the same dimension as the Negative but at the opposite pole and in the opposite way. Mental scientists will no doubt reduce these domains to different states of mind, the Negative to a manically paranoid state, the Positive to a mature healthy state of more carefully articulated intent. To infer the operation of external *forces* here they will see as superfluous. We would claim differently but in any case the description below is centrally empirical.

The Positive Borderline realm seems to build over time, decades or much longer if need be, the Negative destroys, as it has to, as somehow it must do. In the Negative Borderline state one has the mentality of a threatened beast, life is terrifying, portentous, one is hypervigilant, things are happening *fast*, there is little time for reflection, events happen *too fast*. There is a sense of destiny in death as if what one has stumbled across is *forbidden territory* and one's presence there is 'unwanted'.

But with different intent there are no 'kaleidoscopic coincidences' all happening too fast to absorb. Whereas the events of the negative domain feel like Satanic *tricks*, the events of the positive feel *sincere*. Whereas the events of the negative happen just too fast to keep up with, the events of the positive happen in such a way that one has time to use them and learn from them. Whereas the events of the negative are spectacular and showy, the events of the positive are of humble solidity. Table 7.1 gives a full comparison.

The Negative Borderline is a mystical domain of negative implication entwined, it seems, with the psychotic. It is pervaded by coincidence. For example, a person finds that his or her thoughts are racing, but then a couple walk by and one says to the other: 'She'll never keep it up at this pace.' She thinks: 'Where is all this leading?' Enmeshed in another conversation nearby a man says: 'Hell!' These are the genuinely uncanny coincidences, horrific, terrifying, bewildering. The worst such instance I personally ever suffered during the 1979–81 crisis which I think is worth mentioning here in this context was at a time when I was desperately searching myself specifically for the strength to forgive. As if, were I to forgive, my plight would be eased, and perhaps I would be forgiven. I was preoccupied with these thoughts and feelings one day when I happened to be simply browsing in a bookshop in Fulham – a humble enough setting. In exasperation, stupidly needing some 'sign' as if from beyond to guide me, I took down a small black German–English dictionary from a stand and opened it at random. Unseeingly I placed my finger on a word, again at random (I speak no German). The entry read, with the italicised words being *where my finger alighted*:

verzeihen: forgive, pardon, excuse, remit (sins), *nicht zu–*, inexcusable, unpardonable, forgiveness futile.

It must be pretty clear from an example like that that the realm of the Negative Borderline is nothing less than a potential killer. This

Table 7.1 Characteristics of the Positive and Negative Borderline realms

The Negative Borderline	The Positive Borderline
Events feel like Satanic tricks.	Events feel sincere.
Events happen too fast to keep up with.	Events happen so that one has time to use them and learn from them.
Events are spectacular and showy.	Events are of humble solidity.
Events lead one downhill to destruction.	Events enable one to grow and thrive.
Realm terrifies.	Realm nurtures, calms and rests.
Realm confuses and bewilders.	Realm clarifies and illuminates.
Realm paralyses will.	Realm strengthens will.
Realm turns one into a puppet.	Realm turns one into an agent.
Realm presents transient evanescent shocks on which one cannot build.	Realm enables one to consolidate.
Realm induces one to feel that every raw nerve is exposed.	Realm protects and shields.
Realm gives 'signs' or 'directions' that lead relentlessly down.	Realm gives 'directions' which leaves room for personal manoeuvre, choice and decision.
Realm takes one out of life and leads one to trust no one.	Realm takes one into life and leads one to build solid bonds.
Realm destroys all relationships.	Realm enables one to build innumerable new ones.
Realm is fast, sharp, tricky, impressive and empty.	Realm is slow, rounded, sincere, humble and full.
One is at the centre of existence yet totally expendable.	One is a *part* of existence, in place, yet utterly indispensable.

psychophysical dovetailing(?) must have led many to destruction and self-destruction. It is difficult to believe that such events are 'mere coincidence'. We hear of the results only transiently, for example in announcements such as: 'Person under a train at Waterloo' and so on – or in the press as a small item. Ivo remembers the attitude that enhances and facilitates these effects from his days of military service in Germany. After it the slightest provocation would have induced him to violence. His wise solution was to become a conscientious objector.

The way to manoeuvre in the land of the preternatural is centrally via love: love seems to have tangible physical power. To be *able* to manoeuvre needs experience, if one stumbles across the uncanny as I did, as if from the back door it can overwhelm one. But for Ivo *experience* is the only way to grow into a loving being. Rationalising and analysing alone cannot bring about real development. It is necessary not to allow oneself to be drawn into violent or negative experiences. If one is so drawn, then one must step out of them quickly, then conditions will change.

Nevertheless, readers will in the end really have to demonstrate it to themselves at a personal level. One can only test these ideas against one's own experience: eventually the only proof is what works for oneself. For some readers their vitality may lie in total rejection of the above, for others there may be a feeling of 'yes . . . but not yet'. This is understandable. In this realm the time, place and context must be right, and if it is, then all will be well.

ANGER, FEAR AND SEX

It is implicit in the above that Ivo has considerable mastery of the emotions of fear and anger thanks to the development within that his belief system has facilitated during his trade with the world. The attachment of anger and fear to things, people or events, he sees as futile. Nothing can ever really be destroyed; the outcomes of these emotions for him are only illusions. This particular attitude to anger and fear, similar to that in Buddhist and Hindu thought, may well be the source of Ivo's great serenity and calming yet inspirational quality as a man. His practice of Kundalini Yoga, which is embedded in his philosophy, has also induced great tranquillity and self-worth in him, feelings antithetical to anger and fear.

The area of lesser tranquillity in Ivo, as he himself freely admits, is sexuality. At only 35, his Achilles' heel, not surprisingly, is women, particularly beautiful women – and he meets plenty of them in his capacity as a healer. It seems with Ivo's mode of consciousness, the maintenance of lasting relationships is a problem. On this we will have to see what the future holds.

Most psychiatrists regard the prognosis in childhood schizophrenia – the diagnosis which Ivo would almost certainly have received – as poor (Werry *et al*. 1994) – although his basically sound 'pre-morbid' personality would have helped. He would, however, have been put on small doses of anti-psychotic medication in all probability from an early age with the possibility of long-term side-effects always looming as he grew older. Psychotherapists might have probed his 'over-close' relationship with his mother and his attitude to his deceased father, feasibly causing him, in his innocence, even more anxiety and confusion than he already had. He and his mother would have been told that he had a 'serious illness' and the events surrounding his father's death probably would have been totally discounted. All the vital leads could well have been missed. This chapter shows, in a way that my autobiographical chapters do not, that there *are* 'other ways' than traditional mental health approaches, radically different ways, that we in the academy have hardly begun to explore – or even to listen to. This brief biography also reveals a rather subtle feature of Ivo as a person which may well have saved his mind and maybe even his life. As we saw when he was a 'hallucinating' child, he has an uncanny capacity to know or sense when to keep quiet. But now he is talking, and contrary to Thomas Huxley, it is perhaps time that we heard what he and those of his ilk have to say. As we have seen, Ivo is far from his ideal. But he is also slow to reveal himself, at times exasperatingly composed, talks of spirituality on occasion with at least a hint of Germanic mechanical efficiency. Yet he is a man who loves to laugh, who loves to learn and, when all is said and done, is also a man who has a deep capacity to enjoy life. This is a far cry from the escapism practised by so many so-called 'spiritual' people.

REFLECTIONS

Ivo's conception of reality and of the interdependence of matter and mind jars uncomfortably with that of mainstream knowledge – and indeed people such as him are a *threat* to the claims of legitimacy that centrally placed authorities make for that knowledge. Hence it will be imperative that Ivo's 'model of the world' be ignored so that such claims can appear to reign untroubled. This was T.H. Huxley's approach and is still the approach of materialistic science. An alternative strategy is to collapse his claims into intrapsychic psychology and interpret them as illusions or as 'projections'. Hence, on this view, there are *no* 'spiritual forces' eventuating via the situation when a tarot card reading is being done for a troubled mind (to produce even more troubling results). The cards merely are laid out on the table on a chance basis and what is *then* read into them (in a fanciful way) is the source of the distress. Similarly my 'forgiveness futile' event was not the eventuation of a domain of negative meaning into everyday reality but merely an unfortunate coincidence – interpreted by me in a portentous way because of my fearful state at the time.

The 'slicing' of the cognac glasses was a fault in their construction perhaps and Ivo's successes as a healer a pure placebo effect (see, however, reviews by Benor 1990, 1993 and Hodges and Scofield 1995, confirming via controlled trials the effectiveness of healing as a therapy). Ivo's 'travels' when resting or near-to-sleep to other dimensions or 'parallel worlds' could, however, be seen as the products of hypnogogic or hypnopompic forms of *imagery* (Blackmore 1987) and the balls of blue light hovering over his father's grave were (surely?) visual illusions or perhaps even a form of ball lightning. The effectiveness of love rather than fear in taking a person away from the Negative Borderline could be seen by mental scientists as due to its de-arousing properties, which therefore could reduce activation spread through semantic networks and thus reduce magical and 'wild' remote associative thinking. Anger and fear, in turn, could be seen via this scheme of things to have the effects they have only because of their activating properties producing difficulties in the modulation of thought and impairment in the capacity to dismiss 'irrelevant' cognitions.

Ivo presents us with nothing that *demands* our acquiescence to a psychophysical world view. However, just as materialistic science is based on an act of faith that such an approach will produce valid generalisations about the world, Ivo's construction of events is also so founded. He begins from different assumptions, has no interest in *proving* things, evolves techniques that work for him that he passes on to others, and strives for a conception of reality that makes sense out of his experiences and enables him to operate effectively in life. Really his mission is little different in procedure from that of mainstream science and conventional psychology (Kelly 1955), with the exception that he does not search for definiteness. It may, however, be that for these techniques he uses to *work* a psycho-physical conception of the world in the bearer, and a belief in spiritual forces, is *required*. Freud recognised that an external threat is easier for the mind to deal with than one which is internal – hence the use of the defence mechanism of projection (Freud 1911). Also distracting oneself and deflecting attention from the negative, rather than embroiling oneself in it, are now known to be techniques that more successfully make for human happiness (Sackeim 1983; Argyle 1993). Focusing on negative states, although brave, is likely to exacerbate depressive and suicidal tendencies (Nolen-Hoeksema 1987). The intractability of schizophrenic illness, with its frequent religious and spiritual accompaniments, to psycho-dynamic and humanistic therapeutic approaches (Klerman 1984; Mueser and Berenbaum 1990) does suggest that a 'psychologismic' approach in which everything of this genre is collapsed into the mental is seriously defective. Sufferers of spiritual crises do feel that they are being assaulted by forces that emanate from beyond themselves (indeed this was how Jung would describe the spiritual crisis). If this 'externality' is accepted for what it seems to be, counselling of a spiritual nature, taking advantage of the person's belief system and working within it and with it, is arguably a flexible solution of merit (Bilu and Wiztum 1994; Leff 1994).

We are left with the puzzle of why a totally intrapsychic understanding of phenomena of the form that Ivo presents produces so little therapeutic yield, while an understanding that accords the spiritual some reality status is more comforting. There is always the troubling possibility of course that this may be because the latter approach has the greater essential validity. Since the living systems produced by materialistic intelligence and those produced by spiritual intelligence are both grounded in faith and will, eventually we will have to know them and assess them by their fruits in life.

AFTERWORD

Ivo Wiesner is now a practising professional spiritual healer in London. He runs a healing clinic and gives many public presentations on healing at health shows in the capital. He regards the difficulties of the past as having been challenges and learning experiences which have helped him to move towards greater integration, wholeness and inner peace. Further developments in Desmond's and Ivo's quests hopefully will be presented at a future time.

Chapter 8

Deanna
Thunder from 'Elsewhere'

The heart has its reasons which reason does not know.

(Blaise Pascal)

Deanna, 47, tall, slim and trim, I met unexpectedly in London in the autumn of 1986.[1] We met because she answered an advertisement I placed in search of contacts interested in sexual mysticism.

Like Desmond, she had accessed the spiritual through rejection of her body but, paradoxically, felt with Taoists and with followers of the Tantra religion that sensuality and sexuality were perfectly valid routes to enlightenment. This I liked.

Deanna, who hails originally from the North-West, I felt was a 'warm fire' kind of person. She had a pervasive oceanic quality to her, was undoubtedly the most open-minded person I had ever met, and had an imagination that was both ingenious and visionary. This indeed was an aspect of her oceanic quality that acted as such a powerful catalyst to processes in others – from creativity to clairvoyance – that require not frost but sunshine from others to effloresce fully.

Deanna was, however, a dominating presence in any room or gathering. She disliked the role of wallflower, abhorred being overshadowed and quickly took control of conversation by slowing it down, 'deepening' it and jolting it on to issues that preoccupied her. It was difficult to talk small talk with her or to convey 'news' and everyday chatter because the wavelength of her being was so much longer and more undulating than this and hence such sprightly effervescent gossip just evaporated in her presence – as if it was 'shallow and trite'. Deanna, with her rather deep voice and stillness of body language, radiated the message that she was 'here for more important things' – and prattle about trivia was not welcome, at least not for long.

It is difficult to have a relationship with such a person unless you allow them to rule you. If you *don't* give them this licence, meetings with them quickly flare into rows or you find yourself being insulted or in some way belittled for non-acquiescence. Dominant people, by definition, *have* to be 'on top'. Deanna spared me this humiliation in the time we were friends (1986–93) and despite her tendency to orchestrate conversation around herself, I none the less always felt somehow that we regarded ourselves generally as equals – with talents in different areas and with different aims in life.

Deanna's weakness, however, was that for one reason or another she was none the less *paranoid*. She was always highly sensitive to *any* possibility of being 'used' in some way – while freely admitting (without a trace of remorse) to herself 'using' other ('inferior') people if it suited *her* mission in life. So, rather than strengthening our relationship, the latter started actually to be *strained* when Deanna realised that I found her open-mindedness to be a wonderful catalyst of my own creativity. The more clearly she came to realise this muse quality of hers, the less I came to see of her. Not surprisingly, on the EPQ (Eysenck and Eysenck 1975) Deanna's high score on the Psychoticism scale (see later) was largely due to her responses on the seven paranoia items of that scale. Some items on the N scale also indicate anxieties of a paranoid kind and these rocketed the Neuroticism score too.

In this respect Deanna was really her own worst enemy because the fact of the matter was that my wife and I both loved her for the delicate empathic soul that really she was – beneath the mask of cunning, glamour and ruthlessness that she paraded before the world. Her paranoia was embedded within a personality, like my own (pre-psychotically), and Desmond's, that was distinctively schizotypal (see p. 103 and Table 9.1, p. 116). During the seven or so years I knew her, her life revolved around the predictions of clairvoyants, reincarnationist interpretations of her identity, synchronicity, fantastic (and sometimes terrific) ideas, paranoid interpretations of people she did not like, all coupled with a perceptual and empathic social sensitivity that was at times totally 'out of synch' yet at other times truly wonderful. Deanna was a person who resonated to the world like a jelly and who desperately sought that one elusive perfect partner or friend who would complete her life. Her ideals were shining white but she could just not tolerate the petty, messy imperfections of real people in real life without feeling forever wounded and embittered by them. In truth the world was just not good enough for her and everyone in it was a pale imitation of what they ought to be. This incredible sensitivity to unfairness and imperfection coupled with the holding of inordinately high ideals makes for a very socially unstable style of life, as we shall see. But despite it all, beneath this North-West of England high-mindedness in a personality that yearned for triumph and perfection, that poured scorn and contempt on the merely human qualities of ordinary people, lay a delicate, fun-loving sensitive person who would have made a fine therapist or writer had she given up striving for the impossible and faced and accepted the real.

THE REAL DEANNA

This brief introductory sketch of Deanna has had to be incomplete for reasons that will quickly become clear. She had had a career in the police force when younger but this and the nature of her present work – particularly given her present way of life – necessitates a depiction of her which is deliberately rather vague.

You see, Deanna is not a therapist, nor a writer, secretary, probation officer or indeed employed in anything like these professions. She is a 6 feet 1 inch tall male-to-female transsexual prostitute who shares a sadomasochist's brothel with another transsexual in the heart of London's West End. In her male role as Denys (she is pre-operative not post-operative) Deanna works in a security post in the North-East of England and (religiously) commutes between the North-East and London, when leave periodically comes up, to keep the male and female roles safely separate and intact.

Some readers may find all this rather disgusting or unsavoury. Indeed, as she herself says, with 'the petty little middle class suburban value systems' that now pervade our land Deanna may soon not even legally *exist*. It is so easy, as Ryan (1971) has pointed out, to 'blame the victim'. But not only is it easy, these days it is also quite fashionable and acceptable. Alas, Deanna, and her transsexual partner Deborah, are caught in the middle of a vicious catch-22 no-win situation of labyrinthine complexity on all sides. Derided by 'right-minded people', it is extremely difficult for a tall, deep-voiced transsexual, indeed *any* transsexual who is not self-employed and who does not 'pass' *perfectly* in public as a woman, to earn a living outside prostitution. (Telephone reception work is one of a few alternatives.) Unlike the fast disappearing American Indian culture (Plumber 1974) that accepts and respects such people – and where they may even play a shamanistic role – in our technologically advanced but spiritually backward society they are misunderstood and scorned and their experience and identity are devalued. Deborah herself was *sacked* from her job in the male role essentially because of her 'condition' – as indeed many are. Meanwhile, film makers in the West take advantage of the subjective strangeness of the state and the public's prejudice against it and ignorance of it to present absolutely monstrous and sickeningly distorted images of these people in films such as *The Silence of the Lambs* and *Dressed to Kill*.

Denys, the male *alter ego*, has been divorced, has lost the custody of and access to his children and been himself sacked twice, all because of transsexualism. It is not surprising that he is a bitter, society-hating man. 'Them out there!' he says, 'All they know is the law of the jungle: *destroy* that which you do not understand!' This is how he has come to see himself as having been 'used' so many times, then just cast aside when his inner reality became known. Elsewhere and at other times the picture has been so different.

In American Indian culture our male-to-female transsexual is probably represented most closely by the so-called 'alyha' (by Mohave Indians) and the 'berdache' by Crow Indians.[2] The berdache was a biological male who simply chose not to follow the ideal Crow role of warrior. But the berdache suffered neither shame nor scorn for this (Williams 1986) and a Crow warrior who took a berdache as a wife also suffered no contempt or derision.

The Mohave Indians recognised not two but four gender categories with the male, like Deborah, who chooses to live as a woman, referred to as an alyha. Such people would work with women and if they married men this also carried no shame for either party.

This flexibility in the Indian culture was due to the fact that they saw gender as a changeable not a fixed personal quality. They regarded it as a creation of sociocultural conditions. Hence our dualistic categories rooted firmly in the biology of 'the normal' would mean little to them. Alas, Deanna and Deborah are English, not American Indians, and for the most part their lives are a continual fight for their own intrinsic validity. The Christian church has little to offer them either, as the Bible (Deuteronomy, chapter 22, verse 5) refers to such people as 'abominations in the eyes of the Lord'. Statements like that, of course, do not exactly inspire much confidence (see also the dismissals of such people in Christian counselling in Collins 1988).

The scientific legislators and consultants on human personality and sexuality in our society, psychologists and psychoanalysts, also leave them either derided or deserted and stranded. ('The abnormal through normal's eyes' says Deanna.) For example, Stoller (1975) sees symbiotic annihilation and even *hatred* at the maternal slaughter of their male identities as root problems of their ilk and the much venerated psychoanalyst Erik Erikson, in a reference to Stoller (1975), kindly referred to those like Denys as 'far-gone perverts'. If they turn to psychiatrists they find that they can easily end up as fodder for research with little actually being done to help them as the level of knowledge most professionals have of this state is very limited (indeed, many of them state quite explicitly, 'The professionals know nothing'). For surgery they have to prove that they can live 'full-time', as it is known, as a woman (preferably in an earning role) for two years to qualify. But in *our* society and these days that is a tall order. Disputes and recriminations between transsexuals and their psychiatrists are legion – and the more heated and desperate the former become the more seriously unstable (and hence the less suitable for surgery) they are usually *seen* to be (whilst of course they claim it to be all the more reason to *have* surgery!).

Alas, it is difficult to be a very co-operative patient in Great Britain with this condition. Given the circumstances, Deanna's and Deborah's equanimity is remarkable and their source of earnings neither uncommon nor surprising. Its possible future illegality may eventually bring the draw-bridge down even on *this* small arena of personal freedom, expression and function too. I personally have never seen a multiple catch-22 situation of such entanglement before in my life. That transsexuals score highly on psychometric measures of psychosis and psychosis-proneness (Beatrice 1985) is in no way alarming. I find it difficult to believe that an alyha or a berdache, living in the middle of an accepting culture, would similarly present as deranged. Indeed such a control study would be well worth doing. The only saving point in this distressing tale is that Deanna's situation would have been even worse (and the mental state of transsexuals perhaps even *more* pathological) in hardier places such as Scotland, the Shetland Isles and Norway, where the terrain and the climate is tougher and the morality more authoritarian and conservative.

TWO PERSONALITIES

There are no prizes in our society for being a prostitute and certainly none for being a transsexual prostitute. Denys's male personality never received a great deal of positive reinforcement, partly because his feminine tenden-cies distracted from its full expression. This feminine side was, however, the being Denys wanted to become. Having caused Denys problems as a man, it asserted itself as the solution to those very problems. This is a circularity that is endemic in male-to-female transsexuals and it can easily lead the unwary to misinterpret the condition as totally due to 'masculine inadequacy'. What such an interpretation lacks is the answer to why such a harrowing solution as the creation of a female personality should be chosen when so many so much easier solutions, from bodybuilding to rugby, are available. Clearly there must be present some prior genetic or constitutional 'push' for a person to take this extraordinarily tortuous path to inner peace. And it is the latter which has to be explained.

The *existence* of Denys's transsexualism I tentatively will take as rooted in biology[3] and very early childhood experiences (the latter may, however, only be the *occasion* for the *expression* of cross-gender desires rather than the *cause* of them). The form of the female personality itself and the long-term effects on a man's experience of self and of life of having such tendencies within himself are, however, within the realm not of biology but of psychology. The purpose of the rest of this chapter is then to outline the battle that Denys has fought within and the routes he has taken to create for himself *a life*. Denys will never appear in *Who's Who*, he will receive no honours, no recognition, he may indeed die scorned. But beneath this surface skin of disrepute and marginality a tremendous (if quiet) personal struggle has been fought which has required all the (considerable) creative resources of this being to be deployed to enable him/her to survive *at all*.

Despite my own transvestism and rebellious gender-bending escapades (see Chapter 3), there was no doubt that Denys/Deanna was in a psychic place where even I could not go. Indeed Deanna referred to Denys *as experienced* as 'a shell', 'an illusion', 'the living dead' and so on. In fact Denys could only function at all in the male earning role because of the regular emergence of the personality of Deanna, and it was Deanna that was *felt* to be the deeper real self. One might think that if Deanna's male personality, Denys, had received more *rewards*, was positively reinforced more, that if Denys felt liked and respected rather more, he would have gained in strength. But no. All the affection that was given to Denys seemed to have the uncanny quality of 'bouncing off'. It seemed not to be processed, had no impact, was obviously taken to have no value.

But nevertheless, Denys in a psychological sense did live on. Early and then again late in 1987 we explored the personalities and feelings of Denys and Deanna by personality and by mood questionnaires (see Tables 8.1 and 8.2). Early in 1987 Denys referred to his female personality actually as Diana ('the huntress'); in truth the permanent full name of Deanna Beaumont was adopted later that year (see Table 8.2). (The name is taken from the French transvestite nobleman Chevalier d'Eon de Beaumont (1728–1810), who was employed as a diplomatic agent under Louis XV (Ellis 1936).)

From these tables, however, we can see that the male and female personalities early in the career or life of the latter strangely differ very little. The measures of mood from 'Stress' down to 'Startle' are also very similar – with Diana feeling rather more pleasant and alert than Denys. However, the high 'Lie Scores' are revealing. Later in 1987 when Denys completed the questionnaires on a second pair of occasions he wrote to me thus:

Peter,
   From time to time I've said that my male role is an act based upon the behaviour of others. I don't think there are many who have seen me not acting. Today I shut myself away, dropped my act and as my true male self came to the fore started on the forms. You may in the forms' answers catch a glimpse of the true male.
   At the time of doing the forms I had no memory of (a) what I marked last Saturday (*as Deanna (author)*) (b) what I marked last February. My senses tell me this is different. I've had a shock doing it and somehow sense what is/could be happening.
   How long in the light of the attached evidence do you give me??? [The note is unsigned.]

Indeed 'the forms' of late 1987 do tell a very different story – to the extent that I have referred to the Denys who emerged that day as

Table 8.1 Comparison of male (Denys I) and female (Diana) personalities in a male-to-female transsexual early in the 'life' of the female personality

	Denys I (male personality) 21 Feb. 1987 Time: 14.10	Diana (female personality) 21 Feb. 1987 Time: 19.30
Extraversion (21)[1]	6	4
Neuroticism (23)	12	10
Psychoticism (25)	5	5
Lie Score (21)	14	14
Stress (19)	2	1
Arousal (15)	13	14
Aggression (12)	5	8
Concentration (9)	8	8
Deactivation (9)	0	0
Social Affection (12)	12	12
Anxiety (12)	3	0
Depression (9)	6	6
Egotism (12)	0	0
Pleasantness (12)	4	10
Activation (9)	5	7
Nonchalance (9)	3	5
Scepticism (6)	0	0
Startle (6)	0	0

Note:
1 Figures in brackets represent the maximum possible scores on the dimensions referred to. Extraversion, Neuroticism, Psychoticism and the Lie Score are measured by the EPQ (Eysenck and Eysenck 1975); Stress and Arousal by the MacKay inventory (MacKay *et al.* 1978) and the remaining measures of mood from Aggression to Startle by the Nowlis inventory (Nowlis 1965).

'Denys II' (and for me this is the true Denys). Now the Lie Score in the male role drops from 14 to 6, the latter a pretty average score (Eysenck and Eysenck 1975). Extraversion sinks to zero from 6 earlier in the year, Neuroticism lifts from 12 to 18 (a high score) and felt Stress rockets from 2 in February to a maximum score in December of 19! Felt Arousal or Alertness plummets from 13 right down to 0 while felt Scepticism and Anxiety are both considerably lifted. The depressed mood of early 1987 is reflected at the same level late in 1987. Indeed the *real* Denys is far more stressed, anxious and introverted than the Denys the world usually sees. It is clear that Denys I and 'Diana' of early 1987 are a pair of psychologically identical masks dressed simply in different clothes.

The picture Deanna presented, however, was different again. Deanna is a totally different personality from Denys I, Denys II *and* from Diana. While all four selves are slightly aggressive in felt mood, the only personality dimension that receives similar scores across all four personalities is Psychoticism, at a level of 5 or 6. This, alas, is quite a high score (Eysenck and Eysenck 1975, Table 8, p. 27).

Table 8.2 Comparison of male (Denys II) and female (Deanna)[1] personalities in the same transsexual depicted in Table 8.1 approximately eighteen months to two years into the 'life' of the female personality

	Denys II (male personality) 3 Dec. 1987 Time: 14.45	Deanna (female personality) 28 Nov. 1987 Time: 00.47
Extraversion (21)	0	17
Neuroticism (23)	18	3
Psychoticism (25)	5	6
Lie Score (21)	6	19
Stress (19)	19	0
Arousal (15)	0	15
Aggression (12)	3	6
Concentration (12)	6	3
Deactivation (9)	9	0
Social Affection(12)	6	12
Anxiety (12)	12	0
Depression (9)	6	0
Egotism (12)	0	0
Pleasantness (12)	0	11
Activation (9)	0	9
Nonchalance (9)	3	9
Sceptism (6)	6	0
Startle (6)	6	0

Note:
1 She had by this time changed her name from Diana to Deanna.

Denys II has dropped his act and is now allowing himself to feel the pain of a lifetime; Deanna meanwhile is carefree, excited, pleasant, nonchalant, trusting, totally free of any stress and the veritable life of the party with an Extraversion score of 17 (compared to *zero* for Denys II). Her Neuroticism score is merely 3 while Denys II is hitting close to the top of the scale on this. Her colossal Lie Score of 19, which is in fact the highest score I've seen on this scale, could be due (given the wording of the questions) to her inexperience of life and to her having a strong tendency to 'do the right thing' in small everyday affairs rather than to actual lying. On the other hand it could also be that Deanna is the form of an attempt, and thus far a successful attempt by Denys, to create an ideal 'fresh start' personality. However, even a brief glance at the scores in Table 8.2 will show that Deanna is almost a mirror image of Denys II while Diana and Denys I were almost identical! What seems to have happened here is that the false self of Denys I has collapsed and a real self with its unconscious mirror image has actually emerged (as an alternative perhaps to psychosis) with this emergence being facilitated by wearing different garb. This is clearly confirmatory of Jungian theory that the unconscious contains our opposites in a lesser state of development. It is not confirmatory of behaviourist or constructivist ideas because Deanna was (apparently) not modelled on any contemporary woman nor had she been carefully and analytically 'thought out'. She had been 'felt'. Denys had always regarded her as within, 'ready-made', 'waiting' for release. Here with the collapse of a false male and a false female self *two* real selves have indeed blossomed. It is not surprising then that Denys felt (as he did) that he had been 'permeable' to forces from beyond himself, however one construes this (and of course there are many ways of doing this); it is because that is *precisely* from whence Deanna has come.

What of subsequent developments? It is likely that these quite stark scores that Deanna provided me late in 1987 have changed to less idealised levels now as she has gained still more experience of everyday life. Indeed Denys did state in 1993 that intuitively he felt this to be true. Alas, fed up with being interviewed and diagnosed by clinicians, he refused with a laugh my request for a third testing, really vital data thus being lost through our sheer overintrusiveness (and also through Denys's paranoia).

Nevertheless, this possible *later* personality change over more recent years in Deanna is worth bearing in mind. Regular experience of the female role in men I have known who have doubled up in their person-alities in this way does tend to eliminate its dreamy idealised quality. Indeed, after a couple of years the male and female personalities can even converge – and the previously shrouded male personality can start not to disappear but to 'come through' in the female role. In those who practise very sporadic and very secretive cross-dressing this is prevented from occurring by the female role's sheer lack of experience of life. No 'woman' ever learns anything if she never ventures outside the closet. I think it would be extremely valuable for clinicians dealing with transsexuals to monitor their female *and male* personalities over time, say at three- or four-monthly intervals, using inventories in this way. Clearly, if the two personalities *do converge*, as I would suggest they not uncommonly do, the benefits of the female role are beginning to lose their impact and sex reassignment surgery is not indicated. On the other hand if they *diverge* and the female personality seems increasingly strong, healthy and well adjusted over time, then surgery would seem to be a more plausible and viable course of action.

DR JEKYLL AND MISS HYDE

Denys obtained no physical sexual pleasure from dressing as Deanna and stated that his penis was of 'no use' to him. Any sensuous pleasure he obtained was cerebral rather than genital. His appearance as a man was heavily and unambiguously male and the creation of Deanna as a pass-able woman a long-drawn-out, if enjoyable, ritual occupying many hours. Only the most careful (and loving) attention to every minute detail allowed the conversion from male to female to be brought off plausibly at all.

A diagnosis of transsexualism was made in 1971 by an eminent sexologist but strangely Denys was not actually *informed* of this diagnosis. His circumstances at that time did not easily allow the emergence of the female role so he spent no less than *fourteen years* suppressing it – only the music of Richard Wagner gave him any inner peace. These were years that he refers to as 'the void years'. Fourteen years *wasted*. If he had had the diagnosis he might have spent them working towards a productive realisation of what he/she organismically was. It is not surprising that Denys is a bitter person: he has been let down, sacked or rejected not only by his wife but by virtually every societal agent he has ever had dealings with – and all because he is basically a berdache in psychologically naïve Western culture. Western culture, the supposed pride of our planet. A stock comment of his (conventional) ex-wife's that had reverberated maddeningly around his mind ever since was, 'You're not *man* enough for me!'

There is no doubt that Deanna has been set free from or through the unconscious of Denys. But, rather in the spirit of Hyde in Stevenson's *Dr Jekyll and Mr Hyde*, Deanna seemed over the years to be *the stronger personality*. Denys released something that was bigger and more powerful than himself. One can well imagine her in the role of a dominant mistress. Although one could easily see Deanna merely as an escape from Denys's paranoia, shyness, neuroticism, low self-esteem and so on, this would be to take only the obvious and callow path. There was more to Deanna than this, to a degree that was almost eerie. To talk of Denys's inadequacy motives, motives possibly created because of the experiences he has had in our culture with his double-sided nature, is to miss the *capacity* that these motives helped to emancipate and liberate. Simply focusing on the negative and obvious in Denys misses the essential psychological truth of this being. Denys could validly be spoken of as having a double gender capacity rather than a gender identity disorder. In some cultures in India and, as we have seen, in American Indian society, he would easily have found peace and a valid role and function. But not here. Here he was 'disordered' and 'abnormal' (see, for example, Stoller 1969).

It is to this double gender capacity that I will orient this narrative. At one of his (many) visits to clairvoyants he calmly sat down (in the male role) and the woman seer immediately said to him, 'Who is this woman within?' Since Denys as a man looks and behaves far more like the policeman he once was than, say, a feminine male designer or hairdresser, this remark was surprising. But in truth Deanna was a real living force, an ominous, almost sinister presence, of tremendous power within the psyche of Denys. As many transsexuals and transvestites do, he interpreted the existence of 'this woman within' along reincarnationist lines. He speculated that Deanna *was* a woman perhaps from another time using him to live on, to live again. A powerful woman, a woman of bearing inside him, a woman of Borgia-style temperament, who possessed his male body and mind and used them as pawns to seize once again the gift of life.

The clothes, wigs, shoes and make-up had the magical power they had because they gave this woman from the depths *form*. In a way Denys used his body as a kind of scaffold around which to create and build the form of Deanna, a woman who compelled him to do this, a woman who demanded life, *who longed to be.*

MISSIONS POSSIBLE AND IMPOSSIBLE

About a quarter of transsexuals have some fetishistic interest, at least in their early days of cross-dressing. For Denys material fetishism ('material magic') helped to light up this interior feminine field or gestalt. Deanna was in fact a temptress in black satin, the most occult and preternatural of fabrics. The field she radiated can only be described as 'thunder'. Black satin was indeed a symbolic material for Deanna, a veritable gateway to the spirit. It was not a fetish that Denys had, not at all; on the contrary it was a fetish that *had him*. Black satin, via Deanna, was not something that Denys wore, it was something that used Denys as a plaything to show itself to the world. It was a driving force, an electric flash across the mind, compelling him to create this temptress, to give her a personality, an appearance, friends, life experience. To give her *life itself*!

Deanna, in 5" stiletto heels, and thus at 6' 6", and in ball gowns of cascading black satin, was indeed a sight from another time, as if from another dimension. She treated her clients as she treated Denys: as male toys, male slaves, there only for her pleasure, as pastimes to amuse her. It was as if something from 'beyond' had used Denys's weak spot, the very desire over which he (like Wagner) had no power, no control, no *will*, his enslavement to glistening yards of black satin, gradually to insinuate itself over the years into his soul, eventually to blossom in full force as a real living woman. There is no point in talking to Denys about 'dominating mothers and weak passive fathers'. The concept doesn't apply and is irrelevant anyway. What we have here is a *spiritual phenomenon*.

Deanna was Denys's reason for life, *was* his life. Denys was, as he said, just a shell, a biological system which served the needs and desires of Deanna. Of no moment or value in himself, Denys's eyes in the male role were *dead*. In a sense, he was gone, finished. He was a vessel for this being from beyond who, once created, as indeed she had to be, glorified in this bequest of life and in the life of a worshipped woman, a woman who *must* be obeyed. A woman at whose feet men grovelled and whimpered, in chains, in padlocks, powerless, reduced to specks, reduced to *nothing*. This was not Denys, it was not Denys's mother, this was a woman from 'elsewhere'.

Denys was a catalyst-supreme of clairvoyants because of his wonderful receptiveness and open-mindedness. Just as they are able to be 'taken over' by their 'spirit voices' so he too had this capacity, this daring, to be taken over by forces from beyond himself. But the price he paid was a heavy one. When I last spoke to him he was sleeping for eighteen hours a day when on leave. He was a man totally drained, empty, wrung dry. Although this may have been partly due to the draining effect of his heavy smoking, it was also due to his using one body for two lives, an intimidating prospect. But the future may be more positive. Denys has now become semi-politically involved in Deborah's own case and feels, with her, bitter about her sacking and the spoiling and mismanagement of her life by the various authorities she has consulted. Denys, like me, has also done some writing for underground magazines, attempting to dispel myths about his condition and point the way to a better future. As a personality in a psychological sense he still exists even if experientially he feels empty and drained. For me Denys has been brave to dare to give form to this all-possessing fateful force within him. He has risked his mind and his life to do what he *had* to do. To let be what *had* to be. A weaker soul would have shrunk from the task. There are signs that Deanna is receding – or emerging less demandingly. On one recent occasion Denys even said to me that he was 'thinking of doing something else'(!). As Denys becomes more involved in Deborah's 'case' he is developing a new mission and a new purpose that does not entirely revolve around the enslavement to Deanna. In this direction lies the possibility of real progression and a new destiny. Via its political nature, perhaps one day it will help take transsexuals in the direction of what we *all* deserve: freedom and acceptance.

Denys has always been haunted by a sense of inevitability. With this attitude of mind, synchronicity is common, as everyday and not-so-everyday events do *take on* 'meaning' if one interprets them as pointers to one's deeper purpose. What people devoid of meaning do not notice, a 'Man of Mission' will detect – but with this tendency is the danger of over-interpretation. Indeed, at the extreme end of this road lies madness. Now that he is dealing with a more practical and worldly issue, the flights of fancy that synchronicity can compel for Denys are less likely. He is in effect turning away from the Borderline to spiritually calmer waters. But he remains a fighter, one who looks for scraps. This new contest may yet help him to open many closed eyes. In his underground writings, while psychologists are still obsessed with the mummies and daddies of transsexuals and transvestites, Denys has looked well ahead and written of such things as Surrealistic transvestism and abstract transvestism (Watson and Beaumont 1989). In this realm, while the professionals move along slowly seeking facts and mechanisms, people like Denys and Deborah, who really do live where the action is, are disappearing into the blue yonder with far-sighted ideas about the transformational possibilities of transvestism and transsexualism. It is clear from anecdotes like this that the future of the 'Western berdache' is likely to lie with the activities and the campaigning will of the berdaches themselves. In this arena, the academy is in the background. They themselves will do more in ten years by activism and imagination than thirty years or more of scholarship are likely to achieve. This seems, in the circumstances, to be a mission worthwhile – and by no means impossible.

REFLECTIONS

The tall, mysterious Wagnerian presence of Deanna may well by now (1995/6) have disappeared from life. Denys was in his fifties when he entered the world of courtesans and it is a world where the cardinal motto is: 'You'd better not get old.' A being of such fire could also hardly live long without draining its vessel of all life. Had Denys begun his journey into the opposite gender in 1971, things might have been different but in this scenario one needs to be very visually convincing as a woman and able to take off the woman's role with ease. Physically, if not cerebrally, Denys was disadvantaged. To have perhaps a partly female brain in a body that is indubitably male (or vice versa) is one of the greatest tragedies that can befall a human being.

Like most transsexuals and transvestites, Denys was deeply cynical and disrespectful of human scientists – who generally would only interpret him in *their* terms, not in his own. But, as attribution theorists realise (e.g. Hewstone 1983, 1989), it was his own reality and his own attributions that gave the best predictions of him and were what he had to come to terms with and live with daily. At the individual level 'aetiological myths' may indeed be, at times, all that we have to cling to.

Denys's paranoia, odd speech, rapport difficulties and superstitiousness would have been suspect to diagnosticians as evidence of schizotypy but whatever his social problems he was not superstitious without good reason. At one of his many 'sittings' the clairvoyant he was consulting, reacting to something said to him by his 'guide', terminated the session with 'and to prove to you that what I have said is true and will come to pass, twenty minutes into your return journey from here your windscreen wipers will break down'. On the return journey that is exactly what happened, and it was timed exactly. Of course it could have been a coincidence, maybe they had been tampered with, but that was only one incident of many and as such incidents accumulate it is easy to see how they could undermine belief in a purely materialistic world. Given that, before he met her, the layout of Deborah's house was also exactly predicted, as was the special quality of the future relationship, it is hardly surprising that Denys regards scientists as 'merely mortal' and living within 'a petty little middle-class suburban value system'.

Given the likely selective remembering of confirmatory instances of this kind (see Chapter 10 in Sutherland 1992a), it is unlikely that Denys could have convinced any psychiatrist of the validity of his mission in life, his sense of destiny, the inevitability that he felt surrounded him. Scientists are totally dismissive of the methods of clairvoyants (see the rejection by psychologists in Josephson and Ramachandran 1980) and hence could never have established 'joint reference' (Freeman *et al.* 1982) with Denys. He was thus beyond any help or guidance from mainstream authorities and was thus one of the many 'losses to the system' about which we are now becoming so concerned (Newton 1988).

With Desmond comedy is never far away, even in his saddest moments. With Ivo, strangely, romance is about and in my schizotypal years the music was adventure. But with Denys/Deanna the play was a tragedy. Perhaps, when all is said and done, the solution for Denys if he, as a man, survives is to capitalise on inner qualities other than his great anger and his awesome and unearthly anima. 'Deanna' as a personality seems to have little future. But Denys has many other latent qualities which could secure him a viable outlook. As a man he has great powers of integrity, honesty, empathy, dependability and reliability (all catalysed by his training in the police force), and his uncanny sensitivity socially, his imaginative powers and his courage can hardly be let to go to waste. Ironically, he could have made a fine father to his children had he been allowed to and had his anima not been of such daunting and distracting power. One is reminded here of the shamanistic qualities of the berdache (p. 94) and Denys could indeed have fulfilled such a role admirably but for the utter stupidity (and fear) of the agents of western society when confronted with the challenge of the feminine male.

Denys was too independent-minded and cynical of science, psychiatry and psychoanalysis to go to work restructuring and actualising his male identity in other ways in a formal relationship with a therapist. Dominant people are anyway temperamentally unsuited to the passive dependency which is often either required of or inculcated into clients in psychotherapy (on such dependency see Tudor and Tudor 1994). Their heroes, if ever they have any, quickly come crashing down in pieces at the detection of the slightest flaw. No, we are left as before with tragedy, a man born perhaps two centuries too soon and/or into the wrong culture. A visionary imagination and a feminine spirit has been flung into a world of logic circuits and 'tight associations' which reifies the masculine and canonises 'straight' heterosexual behaviour. Like Oscar Wilde (Ellmann 1988, p. 343), Denys was not interested in 'the truth of the professor in the institute'. He preferred his own truth, 'the truth of the dream'. Of this

Oscar was to claim 'of the two truths, the falser is the truer'. Perhaps in this world of the dream, Denys has a future, and can find a truth deeper and more meaningful than all the steel-grey essays on biocognitive engineering could ever provide.

Chapter 9

Reflections on the Borderliners' biographies

The most positive men are the most credulous.

(Jonathan Swift, 1667–1745)

As promised in Chapter 1, the qualitative material presented so far in this book has concentrated on the psychological territory *near* to outright insanity in the hope of validating this style of being as one which is creative, colourful and challenging and also as one which throws light even on the nature of reality itself. The relational structure of reality which is revealed to people near to schizophrenia, because of their less sceptical, less conservative and less associatively tight ways of thinking, is quite different from that entertained by neo-classical science but it is a meaningful pattern, as we have seen, that can be integrated into one's life in functional and effective ways. The Borderliners therefore present psychological pictures which are adaptive in their own terms and hopefully convey an affirmative and constructive impression of the schizophrenia-prone mind.

Here I will concentrate, in reflection, on certain issues which eventuate from these biographies which deserve further mention and deeper 'unpacking'. These are: the experience of synchronicity in sane as opposed to insane people; the sanity and productiveness of Deanna's (perhaps rather outrageous) 'condition' as to an extent one which none the less is 'beyond psychology' and not merely 'roughage for the consulting room'; the costs of the 'process' way of life and the possibilities that these Borderliners hold out for a fusion of esoteric and materialistic knowledge. My purpose here is to separate fact from fiction; to separate psychopathology from that which is not psychopathology and to separate 'caseness' from essential validity. I do not do this in the spirit of a 'New Age' thinker, a postmodernist, a social constructionist, a rhetorician or a discourse analyst; in spirit I am none of those things. I do this in the spirit of being a phenomenological psychologist who does have a belief in objective truth but one who tries also to facilitate possibilities via a deeper understanding of the complex and multifaceted nature of Man. (This is why I describe myself as an 'artist-experimenter' (Chadwick 1996b).) In this role I share neither the negativity of scientists to the esoteric and to the outré nor the unwillingness to *test* ideas that characterises artists. This is clearly a singular identity but one that I would claim is needed if we are to characterise fairly and adequately the essence of the schizophrenic credit.

I will begin here with, I would suggest, a *necessary* careful look at synchronicity – which is an overriding concept in many schizotypals' lives but one which has its dangers as well as its meaningful benefits.

THE LOGIC OF SYNCHRONICITY

When a perfectly sane person has a sense of mission and events occur that subtly facilitate that enterprise, it is common for them to think that these events were 'sent' or 'orchestrated' in some way to help or speed their quest. A job turns up 'just at the right time'; a critical person enters their life 'just when they were close to giving up'. People frequently talk in this way in everyday chatter. 'Meaningful coincidences' of these kinds fuel popular belief in that 'something' which may be beyond the ordinary and indeed Jung (in Jung and Pauli 1955; Jung 1955/1985), in his concept of Synchronicity, gave a kind of verbal form to these experiences. Such events bespeckled the lives of all the biographees here, myself included, but what is the relation between them and the phenomena of delusional madness? How does schizotypal superstitiousness become schizophrenic insanity? I will try to elucidate this transition with reference to seven points which I would claim dismiss a lot of the uncertainty in this area.

1 The coincidences of insanity are less statistically unusual and thus less objectively striking than the coincidences of the stable person and of the schizotypal. Hence the criterion for acceptance of 'reasonable quality data' is lower in the former than in the latter. Jung, for example, remarks on the occurrence of 'fish' in one context or another six times in one day (Jung 1955/1985, pp. 14–15) as an example of an everyday fortuitous series of events of no meaning. In my pre-psychotic state, however, in 1979, coincidences relating to the devil were occurring twenty to thirty times a day. This seemed subjectively strange and ushered in (eventually) outright psychotic thought. In madness, however, psychotics will feel troubled or infer that they are being followed or monitored if they see the same stranger merely three times in a week. Here the criterion for acceptance of data has clearly plummeted. Having said this, however, very striking coincidences can loosen a person's adherence to a material reality and induce an early delusion-like state (e.g. noticing while driving that the car behind has 'followed' one through five turnings). This latter kind of event can easily make a vulnerable (guilt-ridden?) person think that 'something is going on' and hence induce delusional mood. Clearly

here sheer 'instance repetition' is being taken as a quality of the uncanny – and this indeed is a common bias in human cognition – to make judgements based on frequency data rather than on probabilities (Estes 1976).

2 The 'connections' that psychotics make are usually more remote (some would say 'loose') than those of stable people and of schizotypals. For example, my 'unforgivable/unpardonable' incident (p. 85), occurring at the very moment I was contemplating forgiveness as an answer to my anguish, does not require a large inferential leap to connect the event with my mental state. The associative distance is so small that that particular event would probably have been 'disturbing' to anyone (even a positivist). However, in delusional states (to take an actual example) men walking by in dark London Transport uniforms will be seen as 'undertakers coming to kill me'. A piece of lemon peel will be 'significant' because it is 'like the sun'. Here the 'reach' or 'penetration' through the network of associations stored in long-term memory is greater than in superstitious sanity. Hence as we pass from 'first associates' to more remote connections the less 'synchronistic' and the more 'mad' do the interpretations of events seem to be. Because of this (perhaps) facilitation of activation spread through a psychotic's neural network (without a commensurate spread of inhibition), it is common in florid episodes for 'anything and everything' eventually to seem at least *relevant* to their ongoing concerns and thus either to match with thoughts or to *provoke* 'meaningful associates' (e.g. a car accelerates down the road: 'People are eager to get away from me'; a shopkeeper shuts up shop as one walks past: 'All doors are closing on me now'; a young woman throws the end of a cigarette on to the pavement: 'I've reached the fag-end of my life'; or to take a more concrete (and actual) example: 'The "i" has dropped out of the name of the estate on the wall across the road, that means my "eye" is going to drop out').

As the frequency of event occurrence drops, as the associative distance involved increases and as the morbidity of the thoughts increases, the more we tend to regard the cognitions as 'psychotic' rather than 'unusual but reasonable'. (Notice also the tendency shown in examples like this to have difficulty inhibiting attention to basically irrelevant events (Williams 1995).)

3 As the latter examples also show, the intensity of the sense of *meaning* and *significance* to events is greater in psychosis than in schizotypy. Also the inference of some greater external controlling force – be it God, Satan or MI5 – is more intense and securely lodged in the psychotic than in the non-psychotic mind. (Hence more minute and objectively trivial events (such as wind direction) are malignly interpreted than those interpreted by sane suspicious people.) This is the 'top-down' aspect of the feelings of 'relevance' in trivia whereas work on weaknesses in

cognitive inhibition (Beech, Baylis *et al.* 1989; Beech, Powell *et al.* 1989; Beech, McManus *et al.* 1991; Williams 1995) provide the 'bottom-up' aspect.

4 The threshold of consciousness may well be lower in psychotics than in schizotypals – itself likely to impair automatic cognitive inhibition – and hence psychotics have greater access to unconscious and preconscious processes than do sane people (Frith 1979). This can produce a great deal of pseudo-synchronicity: for example, if one is resonant to the preconscious associations going on beneath other people's overt speech, it is elementary that one will think thoughts that they *then say* or think thoughts that their subsequent utterance is a reasonable development from or reply to. The quite common experience in madness of having 'conversations with the radio' or thinking that 'people in the office can hear my thoughts' probably stems from the effects of this threshold drop. These 'matching' or 'reply' associations, however, are emotionally *exceedingly* unsettling and through sheer activation increase to extreme levels may drop the threshold of consciousness even further. They may thus shift criterion placement also still further towards more 'risky' judgements (see Broadbent 1971) whilst possibly damaging inhibitory operations.

5 Enhanced subliminal sensitivity may produce non-conversational coincidences. If one subliminally detects a black cat in peripheral vision, possibly on the basis of colour information alone, then finds oneself *thinking* 'I wish I had a black cat', *then* the very cat involved crosses one's path and is consciously noticed, this 'triangulation' of events could easily pass for synchronicity (the scarab beetle on the window pane in Jung's critical example (p. 3) might itself have similarly preconsciously influenced his patient's dream recall narrative during the session, where- upon he *then* noticed it). I have sometimes found that the headlines or even parts of headlines on newspapers that are lying around in the house can inadvertently set off a train of thought involuntarily and this can *then* be followed by one consciously noticing that headline. For example, a barely noticed headline 'A short step to the abyss' (*Guardian* Outlook 8/9 July 1995), in fact about the fragile peace in Ulster, might subliminally access the level of meaning in long-term memory (see Dixon 1981) and prompt a conversation between myself and my wife about Denys's life situation – *then* one of us might consciously notice the headline and say 'Talk of the Devil!' Much 'talk of the Devil' and incidents of 'syn- chronicity' may involve triangulation with preconscious-to-conscious conversions of this kind.

6 A consensually shareable sane state of mind can be in a sense 'weakened' by a tirade of uncanny coincidences (this is actually what happened to me

in 1979 – see Chadwick 1992, Chapter 4 and 1993b, pp. 244–7). If events from *outside* dovetail with ongoing thoughts and concerns, this facilitates the retrieval of memories and ideas *from within* to sustain the evolving delusional system. Basically the motto is: 'If these incredible things are happening I'd better try and work out what is going on!' Jung himself always recognised that the 'significance' of external events can reveal unconscious or preconscious dynamics (e.g. 'There's an empty milk bottle – that's been put there by the CIA to remind me of how empty I am inside'). Schizotypal superstitious people may actually therefore pass into a psychotic state if a compelling stream of the uncanny does come their way. Sheer frequency of occurrence of the remarkable is therefore weakening of the western rational-empirical mode of thought. Deanna showed tendencies of moderating her rational thought in this manner at times. Desmond would also get excited under such circumstances but was so prone to changing his mind (as pointed out to him by his friend Fred Robinson) that no singular delusional idea ever became entrenched.

7   Once a particular schema is in place and some convincing confirmations of it have occurred (e.g. from numerology or tarot card readings), the person goes into a 'searching mode' and attention is then more heavily focused on events that continue to confirm it (e.g. '16 occurs a lot in your life, you are destined for a strange and terrible fall'). Now the motto is: 'I must miss nothing, even if I make some blunders in what I notice.' If a person thinks 'I am Judas Iscariot reborn – sent to bring havoc to the world', a browse through the bad news of any daily newspaper of the 1990s can provide several dozen 'confirmatory' instances of such a delusion – and *refuting* such a thought would indeed be a tricky business. This acceleration of confirmatory detection (the 'synchronicity of syn-chronicity' (Vaughn 1979)) may be irrational to materialists but what is noticed can in a sense 'cue out' more and more material of psychological significance *within* until one is taken (Jung might say) to the ultimate *inner* reality. Is this confrontation with the ultimate essence of the Self – at the same time as confirmatory coincidences are raining down upon a person – a psychological, psychophysical or existential 'breakthrough' into another dimension of reality or to the deepest strata of mind and matter (Laing/Jung)? It is not surprising that it *seems* to be so when people in this state come to *think* that they have telepathic and precog-nitive powers or may even actually have psychokinetic abilities. But can it be explained entirely by facilitation of associations, tuned attention, amplification of 'confirmatory pickup', selective confirmatory thinking, retrieving and ideation and general 'overactivation' of the pathways subserving thought and feeling? Materialists would undoubtedly give credence to the latter. My belief is that *most* of the 'uncanny' phenomena of insanity can be so explained but that some events occur which jolt even

a cynic. It is my contention that this very openness, even gullibility, that characterises the boldly superstitious mind, this accepting, receptive quality, does indeed permit access to 'the elsewhere'. Most of the phenomena apprehended by such people I believe are illusory but the blurring of boundaries between inner and outer, the receptive confirmation-seeking attitude, the penetration of activation through the neural network, the openness to 'magic' and to 'the impossible' may, I suggest, as we saw in the lives of Desmond, Ivo and Deanna, bring an enlivened and enlarged perception of reality and advantages in spiritual, social and creative life. They may also give us surprising insights into the 'deep structure' of what is. If, then, the schizophrenia-prone mind can be defended partly as outside diagnosis and psychological reductionism – or at least as of an identity and status that is more than mere roughage for psychopathological research – then it can be claimed to have its own intrinsic validity and the claims for a 'schizophrenic credit' will have been upheld.

BEYOND PSYCHOLOGY

Since the framework of this book is essentially psychophysical, it is axiomatic therefore that no psychological explanation of the Borderline could be complete, as that would be to collapse all examination of it into psychologism and the claims of the schizotypal would again be of interest only as pathology.

All of the phenomena of 'the edge' so far discussed do present a challenge to psychology and could indeed partly be outside its purview. If this is so, then insight into the conditions of their origin is therefore not synonymous with the negation of their independent validity. The same is also true of ethics, aesthetics and logic. That mysticism is thus beyond either psychiatric or psychoanalytic reduction has been shown by Deikmann (1966, 1977). The sexual life of Deanna (Chapter 8), perhaps the most unusual in these pages, featuring as it does not only transsexualism but fetishism and sadomasochism, seems indeed to be most poised as fair game for the psychologist (see Gosselin and Wilson 1980) but alas cannot, I would suggest, be explained away quite as easily as one might think. Deanna's life was not an erotic form of hatred (Stoller 1975) but an erotic form of spirituality. It deserves more respect than that. It was not a life of cheap lust but of the sensitive magic of eroticism. Deanna's wish was to dwell in pure femininity – but this cannot be found in one woman or even ten. It requires symbols that embody *an idea*. Such a quest is a search for a platonic style of pure form but of erotic content, a distilled essence, beyond individual human examples with all their flaws. This is rather to be seen as abstract sex, the love of an essential form beyond exemplars, and to regard this as perverse and despicable is surely common and puritanical.

The shunning of human examples in favour of a needed (but for him impossible to find) pure femininity also characterised Keats (Thorpe 1926) and was the reason he did not marry. Oscar Wilde too, in his obsession with youth, was in love chiefly with *an idea.*

While any sexual phenomenon away from the middle ground is static, rigid or compulsive, just a repetitive enslavement, it is indeed fair game for psychoanalytic reductionism (see for example Halberstadt-Freud 1991, p. 6). But when the phenomenon starts to 'move' away from the status of private compulsion and to attract creative life of its own, then psycho-analytic reduction loses its impact. When for example fetishism becomes itself an art form, as in Mimi Parent's Surrealist exhibition (see Alexandrian 1991, p. 227), or when transsexuals start to talk of twenty-first-century developments in eonism (Watson and Beaumont 1989) or when de Sade-inspired sadomasochistic creative imagery emerges (Short 1994, pp. 160–5), we are moving beyond symptomatology and pathology. Outré sexuality is now creating new meanings, becoming of social relevance, becoming a form of art in itself. Now the psychoanalyst is not faced with an inert 'distressing personal problem' but with a semantic system in opposition to his or her own. When the art form attracts some degree of popularity and aesthetic appeal, the analyst is perceived not as refreshing and clarifying but as degrading and trivialising – indulging in what one might call 'psychiatrism'.

It was this desire of Deanna's to take her behaviour to a level that was beyond the talk of the consulting room that in many ways drove her – and to my mind she succeeded, at least in part. It was a tragedy that her real weakness in psychopathological terms was not her cross-gender behaviour or her sexuality but her sensitivity to others' opinions of it – and hence her anger and paranoia. In the end, however, she reoriented this sensitivity away from impotent rage to political activism – providing more than merely a 'case' for analysis but just actions to be reckoned with. This in itself gives her the possibility of the essential validity for which she longed.

DECONSTRUCTING THE DEVIL

It is probably true of all the Borderliners featured here, that they refused to conform to the values and norms of any class, sex role, race or city.[1] Denys and I in particular were classless androgynes, transcending gender role, belonging nowhere. Our truth, as for all of us, was in process. But being a truth seeker in a social reality structured by shared illusions, clichés and stereotypes is stressful, very stressful. Eventually 'total clash' is perhaps inevitable. It is intriguing indeed that a totally free spirit can have *no identity*, as identity is a result partly of social structures and shared values and expectations. If one rejects and undercuts the basis of social roles, structures and norms, one can *only* find one's identity in process:

there is nowhere else to go. And in living as 'personified process' the mystical-paranormal-spiritual way may well on occasion be more available. The very clouding of that 'way' could be partly due to the creation of organised society as such – which demands that people be a type and play a certain set of dominant roles within a political-economic framework. Only at the fringes of life does one discover alternative undercurrents and possibilities.

The whole kaleidoscopic interweaving of epistemological ideas about truth, the nature and conduct of science, the validity of the foundations of society, the bases of communal living and the origin of identity is there and these questions are all brought into macrocosmic relief in the various Borderliners' biographies. Does democracy need real independently validated foundations? Is science a pawn of a basically machismo value system? Is truth-seeking the only responsibility of a free spirit? Every Borderliner is faced explicitly or implicitly with these questions. Clearly in my own case I thought myself and acted myself into a state where the idea of being 'cast out' became very available to me – as was the idea of being a destroyer of society, with its mountain of merely 'shared biases' (something I also studied in my formal research, e.g. Chadwick 1975a, b). The idea of being 'no one', 'hell bent' on the violation of all 'arbitrary' social norms in the interest of 'truth', may well have been an attitude congruent with the general thrust of my research in the 1970s but it was very easily transformed into the idea that 'I' do not *exist*, I *am* a real destroyer of this world, deserving indeed to be 'cast out' because I am or am possessed by Satan! What was a marvellous culmination-in-Nirvana of a free spirit research adventure suddenly flip-sided into an Old Testament abomination.

Society (and even science itself) is importantly cemented not only by faith and trust but by traditions, clichés and shared biases. Try and live beyond and outside them and one risks living in a void. As we know from work on visual illusions (Chadwick 1977) and on the many self-protective and distortive deceptions we use (e.g. Nisbett and Ross 1980), all can agree or behave in the same way yet all be in a sense wrong. In the end the final justification for behaviour in a certain context often seems to be, 'Well it's just the way we've all decided to do things round here and this is the way it's always been done.' If, rebelliously, one tries to dig beneath this to see 'bedrock truth', one risks either profound loneliness and depression, the label of psychopath or outright insanity. There therefore is a warning sign at the gate of 'The Garden of Answers', which reads: 'See reality and suffer.'

EXTENDING THE BOUNDARIES OF SCIENCE AND ART

At death, science stops. As experience grades into insanity, science starts slipping. When mind starts to influence matter, science turns cynical. This is a tragedy. The realm of the poet and that of the scientist essentially meet at the Borderline and it is my contention that each has something to say to the other (see Chadwick 1996b). Science traditionally requires a cautious, rather narrowly focused, aggressive logical attitude; to apprehend the uncanny one needs, however, to be more risky, open, loving and poetical. This really is the barrier to the fusion of scientific and esoteric knowledge. It is an attitude barrier.

I would suggest that it is not enough to collapse all the phenomena discussed so far in this book back into either the physical world or the individual unconscious. We are dealing here with *psychophysical* phenomena not 'derivatives of the unconscious', even though the power of unconscious processes is not denied. When we deal with psychophysical phenomena we cannot expect the exactitude and perfect reproducibility so prized by classical science. There is pattern, harmony and order to be found but it is not rigid; actualisation of the uncanny is partly a function of mind. To understand this realm we have to tread honestly, bravely, sincerely, as we do in the materialistic realm. But we must also be loving, caring, open, reaching somehow higher and beyond ourselves. An attitude of aggressive cynicism will lead to the door being *instantly shut*.

The very attitude we encourage in the West – towards autonomy, independence and subject–object differentiation is the very antithesis of the empathic attitude which 'enables' the uncanny. The close bond between mother and baby, therapist and patient and between some identical twins (see for example Ehrenwald 1972) may be able to facilitate mind–mind and mind–matter interaction, as may the diffusion of boundaries in psychosis and in borderline states. The fragility of identity of all Borderliners (and this was true also of Keats (Thorpe 1926)) is precisely *because* of their cellophane-thin boundaries which, even though we only know of this as an *experienced* state, seem to have none the less distinct physical consequences as well as consequences for creative life.

As we glide beyond the Borderline I would suggest that we gradually change our attitude in order to be able to discover and understand the regularities and order that *do* exist in this territory. The territory is of powerful, perhaps awesome, potential. It can only be negotiated safely and non-self-destructively in *love*. One's conscious attitude is even more important than one's unconscious 'reality' – which may well be better dealt with by forgiveness than by 'ventilating and purging'. A mind that has never known love and forgiveness will not survive beyond the Borderline, but most such minds will (self-protectively) never venture there. This in itself is perhaps a spiritual law or regularity which prevents too many catastrophes.

SCHIZOTYPY, CREATIVITY AND HEALTH

As can be seen from Table 9.1, all the biographees here documented would be seen as disordered by standard-minded clinicians. The trait scores and symptom check-lists present pictures far removed from conventional models of mental health. Whatever our enjoyments of the flesh the two most vulnerable 'cases', I myself pre-psychotically and Denys/Deanna suffered most, however, not from our sensuality but from our own *anger*. Denys's vulnerability as I saw it stemmed particularly from his immersion in cunning and suspicion (the latter particularly of psychiatrists). Desmond and Ivo, however, seem to retain greater stability, not through sexual purity but through their continual orientation to the positive (and this despite everything). Ivo is an excellent example of a productive personality who none the less hears voices (see Romme and Escher 1993 on this). Desmond, meanwhile, is productive despite his paranoid ideation concerning his appearance (this, however, is an anxiety quite common among comedians who often use their trade to turn their odd appearance to their advantage).

All of these people stand as exemplars of the profit to be gained from the *non*-standardisation of mind – be that via Prozac, Clozapine, cognitive therapy or whatever. In a way we have all turned our abnormalities to our advantage and tried to turn them to the advantage of others. This of course has been a challenge to our creativity operating thus at the introverted individual level of personal coping rather than at the more universal extraverted level of published work by recognised figures. This more private challenge to reshape an extremely aberrant endowment into a socially useful and inwardly harmonious form is not, however, an insignificant one. In the empirical sections of this text which now follow we will see whether schizotypal and paranoid tendencies facilitate, dampen or have no effect on creativity and also see whether the qualities of empathy, risk and gullibility really *do* characterise the schizophrenia-prone mind. It may be that the latter does have a particular emotive and cognitive style which is benign in its influence on creative life and indeed it also may be that the general psychology of the schizotypal is better suited (in a sense 'through and through') to a different conception of reality than is marketed by cognitively more inhibited, less emotive and more sceptical thinkers. If this is so then the schizotypal mind and lifestyle offers a self-consistent alternative and a challenge to those of the middle ground with their belief solely in a materialistic reality. Rather than merely diagnosing the schizotypals and offering them pills, it could be argued that they embody a mentality and an epistemology which – though it jars with mainstream society and thus provokes (sometimes extreme) stress – is coherent, harmonious and integrated in its own terms and capable of being functional in its deployment in life.

Table 9.1 Characteristic features of the four biographees

	PKC (pre-morbid, i.e. pre-psychotically)	Desmond	Ivo	Deanna (as Denys II)
Schizotypy				
1 Ideas of reference	✓	✓	x	x
2 Belief in telepathy	✓	✓	✓	✓
3 Belief in clairvoyance	x	✓	✓	✓
4 Belief in psychokinesis	x	✓	✓	✓
5 Superstitiousness	✓	✓	✓	✓
6 Unusual perceptual experiences	✓	✓	✓	✓
7 Odd speech	✓	✓	x	✓
8 Suspiciousness or paranoid ideation	✓	✓	x	✓
9 Inappropriate feelings	✓	x	x	✓
10 Odd behaviour	✓	x	x	✓
11 Lack of close friends or confidantes	✓	x	x	x
Paranoia				
12 Excessive social anxiety of a paranoid kind	✓	✓	x	x
13 Suspects exploitation	x	x	x	✓
14 Doubts friends' loyalty	✓	x	x	✓
15 Reads hidden meanings into benign remarks	x	x	x	x
16 Persistently bears grudges	✓	x	x	✓
17 Feels character is under attack	✓	x	✓	✓
18 Doubts sexual partner's fidelity	✓	x	x	✓
Schizoidism				
19 Does not desire or enjoy close relationships	x	x	x	x
20 Solitary life and activities	✓	x	x	x
21 Emotionally cold	x	x	x	x
22 Indifferent to praise or criticism	x	x	x	x

Chapter 10

Experimental studies
The rationale

What is first in mood is last in form.

(Oscar Wilde, *de Profundis*)

The purpose of the experimental investigations reported here is chiefly to examine the relationships between psychosis-proneness and creativity in very intelligent subjects. It is possible that a combination of schizotypy or psychoticism with high intelligence facilitates creativity more clearly and unambiguously than is the case with less intelligent participants. It is also my purpose to examine the role of non-conformity in creative performance and to assess the *empathic* capabilities of psychosis-prone people. It may also be that the 'looser' cognitive style of schizophrenia-prone individuals can be captured by certain experimental empirical measures and the positive purchase of this looseness and unconventionality then evaluated.

PSYCHOSIS-PRONENESS AND CREATIVITY

To examine the creativity of schizophrenia-prone individuals two experimental investigations will be reported. The first, which I will refer to as 'The London Block', involved the participation of 59 working or unemployed people resident at the time in London: 17 recovering mainly from schizophrenia and schizoaffective disorder; 21 people who scored high (> 12) on Neuroticism on the EPQ (Eysenck and Eysenck 1975) and 21 people who were low on this scale. They were administered three tests of (more generally schizophrenic) psychosis-proneness, the Eysenck P scale (P^E), and two questionnaires I devised myself as research instruments, the P^C and P^A scales, the latter being a brief measure of paranoid tendencies[1-3] (see Tables 10.1 and 10.2). They were also administered five tests of creativity. These were: a Uses test (uses of a brick (Christensen *et al.* 1960)) but with a time limit of two minutes, scored for fluency and originality; a word fluency test (how many words could the participant think of in two minutes that began with the letter S?); the Drawing Completion Test (DCT) of Barron (1962), where the participant is given a fragment of a pattern and has to complete it or 'make something out of it' (Figure 10.1 and scored for originality); and two tests of word finding. The latter two tests were based on Mednick's (1962, 1967) Remote Associations Test and were called the '2–3' and '3–4' tests (see also p. 180 on the latter). They involved presenting participants with two (2–3) or three (3–4) words and asking them to find a further word which was an *associate* of the previous words in the 2–3 test (e.g. 'Head, Box': answer 'Letter') and a more generally connected word in the 3–4 test (e.g. 'Record, Theatre, Doodle': answer 'Play').

Table 10.1 P^C psychoticism scale (all responses scoring for psychoticism were 'Yes')

1 (Filler item)
2 (Filler item)
3 Are you interested in astrology and the occult?
4 Are you unhappy because you are not famous?
5 (Filler item)
6 Do you often think that you have a mission to fulfil?
7 (Filler item)
8 Do you sometimes worry that people can read your thoughts?
9 Do you believe in Fate?
10 (Filler item)
11 Do you ever worry about the end of the world?
12 (Filler item)
13 Are you sometimes afraid that you might kill somebody?
14 Are you afraid of boredom?
15 Do you often have nightmares?
16 (Filler item)
17 (Filler item)
18 Do you often think that the neighbours are 'listening in' on you?
19 Do you like science fiction?
20 (Filler item)
21 Do you sometimes think that you are a special person?
22 Do you often feel that too much is happening around you for you to concentrate?
23 (Filler item)
24 Do you often find it difficult to control your own excitement?
25 (Filler item)
26 Are you superstitious?
27 (Filler item)
28 Are you a dreamer?
29 Are you afraid of losing control?
30 Would you call yourself a religious person?
31 (Filler item)
32 (Filler item)
33 Do you sometimes think you are being followed?
34 (Filler item)
35 Do you often worry that you might go mad?
36 Do you get easily upset by noisy surroundings?

37 (Filler item)
38 Do you often have difficulty making decisions about the simplest things?
39 Are you ever afraid that you might blurt or shout out something unpleasant that you are thinking?
40 Are you easily distracted?
41 Do you sometimes think that you are running away from yourself?
42 (Filler item)
43 Do you often feel suicidal?
44 Do you tend to rush things?
45 Do you find classical music disturbing?
46 (Filler item)
47 Is a lot of emotion expressed in your home?
48 (Filler item)
49 Do you often think that things that happen were somehow meant to be that way?
50 (Filler item)
51 Do you often feel that your mind works quite differently to other people's?
52 (Filler item)
53 (Filler item)
54 Are you ashamed of your thoughts?
55 Do you sometimes feel really elated and optimistic about things for no good reason?
56 (Filler item)
57 Do your family criticise you a lot?
58 Do you often feel that your personality is false or a put-on?
59 Do a lot of uncanny coincidences happen to you?

Table 10.2 Short paranoia scale (P^A)

Question	Response scoring for paranoia
1 Do you lock up your house carefully at night?	Yes
2 Do you often worry about things you should not have done or said?	Yes
3 Are you often troubled about feelings of guilt?	Yes
4 Do you have enemies who want to harm you?	Yes
5 Do you have many friends?	No
6 Do you worry about awful things that might happen?	Yes
7 Do you like mixing with people?	No
8 Are there several people who keep trying to avoid you?	Yes
9 Would you like other people to be afraid of you?	Yes
10 Do people tell you a lot of lies?	Yes
11 Are you touchy about some things?	Yes
12 Do you often think you have a mission to fulfil?	Yes
13 Do you sometimes worry that people can read your thoughts?	Yes
14 Are you sometimes afraid that you might kill somebody?	Yes
15 Do you often think that the neighbours are 'listening in' on you?	Yes
16 Do you sometimes think that you are a special person?	Yes
17 Do you sometimes think that you are being followed?	Yes

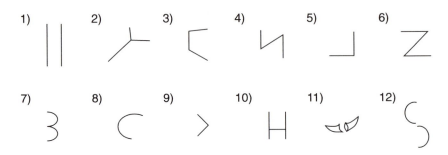

Figure 10.1 Patterns used in the Drawing Completion Test (DCT)
Source: After Barron 1962

The justification of the validity of these creativity measures is clearly of critical importance so I will here anticipate the results section a little in dealing with this. Some of the volunteers had already demonstrated real world creative effectiveness: one had written a novel; another a Ph.D. thesis in chemistry; another had produced publishable work in theoretical physics and was a talented and creative carpenter; another was a professional writer, one a freelance interior designer and so on. I therefore distilled out eleven volunteers who were unambiguously creative. These included two previously psychotic participants reported in Chadwick (1992): Chris (Chapter 7 in that work), who had produced a number of remarkable drawings published as illustrations accompanying articles, and Alana J (Chapter 6 in Chadwick 1992), whose abstract art bore a striking resemblance to the work of the prizewinning sculptor Paul Neagu. I then compared all their test scores with those of the remaining volunteers. The results are shown in Table 10.3. All measures except the originality score on the Drawing Completion Test correlate significantly with criterion, the fluency score on the Uses test being the most successful measure despite the fact that performances on this were done with a time limit.

The results are obviously not conclusive proof of the validity of these measures but they do tend to suggest that the pessimism concerning the validity of measures of ideational fluency and flexibility and especially about the Uses test in this context, expressed by Kogan and Pankove (1974); Mansfield and Busse (1981) and Perkins (1988), is not justified. I therefore conclude that the measures of ideational fluency and flexibility deployed in this experiment are reasonable measures of creativity.

The correlations *between* creativity measures were also all positive and were found to be usually higher than +0.3 and often higher than +0.5. Those having the highest mean correlations with the others were the 3–4 test (+0.49) and the fluency score on the Uses test (+0.43). The DCT seemed to be the lowest in validity of the tests deployed here.

Table 10.3 Correlations of creativity with criterion (real world creative effectiveness: creatives versus non-creatives (London Block))

Test	r phi	t	p (one tailed)	df
S test (Fluency)	+0.344	2.744	< 0.005	56
Uses (Fluency)	+0.401	3.280	= 0.001	56
Uses (Originality)	+0.228	1.753	< 0.05	56
2–3 score	+0.227	1.757	< 0.05	57
3–4 score	+0.274	2.128	< 0.025	56
DCT (Originality)	+0.113	0.859	NS	57

Verbal intelligence was also assessed in the London Block by the Definitions and Synonyms scales of the Mill Hill Vocabulary Test, Form 1 Senior (1977 and 1994 revisions; Raven 1976; Raven *et al.* 1994). As it is generally felt that creativity shows little or no relation with intelligence above an IQ of 120 (Canter 1973; Heansley and Reynolds 1989), the data presented in Chadwick (1988, 1992) were therefore reanalysed to compute the correlations between creativity and psychoticism[2,3] for those participants scoring higher than this in intelligence. The data of 21 subjects were extracted. Their mean Mill Hill score scaled by age as a percentile was 90.99 per cent with a range from 78 to 97 per cent. This is clearly a very high verbal IQ sample. In the London Block we are therefore looking, as did Woody and Claridge (1977) with Oxford undergraduate and postgraduate volunteers, at the correlations between creativity and psychoticism of schizophrenic style[2] at a level of IQ where intelligence should complicate the picture less. (It is worth noting here, however, that the highest scores in the whole 1988 sample on the Mill Hill were actually provided by a recovering male psychotic and by a female who was the highest Neuroticism scorer on the N scale of the EPQ.)

In the second experiment many participants were Open University mature students of high grades resident in the Cambridge–Anglia region of that establishment. This investigation I will therefore refer to as 'the Cambridge Block'. Again, participants with high IQ were recruited (N = 42), their scores being checked by the use of the Synonyms scale of the Mill Hill. (It was found in 1988 that this scale correlated +0.94 with the Definitions scale of that test and was considerably quicker to administer (Chadwick 1988, p. 296).) The volunteers also were asked to complete the STQ of Claridge and Broks (1984) and Jackson and Claridge (1991). This scale assesses schizotypal tendencies via the STA scale and borderline personality tendencies (in the medical sense of the term (DSM III, 1980)) via the STB scale. Factor analysis of the STA (Hewitt and Claridge 1989) revealed three distinct factors referred to as 'magical ideation', 'unusual perceptual experiences' and 'paranoid ideation and suspiciousness'. In the present experiment scores on these components will also be computed and related to creativity. By subtracting scores on the paranoia component of the STA scale from the total STA score a measure of 'non-paranoid phenomena' will also be obtained to see whether the paranoid or the non-paranoid scores correlate more highly with creativity. On the basis of the work of Keefe and Magaro (1980) and of Chadwick (1992) on the full London Block sample it would be expected that paranoid tendencies are detrimental to divergent thinking styles of creativity.

A Lie Scale derived from the EPQ is also included in the STQ and it is reasonable to infer that this is an indirect measure of non-conformity. Questions such as 'Are *all* your habits good and desirable ones?' may be answered in the affirmative by more socially conforming people and indeed Lie Scale scores are higher, as would be expected, in females and older people, increasing with age (Eysenck and Eysenck 1975). It will be expected, then, that Lie Score could well correlate negatively with creativity, lower scorers being more creative. Non-conformity has previously been so related to creativity by Schuldberg *et al.* (1988).

To assess creativity in the Cambridge Block, first two creativity measures from Wallach and Kogan (1965) were administered: 'Pattern Meanings' (see Figure 10.2), where the participant is asked to write down as many things they can think of that a pattern *could be* (scored here for fluency, originality and subjective strikingness, untimed), and the Similarities Test (see Table 10.4), where a series of object pairs are given and the volunteer has to think of as many ways as possible the two could be regarded as similar. This was untimed and scored here for fluency and strikingness. These two tests were the most successful instruments in the study by Woody and Claridge (1977). All participants were requested to do the question-naire and tests in their own time, handing the results to me within or after about six or seven weeks. Instructions in the test booklet given to them encouraged a permissive and relaxed attitude to the tasks, emphasised as necessary by Wallach and Kogan (1965). Although the tests were untimed, participants were asked to record roughly how much time they had spent on each item and all were strictly requested to ensure that their responses were *entirely* their own work. In addition and finally, the Uses test was also administered to the Cambridge Block (uses of a brick), scored for fluency, originality and strikingness, giving a total of eight creativity scores in all.

CREATIVITY, RISK AND 'INNER PERCEPTION'

It has been known for some time that strong critical tendencies interfere with creative thought (Torrance *et al.* 1958). It is also known from research in the theory of signal detection that a risky criterion maximises 'hits' or true positives – but at the cost of an increased number of false alarms (McNicol 1972). Give that there are similarities in process between

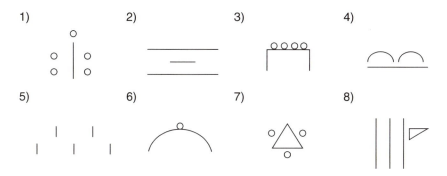

Figure 10.2 Patterns used in the Pattern Meanings Test
Source: After Wallach and Kogan 1965

Table 10.4 Similarities Test

Guidance: 'Write down all the ways in which an apple and orange *are alike*.' Possible answer: 'Both round, sweet, have seeds, are fruits, have skins, grow on trees. Both can be used as tennis or golf balls, both can be stuck on a pole, both can have faces painted on them, both can be used in Hallowe'en barrels, both go rotten, open – both can be used to stub out cigarettes safely, etc.'

The test: Write down all the ways in which the following *are alike*:

1 A potato and a carrot
2 A cat and a mouse
3 A train and a tractor
4 Milk and meat
5 A grocery shop and a restaurant
6 A violin and a piano
7 A radio and a telephone
8 A watch and a typewriter
9 A curtain and a rug
10 A desk and a table

Source: After Wallach and Kogan 1965

perception of the external world and internal image scanning (Kosslyn 1976, 1978, 1980), it is at least feasible that people who demonstrate a risky criterion in a signal detection task will therefore be more creative as they may be less likely preconsciously to censor potential ideas and thus may retrieve more. This was tested on the London Block by also administering, in addition to the creativity tests, a Slide Viewing Task (SVT), in which participants had to guess the identity of seven initially out-of-focus slides as they were gradually brought into focus but also to give a measure of confidence in their decisions at each stage from 0: 'Pure Guess', through to 5: 'Certain'. Treating low-confidence correct decisions as 'misses' and high-confidence incorrect decisions as 'false alarms', this enables measures of sensitivity (d'_e and $\triangle_m$) and bias (B index) to be computed (McNicol 1972) – where a high B index value would represent riskier judgement. The relation between confidence and creativity could also be assessed from this rating scale task as mean confidence levels were computed for each participant. The critical measure here was thus to be the correlations between the B index and particularly the fluency scores on the S test and the Uses test.

Creativity, to the extent that the concept has any unitary status at all, is axiomatically a constructive and evaluative rather than a detection process. None the less, some degree of conscious sensitivity to the products of unconscious and preconscious processes could arguably be involved in a manner roughly analogous to sensitivity to externally presented patterns. If a strict criterion (low B index value) interferes with pattern detection externally, it feasibly could do so internally, and indeed measures of perceptual accuracy computed from perception of unclear external patterns – as given in the SVT – might well correlate with creativity if external perception maps positively *or indeed negatively* on to insight processes to any significant degree. Researchers have of course been warned for some time against comparing external perception to the much vaguer concept of 'internal perception' (Hebb 1949). None the less, the experimental tasks presented to the London Block participants do offer a rare opportunity to see whether measures of perceptual bias, sensitivity and accuracy at all relate to divergent creativity in any consistent way (be it positive or negative). Hence it would be unwise to miss the opportunity that this experiment provides. Apart from the usual measures contributed by the theory of signal detection (d'_e and $\triangle_m$) it is possible to compute perceptual accuracy on the Slide Viewing Task (SVT) from the mean focusing position (from 7 (very out-of-focus) to 0 (in focus)) at which the out-of-focus slides were correctly identified. Accuracy is clearly greater the higher numerically is the focusing position at correct identification. This mean value will be referred to as the 'recognition position'. All the slides depicted non-social and non-threatening familiar everyday objects (e.g. a roundabout; a stapler; a bowl of fruit and so on) so as to be less likely to activate specific paranoid experiences in the experiment itself. This makes the task arguably better at tapping general dispositional features of processing rather than processes which eventuate because of a previous delusional episode.

EMPATHY

Although the empathic powers of neurotic and psychotic patients are known at anecdotal level by group home staff and residential social workers and the like, and were particularly evident in Desmond, Ivo and Deanna, is it the case that psychosis-prone people demonstrate high empathy on tests designed to measure this? Using the P^E, P^C and P^A scales taken by the

London Block mentioned earlier, I decided in this study to examine their correlations with scores on the I_5 empathy scale of Eysenck and McGurk (1980). A comparison of the empathy scores of the recovering psychotics in the London Block with the high N and low N samples was also to be undertaken by ANOVA. Since measures of current mood at the time of testing were also taken from all the London Block participants via the Nowlis (1965) check list, it will also be possible to see whether the volunteers with a more diverse range and intensity of feelings are also more empathic.

SCHIZOPHRENIA, SMOKING AND CREATIVITY

It may seem strange to introduce the issue of tobacco smoking at this late stage but it is a topic that should be addressed, if only as an aside. It is well known that schizophrenic people smoke more; indeed, in one sample of eighty such patients being tested at Charing Cross Hospital in the 1990s only *one* was a non-smoker (Keith Laws, personal communication 1991). Smoking is a well-known stimulant and increased arousal is also well known both to narrow the attentional field (Easterbrook 1959) and increase rigidity of thought (Maher 1957; Glucksberg 1962, 1964). Recovering schizophrenic people such as those who performed so poorly in Rothenberg's research on creativity (Rothenberg 1973a, b, 1983, 1990) may, I would suggest, be disadvantaged in such tests by their (probable) smoking. This, however, needs to be checked. As I possessed data on whether the London Block participants were smokers or non-smokers I have decided in this study to investigate and report on whether smoking did impair performance on the creativity tests used there and, incidentally, to see if it has any interesting correlations with other relevant personality, state and performance variables. In this context measures of mood and arousal (Nowlis 1965; MacKay *et al.* 1978) were employed to assess participants' state at the time of testing (volunteers, however, were requested not to smoke while actually completing these check-lists).

CONFIRMATION BIAS AND CREATIVITY

It was a feature of all the schizotypal subjects reported in the qualitative section of this book that verificationist tendencies dominated their thinking and perceiving. This was especially so of Deanna. Information that *confirmed* an ongoing scheme was assimilated to a degree far higher than was information that discredited it. This of course in itself is not an abnormal bias (Garety and Hemsley 1994) but the degree to which it is demonstrated in recovering psychotics has been suggested to be more extreme (Chadwick 1992, Chapter 12). In one recovering patient I was friendly with in 1980, a young Nigerian man called Harry, he demonstrated this loose verificationist thinking very clearly one day (when he was actually floridly psychotic) as we were both leaving Wood Lane hostel in Shepherds Bush to go to see some friends of his on the other side of London. Harry was sure he was going to be *killed* soon, so I accompanied him for support on the trip. But as we were coming out of the door of the hostel he noticed a group of men coming out of the London Transport Training Centre then located on the opposite side of Wood Lane. He was alarmed and said 'Oh No! Men are coming for me!' Then he noticed they were all wearing dark (nearly black) clothes and exclaimed 'Yes! Look! Black suits! They're all funeral attendants, I am going to be killed! We must move fast!'

This 'overconnectivity' of psychotic thought has of course been known for some time (Schneider 1959; Frith 1992) but I would suggest, having suffered positive symptom psychosis myself, that it is more central to the psychotic experience than is generally realised. The process of frenziedly 'fitting things in' was the single most marked quality of the psychotic experiences of all the recovering patients I mixed with in the years of my own recovery in London and greatly outweighed failures in metarepresentation, which has been made so central by Frith (1992) – although it must be admitted that Frith's theory seems to have strong relevance for negative-symptom patients. Indeed, to the extent that patients who are either ill or recovering do have difficulty in reflecting on their own cognitions, this, I would claim, could partly be *due* to the overwhelming effect that compulsive assimilation has on their capacities to detach themselves from their experienced content of consciousness in the effort to gain any measure of control or regulation over it. This surely must involve a breakdown of perhaps already fragile inhibitory processes.

'Confirmation bias' (Wason 1960) is perhaps a better term than 'overconnectivity' in this context as it has a *directional* 'If–Then' quality to it that mere associative looseness in semantic networks does not have. Confirmation seeking is, however, a useful problem-solving as well as creative strategy (Tweney *et al.* 1981) and Eysenck (1981) has suggested that it *should* be used as a means of theory building at least in the early stages. Refutation-seeking, so favoured by Popper (1959), is ironically a poor strategy to adopt in experimental 'breadth search' then 'depth search' problem-solving tasks (Tweney *et al.* 1981).

It seems likely then that tendencies towards confirmation-seeking will facilitate creativity. The creativity tests mentioned earlier were the ones used in this analysis and the Slide Viewing Task also enabled a measure of confirmation seeking to be obtained as it was possible to compute the number of *focusing position changes* through which hypotheses were 'hung on to' rather than given up as new data became available. This was recorded as 'visual confirmation bias score'. *Verbal* confirmation bias score was assessed by the tendency of participants to think of solution words on the 3–4 test which 'fitted' with two of the given words but not the third. In these cases the volunteer is, so to speak, 'forcing a connection' between the hypothesised solution word and the third word (as in atomic, sex, shell: answer 'nucleus' rather than 'bomb' or perhaps 'war'). This is rather like Harry's remote connection-seeking behaviour mentioned above but demonstrated in a context outside the person's delusional concerns. In this respect such tests may reflect more general features of processing rather than merely tapping the delusional system by activating it in the experiment. The 3–4 test is also in practice a hypothesis-testing task (Perkins 1988) as well as an associative network search task – and this is also the case with the Slide Viewing Task (Bruner and Potter 1966). In the 3–4 test volunteers serially *test* potential solution words against given words as data and then 'exit' when they have a match for all three. Clearly confirmation seekers are 'exiting early' but it is possible that this could be due sometimes to their finding a remote connection not easily appreciated in scoring. In one case they are thinking what they want to think and in the other they are being somewhat poetic. Either way the test is a useful probe of schizotypal styles of thought which I would recommend to other researchers (see Appendix II) and I would suggest it is not best regarded simply as a test of 'associative thinking', as stated by Bentall (1992).

The two experimental blocks will inevitably reveal other and unexpected patterns of interest in their data. These I will report. The London Block has the greatest range of variables (167 in all) but with only 59 participants factor analysis is not indicated as the matrix is not even square. It will, however, be interesting to see whether attitude and cognitive style variables such as empathy, non-conformity, riskiness and perceptual sensitivity mediate creativity, greater similarity perception and meaning seeking. If so, we have here some empirical backup for the oft-made claim that stylistic features of pathology have functional advantages. Whilst the twentieth century has been dominated by cynicism, logic, facts and 'fun', it could be that schizotypals and their ilk can point a way to a twenty-first century characterised by empathy, belief and meaning. Clearly the account of reality derived from the looser and more non-conforming schizotypal style (as we saw in Chapters 3 to 8) is very different from that of a conservative positivist yet we have no guarantee that the most cautious model of what is the case is indeed the correct one. In seeking the intrinsic validity and dignity of schizophrenia-prone people we may find that they have tendencies and competencies that indicate that their way of life and view of self and of reality, usually an occasion prompting medical diagnosis, instead deserves to be regarded with respect.

Chapter 11

Experimental studies
Results and analyses

> As far as I can remember, there is not one word in the Gospels in praise of intelligence.
>
> (Bertrand Russell, 1872–1970)

It is clearly essential that I commence here by providing some descriptive statistics about the people who actually took part in these experiments – and to take this opportunity to thank them for consenting to participate. The London Block study was particularly demanding as it required about three hours to obtain all the necessary data. The Cambridge Block booklet was also quite challenging.

From Table 11.1 it can be seen that the experimental subjects tended to be about 35 years of age, the Cambridge Block subjects being slightly older (39.48, SD 10.07). The Cambridge Block was predominantly female, the F:M ratio being 3.67, while the London Block was predominantly male, F:M ratio 0.64. The London Block participants ranged widely in age from 19 to 64 (SD 11.03), as did the high verbal IQ subgroup (from 22 to 59 (SD 10.83)). The Cambridge Block subjects meanwhile ranged in age from

Table 11.1 Characteristics of participants in the experimental studies

	Total N	Males	Females	Mean age	SD
London Block					
Recovering psychotics	17	12	5	35.91	10.83
Paranoid patients	9	7	2	37.59	10.52
Non-paranoid	8	5	3	34.05	11.58
High N group	21	12	9	35.42	10.20
Low N group	21	12	9	34.88	12.42
High IQ subgroup	21	11	10	35.21	10.83
All subjects	59	36	23	35.37	11.03
Cambridge Block					
All subjects	42	9	33	39.48	10.07

25 to 63 (SD 10.07). The Cambridge subjects, as expected, did prove to be highly intelligent and had a mean Mill Hill age-scaled percentile score of 83.74 (SD 16.86). The specially selected high verbal IQ London Block subgroup's score here was 90.99 (SD 5.84). The full 1988 London Block sample of 59 participants was, as expected and hoped for, close to the average with an overall age-scaled percentile score of 53 per cent, and their SD was 16.64. It would seem from these values that the full London Block of 59 participants was a fairly representative sample of the population, at least in terms of verbal intelligence.

CREATIVITY AND PSYCHOSIS-PRONENESS

The Cambridge Block provided the most interesting data here so I have chosen to discuss it first in this context. As was stated in Chapter 10: the STQ comprised STA, STB and Lie Scale scores. It was also decided (see Chapter 10) to subdivide the STA into Magical Ideation; Perceptual Aberration; Paranoia and a total 'Non-paranoid phenomena' score. The items chosen for these latter four subscales are given in Table 11.2. The overall pattern of scores on these dimensions are given in Table 11.3. The scores are closely comparable to those reported by Jackson and Claridge (1991) in their validation study of the STQ.

Referring to the eight creativity measures described in Chapter 10, their correlations with STA (Schizotypy) are presented in Table 11.4 (all significances are 2 tailed). Table 11.4 gives the correlations with the raw

Table 11.2 Subdivision of the STA Scale

Component	Items used
Magical Ideation	16, 25, 32, 47, 54, 67, 72, 74, 75 (N = 9)
Perceptual Aberration	10, 13, 19, 20, 22, 33, 40, 46, 49, 52, 65, 70 (N = 12)
Paranoia	5, 8, 21, 29, 56, 63, 73 (N = 7)
Non-paranoid phenomena	Total STA score minus Paranoia score

Table 11.3 Patterns of scores on the STQ (Cambridge Block)

	Mean	Median	SD	Range
STA	16.38	16.50	7.21	1–34
STB	5.93	5.00	3.69	0–16
Lie Scale	4.83	4.00	3.56	0–16
Magical Ideation	4.47	5.00	2.32	0–9
Perceptual Aberration	5.38	6.00	2.79	0–12
Paranoia	2.52	2.00	1.78	0–7
Non-paranoid phenomena	13.86	14.00	6.17	0–28

Table 11.4 Correlations of creativity with personality variables and intelligence

	Uses F	Uses O	Uses G	PMF	PMO	PMG	SIM F	SIM G
STA	0.378 (p = 0.014)	0.299	0.252	0.139	0.110	0.066	0.051	0.164
STB	0.229	0.184	0.230	0.134	0.097	0.109	0.012	0.122
Lie Score	-0.254	-0.344 (p = 0.026)	-0.315 (p = 0.042)	-0.231	-0.081	-0.174	-0.341 (p = 0.027)	-0.329 (p = 0.034)
Mill Hill (raw scores)	0.302	0.411 (p = 0.007)	0.427 (p = 0.005)	0.035	0.382 (p = 0.013)	0.267	0.147	0.284
Magic id.	0.345 (p = 0.025)	0.324 (p = 0.037)	0.152	0.158	0.168	0.094	-0.011	0.128
Percept Ab	0.392 (p = 0.01)	0.388 (p = 0.011)	0.304 (p = 0.05)	0.127	0.081	0.066	0.169	0.284
Paranoia	0.228	-0.074	0.081	0.023	-0.041	-0.087	-0.011	-0.136
(Transformed Paranoia scores)	0.178	-0.086	0.066	0.037	-0.073	-0.104	0.063	-0.108
Non-paranoid phenomena	0.376 (p = 0.014)	0.371 (p = 0.016)	0.271	0.156	0.141	0.102	0.062	0.231
Assoc Flu	0.239	0.277	0.261	0.192	0.252	0.224	-0.003	0.229
Soc RP	0.091	-0.105	0.070	-0.025	-0.114	-0.097	0.034	-0.062
Age	-0.127	-0.025	-0.043	-0.176	0.071	-0.118	-0.325 (p = 0.036)	-0.084

Mill Hill (age scaled to percentiles)	0.308 (p = 0.047)	0.387 (p = 0.011)	0.505 (p = 0.001)	0.188	0.462 (p = 0.002)	0.389 (p = 0.011)	0.160	0.260
Mill Hill (scaled and transformed scores)	0.370 (p = 0.016)	0.449 (p = 0.003)	0.488 (p = 0.001)	0.119	0.365 (p = 0.017)	0.350 (p = 0.023)	0.301 (p = 0.053)	0.373 (p = 0.015)

Key
Uses F: Uses Fluency
Uses O: Uses Originality
Uses G: Uses Graded Measure
PMF: Pattern Meanings Fluency
PMO: Pattern Meanings Originality
PMG: Pattern Meanings Graded Measure
SIM F: Similarities Fluency
SIM G: Similarities Graded Measure

The Graded Measure is a subjective measure, on a 4-point scale, of the strikingness or novelty of the responses.

Magic id: Magical Ideation
Percept Ab: Perceptual Aberration
Assoc Flu: Associative Fluency/Access to primary process modes of thought (see text)
Soc RP: Social relationship problems (see text)

creativity scores for completeness and Table 11.5 gives the correlations with creativity scores transformed to reduce skewness.[1] Contrary to the arguments of Kessel (1989), Rothenberg (1990) and Jamison (1993), there is no evidence whatever from either of these tables that schizophrenia-proneness is damaging of creativity. The correlations of all eight measures with STA score are positive, *none* are negative and the correlations of Uses Fluency (both raw and transformed data) with STA are highly significant. Uses Fluency and Uses Originality also show positive correlations with Magical Ideation, Perceptual Aberration and Non-paranoid phenomena. *All* of the six possible correlations here are significant (see Table 11.5).

The general pattern of correlations with Lie Score (as a measure of non-conformity) are also as predicted. With low Lie scorers expected to be more creative, *negative* correlations with creativity should be obtained, and indeed they are, with all measures. Two of the five correlations with transformed data are significant (Table 11.5).

Despite the high verbal IQ of the Cambridge Block sample and the permissive and relaxed attitude I tried to encourage by the wording of the test instructions, Mill Hill score is still a powerful predictor of performance on all the creativity measures used here. In Table 11.4 the correlations of raw Mill Hill scores and also of scaled and transformed Mill Hill scores with raw creativity scores are given. In Table 11.5 the correlations of scaled-by-age percentile Mill Hill scores with transformed creativity scores are presented. From both these tables it is clear that verbal intelligence has a strong relationship with creativity even in highly intelligent subjects (the *median* scaled percentile score for the Cambridge Block participants was in fact 91 per cent, well above an IQ of 120).

Confirming the superiority of non-paranoid subjects to paranoid subjects on divergent thinking tests, as found both by Keefe and Magaro (1980) and by Chadwick (1992) on the full London Block sample, the correlations in Tables 11.4 and 11.5 virtually always show that non-paranoia scores correlate more highly with creativity than do paranoia scores. Of 21 possible comparisons no less than 20 are in favour of the contribution of non-paranoid states over paranoid states. Other than paranoia, the only measure consistently correlating negatively with divergent creativity score is (sadly) age.

As an aside, it was also considered worth while to examine whether general 'associative fluency' and access to primary process (as revealed for example by good dream recall or by repeatedly having disturbing dreams) might correlate with creativity. Associative Fluency of this kind was measured by items 24, 41, 43 and 76 on the STQ. As can be seen from Table 11.5, all the correlations are positive but alas none are significant. Correlations of creativity with another component, 'Social Relationship Problems', measured by items 3, 35 and 37, were either extremely low or negative. In the Hewitt and Claridge (1989) factor analysis, these three

Table 11.5 Correlations of personality variables with creativity scores transformed to reduce skewness

	Uses F	Uses O	PMF	PMO	SIM F	Uses (time on test)
STA	0.403 (p = 0.008)	0.286	0.170	0.079	0.069	0.275
STB	0.240	0.163	0.117	0.155	0.008	0.251
Lie Score	-0.262	-0.371 (p = 0.016)	-0.208	-0.145	-0.349 (p = 0.023)	-0.103
Mill Hill Age-scaled percentile scores	0.414 (p = 0.006)	0.447 (p = 0.003)	0.150	0.336 (p = 0.03)	0.302 (p = 0.052)	-0.275
Magic id	0.368 (p = 0.017)	0.319 (p = 0.04)	0.196	0.098	-0.005	0.283
Percept Ab	0.415 (p = 0.006)	0.382 (p = 0.013)	0.158	0.048	0.185	0.333 (p = 0.031)
Paranoia	0.228	-0.072	0.009	-0.007	-0.010	0.087
(Transformed paranoia scores)	0.177	-0.072	0.018	-0.024	0.050	0.084
Non-paranoid phenomena	0.405 (p = 0.008)	0.355 (p = 0.021)	0.196	0.094	0.084	0.296
Assoc Flu	0.284	0.263	0.231	0.213	0.016	0.187
Soc RP	0.089	-0.127	-0.034	-0.056	0.046	0.038
Age	-0.132	-0.062	-0.161	0.025	-0.377 (p = 0.029)	0.019

Note: For key, see Table 11.4

items loaded on the 'paranoia and suspiciousness' factor so these negative findings are in line with those from the correlations of paranoia with creativity.

Judging from the general pattern of correlation coefficients, the most successful test in the Cambridge Block analysis clearly is the Uses test. This also performed well in the London Block validity study (Chapter 10, Table 10.3). Pattern Meanings and Similarities performed less well but of the 30 possible distinct correlations of their scores with STA, STB, Magical Ideation, Perceptual Aberration, Non-paranoid phenomena and Associative Fluency, over both Tables 11.5 and 11.4 (which contain the Graded Measure results) no less than 29 are positive. This is at least encouraging.

To examine the effects of combinations of variables: multiple regression and ANOVA analyses were also performed on the transformed Cambridge Block data. For the purpose of the ANOVA the Lie Score split (High/Low) was ≥ 5 for High Lie and < 5 for Low Lie; the STA split was ≥ 18 for High STA and < 18 for Low STA and the Mill Hill split was ≥ 91 for 'higher intelligence' and < 91 for 'lower intelligence'. It should be emphasised, however, that this 'lower intelligence' group are still well above average, with a mean IQ in the vicinity of 120. The higher intelligence group have IQs generally above 140 so we are comparing two very intelligent groups here.

MULTIPLE REGRESSION ANALYSES

Entering STA, Lie Score, Age, Sex and Mill Hill (scaled and transformed) Score, multiple regression analysis revealed that Lie Score ($F = 5.548$, $p = 0.024$) and age ($F = 6.926$, $p = 0.0027$) predicted Similarities Fluency Score and both STA ($F = 7.687$, $p = 0.0015$) and scaled and transformed Mill Hill Score ($F = 8.2609$, $p = 0.065$) predicted Uses Fluency. Lie Score was also close to predicting Uses Originality ($p = 0.0645$). Mill Hill Score predicted Pattern Meanings Originality ($F = 5.088$, $p = 0.0296$) and all three Graded or 'Strikingness' measures. This measure, also used by Keefe and Magaro (1980) (see Chapter 2), correlated highly here with the other creativity measures (fluency and originality), as can be seen from Table 11.6. Its power, however, may come from having a strong loading on an underlying factor associated with intelligence.

ANALYSES OF VARIANCE

Examining STA, Lie and Mill Hill Scores as described above (High/Low), it was found that a strong STA and Mill Hill interaction ($F = 7.224$, $p = 0.011$) occurred for Similarities Fluency (see Table 11.7). The means of Groups 1 and 3 are significantly different from that of Group O (Newman-Keuls

Table 11.6 Correlations of Graded Measure scores with other creativity scores – the latter transformed to reduce skewness

	Mill Hill (scaled and transformed)	Uses F	Uses O	PMF	PMO	SIM F
Uses Graded Measure	0.488 (p = 0.01)	0.692 (p < 0.0001)	0.761 (p < 0.0001)	0.427 (p = 0.005)	0.357 (p = 0.02)	0.497 (p = 0.001)
Patterns Graded Measure	0.350 (p = 0.023)	0.324 (p = 0.036)	0.356 (p = 0.021)	0.818 (p < 0.0001)	0.803 (p < 0.0001)	0.466 (p = 0.002
Similarities Graded Measure	0.373 (p = 0.015)	0.293 (p = 0.06)	0.560 (p < 0.0001)	0.386 (p = 0.012)	0.220	0.694 (p < 0.0001)

post hoc test, $p < 0.05$) and hence STA score enhances the creative performance of people in the lower intelligence group (IQ ~ 120) while having no effect on the creativity of the subjects of very highest intelligence. Schizotypy, however, does not impede the performance of the latter. This general pattern was also found for Uses Fluency (Table 11.8) (STA × Mill Hill: $F = 4.708$, $p = 0.037$), where Group O differs from Groups 1, 2 and 3 (Newman-Keuls, $p < 0.05$). Again schizotypy helps the creativity of the group of lower intelligence while not impeding the subjects of highest intelligence.

Interactions between STA and Lie Score were found for Uses Fluency and Uses Originality. In the former (STA × Lie Score: $F = 6.370$, $p = 0.016$) the highest creativity was found for High STA and Low Lie Scores (Table 11.9). There are significant differences between Groups 1 and 0, 2 and 3 (Newman-Keuls, $p < 0.05$). In the latter (Uses Originality) the above pattern was somewhat similar and an STA × Lie Score interaction very nearly reached significance ($F = 3.848$, $p = 0.058$). There was, however, here no significant difference between Low Lie/High STA and Low Lie/Low STA, using a more conservative Scheffe *post hoc* test. Both of these groups, however, did outperform the two High Lie cells.

The ANOVA did not reveal any three-way STA × Mill Hill × Lie Score interactions. Pairs of these variables seem to exert their effects in different tests but it was not found that they exert their effects in tandem on any of the tasks involved here. Of the variables studied, Lie Score emerged as a particularly powerful predictor. As well as featuring in the above analyses and interactions it was, in its own terms, significantly associated with Uses Originality ($F = 6.051$, $p = 0.019$), Uses Graded Measure ($F = 6.696$, $p = 0.014$) and Similarities Graded Measure ($F = 5.066$, $p = 0.031$). The Mill

Table 11.7 Contribution of STA Score and Mill Hill Score to Similarities Fluency Score (ANOVA) (creativity scores transformed to reduce skewness)

	Lower intelligence group	Higher intelligence group
Low STA	0.74(0)	1.05(1)
High STA	0.98(3)	0.87(2)

Table 11.8 Contribution of STA Score and Mill Hill Score to Uses Fluency Score (ANOVA) (creativity scores transformed to reduce skewness)

	Lower intelligence group	Higher intelligence group
Low STA	3.22(0)	4.30(1)
High STA	4.50(3)	4.48(2)

Table 11.9 Contribution of STA Score and Lie Score to Uses Fluency Score (ANOVA) (creativity scores transformed to reduce skewness)

	Low Lie	High Lie
Low STA	3.83(0)	3.40(3)
High STA	5.04(1)	3.63(2)

Hill did not feature as prominently as expected as a main effect except for predicting Similarities Graded Measure (F = 5.066, p = 0.031) but this may have been because of higher variance existing in the higher intelligence sample.

The Pattern Meanings Test did not produce any significant main or interaction effects and was generally the least successful measure used.

REFLECTIONS ON THE CAMBRIDGE BLOCK ANALYSIS

The analysis clearly produced encouraging results which were in line with previous findings by Schuldberg *et al.* (1988) and Poreh *et al.* (1993), assuming that we can reasonably regard the Uses test as tapping visual and spatial creativity more than verbal creativity. Schizotypy and its components were in general found to be associated with creativity, as was non-conformity as assessed by the Lie Scale. The results were marred, however, by the poor performance of the Pattern Meanings Test but the general complexion of the results is reasonably bright. The contribution to creativity of schizotypy, intelligence and non-conformity that was so in evidence in the lives depicted in the biographical sections of this book (Chapters 3–8) was generally reflected and confirmed in this empirical study, although the impact of these variables, both singly and in inter-action, did vary across different creative tasks.

LONDON BLOCK ANALYSES

Measures of psychoticism from the full London Block sample of 59 participants did not correlate to any notable degree with creativity (Chadwick 1992, Table 11.3, p. 122). A reanalysis of these data using only the 21 participants out of 59 at the 79th percentile and above on the Mill Hill vocabulary test sadly failed to produce any differences to this pattern. Correlations were extremely low or negative and all non-significant. It is clear that, if schizophreniform psychoticism *is* related to creativity, it is the STA Scale and *not* the three tests (P^E, P^C and P^A) deployed in the London Block study that measures it. The Eysenckian P scale (P^E) may indeed relate more to negative symptom patterns while my own instrument (P^C) may in fact be measuring neuroticism, with which it correlated +0.735 (p < 0.001).[2] Kubie (1958) has argued for a detrimental effect of neuroticism on creativity. Paranoia, as has previously been stated, generally does also correlate negatively with divergent thinking scores.

It is clear then that if we are to find connections between schizophrenic tendencies and creativity it is necessary to move on to alternative tests of this construct and the STA Scale looms large as a useful instrument. The *creativity* tests, however, that were used in the London Block do appear to have validity and will be deployed here in other contexts.

The relationships of creativity with other variables appear more pro-mising. Tables 11.10 and 11.11 provide the correlations of creativity test scores with Lie Score and Intelligence (Table 11.11) and with perceptual, cognitive and mood variables (Table 11.10). Low Lie Scores again appear to predict high creativity, as they did in the Cambridge Block analyses, while high perceptual sensitivity (d'_e and $\triangle_M$) and decisional cautiousness have *tendencies* to be associated with creativeness (Table 11.10) although all the correlations involved are low. Alas, there is no evidence that risky perceivers (high B index values) are more creative on Fluency measures; if anything, the reverse is the case. This experiment therefore tends to suggest that divergent creativeness is higher not in more gullible confident people but in those who are sensitive and cautious perceivers.

With reference to measures of confirmation bias it seems that it is *visual* confirmation bias that most consistently relates to creativity[3] while, surprisingly, stress does not seem to have any consistent positive or negative effects (Table 11.10). The data for positive mood are also conflicting, with, if anything, positive mood having a slight facilitative effect. Again, however, the values involved are low. As in the Cambridge Block analyses, Mill Hill Score is powerfully related to creativity (Table 11.11), the correlations with all tests except the DCT being highly significant.

Table 11.10 Correlations of creativity (full London Block) with perceptual, cognitive and mood variables

With observational accuracy

		B index	d'_e	$\triangle_m$	Recognition Position
66	S test (fluency)	−0.019	−0.111	+0.161	+0.085
67	Uses test (fluency)	−0.132	+0.125	+0.015	−0.019
68	Uses test (originality)	−0.313	+0.104	+0.194	−0.120
72	2–3 test	+0.146	+0.052	−0.185	+0.141
87	3–4 test	−0.188	+0.104	+0.098	−0.046
170	DCT (originality)	−0.129	−0.211	+0.040	+0.282

With confirmation bias

	Verbal CB	Visual CB
S test (fluency)	−0.131	+0.008
Uses test (fluency)	−0.246	+0.226
Uses test (originality)	−0.490[1]	+0.140
2–3 test	−0.425[2]	+0.058
3–4 test	−0.504[1]	+0.175
DCT (originality)	−0.112	−0.275

With stress variables

	Stress	Anxiety	Depression	Aggression
S test (fluency)	−0.183	−0.166	−0.193	+0.097
Uses test (fluency)	+0.077	+0.013	−0.008	+0.247
Uses test (originality)	+0.173	+0.047	−0.025	+0.085
2–3 test	+0.129	+0.161	+0.105	+0.096
3–4 test	−0.135	−0.246	−0.196	−0.082
DCT (originality)	−0.239	−0.337	−0.037	−0.137

With positive mood

	Social Affection	Pleasantness
S test (fluency)	+0.093	+0.017
Uses test (fluency)	+0.205	−0.059
Uses test (originality)	+0.071	−0.125
2–3 test	+0.166	+0.130
3–4 test	+0.051	−0.110
DCT (originality)	−0.066	+0.009

Notes:
1 $p < 0.01$, 2 tailed
2 $p < 0.02$, 2 tailed

Table 11.11 Correlations of creativity (full London Block) with Lie Score and intelligence

With Lie Score (lower scores denote less conformity)

S test (fluency)	−0.001
Uses test (fluency)	−0.266
Uses test (originality)	−0.349[1]
2–3 test	−0.286
3–4 test	−0.012
DCT (originality)	+0.217

With Verbal Intelligence (as assessed by the Mill Hill VS)

S test (fluency)	+0.557[2]
Uses test (fluency)	+0.600[2]
Uses test (originality)	+0.600[2]
2–3 test	+0.420[3]
3–4 test	+0.566[2]
DCT (originality)	+0.032

Notes:
1 $p < 0.05$, 2 tailed
2 $p < 0.002$, 2 tailed
3 $p < 0.002$, 2 tailed

Smoking, as predicted, does indeed seem to correlate negatively with divergent styles of creativity, the correlation with Uses Originality being significant (Table 11.12). It also tends to relate to low perceptual sensitivity and (possibly) a decisional attitude of slight risk – themselves feasibly associated with lesser creativity, as we have seen previously. There is a suggestion that smokers are less depressed, anxious and aggressive than non-smokers (and feel more pleasant) but the correlations are all less than 0.2. Smoking is, however, associated more strongly with Paranoia ($+0.405$, $p < 0.02$, 2 tailed) and with Chadwickian Psychoticism ($+0.345$, $p < 0.05$, 2 tailed) – and, strangely, with Empathy ($+0.423$, $p < 0.02$, 2 tailed) (Table 11.12). The psychological significance of these latter correlations clearly is debatable as regards direction of causation. The present analysis does not enable a choice to be made on this matter but the topic is worthy of further research (Chadwick 1988, 1995a).

EMPATHY

Empathy does not appear to facilitate the kind of creativity assessed on divergent thinking and word finding tests (see Table 11.13). Its helpfulness is more likely to be in interpersonal domains, as discussed by Gardner (1985). Empathy also has no relation with perceptual efficiency, at least of the non-social stimuli used here in the London Block experiment. This is perhaps understandable. Empathy does, however, correlate significantly with paranoia, with my own measure of psychoticism and with Eysenckian

Table 11.12 Correlations of smoking (full London Block) with personality, state and performance variables (25 smokers, 34 non-smokers)

With personality measures		*With state measures*	
Extraversion	−0.294	Anxiety	−0.173
Neuroticism	+0.325	Depression	−0.148
Psychoticism (P[E])	+0.148	Egotism	+0.162
Lie Score	+0.042	Pleasantness	+0.143
Impulsiveness	+0.220	Nonchalance	+0.124
Empathy	+0.423[1]	Scepticism	+0.048
Venturesomeness	−0.279	Aggression	−0.170
Psychoticism (PC)	+0.345[2]	Social Affection	−0.218
Paranoia (P[A])	+0.405[1]	Concentration	−0.278

With creativity measures ·		*With other performance measures*	
S test (fluency)	−0.130	B index	+0.021
Uses test (fluency)	−0.272	d'_e	−0.197
Uses test (originality)	−0.421[1]	$\triangle_m$	−0.395[2]
2–3 test	+0.010	Recognition Position	−0.182
3–4 test	−0.093	Verbal confirmation bias	+0.225
DCT (originality)	+0.205	Visual confirmation bias	−0.361[2]

Notes:
1 p < 0.02, 2 tailed
2 p < 0.05, 2 tailed

Table 11.13 Correlations of Empathy (full London Block) with personality and performance variables

With other personality variables		*With creativity*	
Extraversion	−0.311	S test (fluency)	−0.235
Neuroticism	+0.557[1]	Uses test (fluency)	+0.074
Psychoticism (P[E])	+0.001	Uses test (originality)	+0.142
Lie Score	−0.274	2–3 test	+0.103
Impulsiveness	+0.051	3–4 test	+0.188
Venturesomeness	−0.112	DCT (originality)	−0.090
Psychoticism (P[C])	+0.431[2]		
Paranoia (P[A])	+0.439[3]		
State 'Fluency'	−0.194		

With observational variables	
B index	−0.034
d'_e	+0.140
$\triangle_m$	−0.281
Recognition Position	−0.106

Notes:
1 p < 0.002, 2 tailed
2 p < 0.02, 2 tailed
3 p < 0.01, 2 tailed

neuroticism (see Table 11.13). There is no evidence that people who report a wider range and more intense level of *feeling* in the mood check-lists used here (referred to in Table 11.13 as 'State Fluency') are more empathic. Hence it is not valid to assume that empathic people 'feel more', as is commonly taken to be the case. ANOVA analysis of the three London Block groups did not reveal significant differences in empathy (F = 2.848, p = 0.067), although there was a tendency for the stable (low N) group to be less empathic.

CONFIRMATION BIAS

Confirmation- and, in turn, refutation-seeking styles of thought appear to be associated with greater left and right hemisphere activation respectively (Drake 1983; Drake and Bingham 1985). Hence high confirmation-seeking cognition would be expected to involve high left and low right hemisphere activation. *High* right hemisphere activity levels are therefore to be associated with *low* visual confirmation bias scores (see Chadwick 1992, chapters 10 and 11). The Slide Viewing Task (SVT), with its involvement of very blurred 'low spatial frequency' information (see Sekuler and Blake 1985), will probably recruit the right hemisphere as that hemisphere preferentially processes low spatial frequencies (Sergent 1982, 1983). Word finding tasks such as the 2–3 and 3–4 tests are more likely to activate the left (language) hemisphere, particularly in a predominantly right-handed sample. (The full London Block contained 57 right-handers and only 2 left-handers and was also predominantly male.)

The correlations of verbal and visual confirmation bias with measures of arousal and with dimensions likely to involve high arousal (such as State Anxiety, Trait Neuroticism, Smoking, etc.) are given in Table 11.14 and, as expected, the correlations are positive (in fact exclusively so) with verbal confirmation bias, and negative (with one exception) with visual confirmation bias (CB). This is what one would expect to obtain if these conditions did activate *both* hemispheres and generally confirms Drake's (1983) theoretical work.

The pattern *reverses*, however, when the confirmation bias scores are correlated with (autonomically mediated) pulse and blood pressure readings – which were also taken from the London Block participants for purposes other than those central to this report (see Chadwick 1988, chapters 10 and 12). Although the correlations are not strong, the general pattern in Table 11.14 is unmistakable but its full meaning is obscure. It could be that the semantic and associative processing involved in the 3–4 test (see also Appendix II) is a more *introverted* task which arouses the cortex but subdues the autonomic system. In turn, confirmation seeking on the more externally oriented Slide Viewing Task may subdue the right cortex but activate at autonomic levels. Confirmation-seeking therefore

Table 11.14 Correlations of confirmation bias (full London Block) with felt stress and dispositional pathology and with autonomic measures

		Verbal CB	Visual CB
MacKay	Stress	+0.037	−0.109
	Arousal	+0.210	−0.305
Nowlis	Activation	+0.031	−0.135
	Anxiety	+0.163	−0.195
	Depression	+0.139	−0.011
Paranoia (P^A)		+0.176	+0.005
Neuroticism		+0.115	−0.177
Psychoticism (P^E)		+0.114	−0.191
Psychoticism (P^C)		+0.095	−0.050
Smoking	·	+0.225	−0.361[1]
Correlations with autonomic measures			
Resting pulse		−0.089	−0.044
Mean pulse		−0.045	−0.051
Pulse during 3–4 test		−0.171	+0.117
Pulse after 3–4 test		−0.023	+0.023
Resting systolic BP		−0.158	+0.117
Mean systolic BP		−0.287	+0.154
Systolic BP during 3–4 test		−0.335	+0.197
Systolic BP after 3–4 test		−0.371[1]	+0.154
Resting diastolic BP		−0.181	+0.034
Mean diastolic BP		−0.322	−0.020
Diastolic BP during 3–4 test		−0.370[1]	+0.111
Diastolic BP after 3–4 test		−0.388[1]	−0.122

Note:
1 $p < 0.05$, 2 tailed

may involve specific neuropsychological activity patterns and it could well be that the frenzied enhancement of this strategy in positive-symptom psychosis involves a see-saw activity between cortical and limbic areas in which cognitively introverted then extraverted strategies are deployed continually to prevent excessive activation of either system and hence to 'titrate' the general cerebral state.

It is perhaps understandable, however, that the very serial, linear, perseverative style of thinking associated with verbal confirmation bias, at least as measured here, would correlate negatively with *divergent* styles of creativity which demand that one break out of familiar ruts in one's ways of thinking. In this context the correlation of −0.490 ($p < 0.01$, 2 tailed) between verbal CB and the Uses Originality score (Table 11.10) makes sense – as does the positive relation between both visual and verbal CB and paranoia (Table 11.14) – itself a very perseverative mode of cognition (Magaro 1981). The correlations of visual confirmation bias with creativity are more positive (Table 11.10), except with the least valid test, the DCT, but this study does not generally involve results which sustain in any great strength a connection between confirmation bias and creativity. It is possible, however, that more 'serial' styles of creativity in which singular lines of thought are pursued with great vitality could be more available to paranoid individuals (see Chapters 2 and 3 in Chadwick 1995a).

REFLECTIONS ON THE EXPERIMENTAL STUDIES

The findings reported here present somewhat mixed but generally positive support for the expectations raised in Chapter 10 and indeed throughout this book. From both this and previous research (see also Rust *et al.* 1989) there does seem to be a contribution from schizotypy in the direction of enhancing creativity. The contribution from intelligence seems greater but schizotypy in no way impedes the creativity of highly intelligent subjects and for those of non-conforming type may well enhance it. Schizotypy also seems to enhance the creativity of participants just below the highest levels of intelligence.

Empathy, generally regarded as a desirable trait, seems more in evidence in those of somewhat pathological disposition, though the direction of causation is obscure. The tests used in the present investigation do not really enable us, alas, to assess whether or not empathy is facilitative of creativity or of true interpersonal sensitivity. It is always possible that empathic individuals are not as accurate in the interpersonal domain as they intuitively feel themselves to be.

The effects of attitude and cognitive style on creativity, in this study, were difficult to assess as the correlations involved were all so low. Perceptually sensitive, non-conforming people and those prone to confirmation-seeking, at least in the visuo-spatial sphere, appear to be more creative. But a prudent man would probably be forced to adopt the position that many cognitive styles and emotive stances could be enhancing of creativity in different circumstances and domains. The present study does not really allow a definitive conclusion to be drawn on this.

All of the biographees reported in this text were undoubtedly intelligent, non-conforming, sensitive, creative and yet schizophrenia-prone. It is encouraging that these components of a person's psychological make-up were indeed shown in this empirical study to enter into meaningful relations with one another. In this respect continuity is thus also preserved between the qualitative and quantitative aspects of this enquiry and this is clearly reassuring.

Chapter 12

Implications for therapy I
Learning from patients and the public

When an architect examines a Gothic structure by Grecian rules, he finds nothing but deformity.

(Richard Hurd, 1762)

This chapter, rather than being theoretical and discursive, will be one that is intended to be entirely practical and succinct. In the first two sections I will present additional therapeutic hints that have emerged from discussions with Desmond, Ivo and Deanna; from visitors to the Borderliners group (see Preface) and from the group itself and from students at Birkbeck College and the Open University. Then I will go on to outline briefly how my own recovery from psychosis, *in the long term*, was brought about; then give some hints about the same issue from other patients I mixed with between 1979 and 1988 (some 33 people in all). Finally, I will provide some 'gut feelings' about recovery from schizophrenia and schizoaffective psychosis and conclude with a comment about the intrinsic validity of schizotypy.

HINTS FROM OTHER BORDERLINERS

A broad metaphysical perspective, although outside a naturalistic framework, was found by all of us to be a valuable horizon to steer by – beyond the pilot's 'levers, switches and dials' of logic and cognitive engineering.

Delusions and hallucinations we feel are best regarded also as having *some* truth value. Perceiving them as 'utter nonsense', apart from being humiliating, is an impediment to recognising and incorporating their existential meaning (see also Romme and Escher 1993).

Since science is not able to explain all the facets of human experience, an irrational, even self-deceptive, model which goes outside the boundaries of science can give enhanced motivation, self-esteem and act as a usable framework by which to live and cope. (See also Sackeim (1983) on this.)

Rather than grasping at mechanistic answers, the cultivation of the quality of *being* with one's ignorance, facing the fact that one does not know, John Keats's 'Negative Capability' (Gittings 1978, pp. 40–1), is something we have found strengthening rather than weakening. (Smith (1990, p. 29) also stresses the importance of this in psychoanalytic therapy.)

Whilst being cautious of the value of mechanistic thinking, it is best not to be *too* romantic or expectant about love. Although, as Desmond and I particularly have found, the power of love cannot be denied, the idea that the patient is cured by the love of the analyst (Freud) is in real life generally unrealistic. Very few therapists genuinely love their clients, although they usually care about them and (maybe) like them. The idea of 'finding love in therapy' sets up improbable expectations in the minds of potential service users. One senior member of MIND encouragingly said to a friend of mine who was contemplating therapy, 'You will love your therapist and your therapist will love you.' The therapy was a disaster.

The client needs a model of reality that is congruent, at least in a general sense, with their experience. This provides a foundational base so that accommodatory manoeuvres are not too stressful. Cognitive-behavioural therapy may be too narrow and tight for some people who need a broader framework to find meaning in their lives. Recent more outré therapies (Rowan and Dryden 1988) may satisfy this need – although there is no reason why cognitive reframing should not also be used with the latter.

To stop highly superstitious thinking turning (perhaps via the person suffering a remarkable tirade of coincidences) into *schizophrenic* thinking, it is valuable to notice when there is a *lack* of correlation between what one is thinking and what is going on externally. It is also useful to avoid 'projection-tempting' activities such as ouija boards, tarot cards and pendulums and to search for mundane rather than spectacular interpretations of unusual coincidences. Fear seems to be an emotion particularly facilitative of the uncanny – it is vital to fight fear back, to focus on *positive* affirmations (see S. Wilde 1987) and to focus on everyday events and positive memories rather than painful memories, distressing emotions and catastrophic 'grand scale' thinking. Clearly all of the above requires considerable discipline, sometimes acquired over years, so that young people can easily move from superstition to insanity in the absence of coping techniques. It is also valuable to notice, however, that one may *seek* this altered state of consciousness for its excitement value because, in one's heart, one is depressed or feeling low about oneself. Usually the payoff is a worse situation than the one from which one came. It is helpful then, in a preventative situation, to be honest with oneself about one's motives – and here a sense of humour is an advantage. Many people have said: 'I thought I might be the Messiah – but laughter prevented it'.

THE THERAPEUTIC VALUE OF WRITING

All of the biographees in the qualitative part of this work involved themselves (as have many students of mine) therapeutically, to a greater or lesser extent, in writing – as did of course outstanding creatives of schizophreniform disposition such as Wittgenstein and Joyce. To use one's own struggle to enrich one's creative work is, for many people, to labour within the Kierkegaardian tradition. This stresses knowledge from passion and understanding from being (see Chadwick 1996a). The writer who toils in this vein seeks to avoid the middle ground and the tyranny of domestic virtues and standards to pursue uniqueness and intensity. The equivalent of bourgeois categorisation in academia, diagnosis, is really the enemy of the writer and of the artist who seeks beauty and poignancy everywhere, even in ugliness and deformity, and especially away from the centre. The pen is undoubtedly a tool through which to realise one's own intrinsic validity and with which to define and express the Self as secure in its own terms.

Writing is particularly refreshing, revealing and liberating, as so much new material from within becomes available to consciousness through the characters one creates. Oscar Wilde used to say, 'Give a man a mask, and he will tell you the truth.' By writing as *someone else* (see also Hudson 1966), one can plummet oceans which cannot at all be easily accessed in either analysis or self-analysis, where one must 'own' every word or thought. In analysis one sometimes cannot dare to scrutinise certain ideational strands until one is morally or intellectually ready for them (see Horney 1942). By creating characters (masks) one can allow all strands freely to come to the surface, one can *play* with possibilities, *rehearse* thoughts, build much faster and 'own', if necessary, at a future time. In writing, and unlike in science and psychoanalysis, one can indeed *use* all of one's experience through to the most remote trivia in a manner that has a freshness and openness about it that contrasts with the self-consciousness and stiffness ('analysis paralysis') that can so easily be evoked by intense dyadic therapy.

Writing, however, need not be for others. Via the keeping of a *journal* all manner of thoughts and experiences can be ventilated and problems genuinely worked through and solved. Journal writing testifies to the possibility of effective therapy without transference. A journal has many advantages. For example, it sets no time limit to your verbal delivery. It never gets exasperated or bored, nor does it ever criticise or rebuke you. It never forgets anything, its cost is minimal, it can travel with you and it demands nothing from you other than that you fill it with meaningful useful writing so that in a way it is 'allowed' to fulfil its function. It allows *you* to find your own interpretations, never chides you for lack of motivation or evasiveness and it never misunderstands you or gets romantically or sexually involved with you. It never probes or questions you if you are 'late' and it is never shaken by outbursts of emotion – all that happens is that the pen is more indented into the page. It allows you to be yourself completely and it will receive what you say faithfully at any time of the day or night. The deficiency, of course, is that there are none of the challenges or the positive consequences of a relationship – and none of the positive spin-offs of criticism or of the sense of *development* of a relationship.

HINTS AND GUIDELINES CONCERNING HOW MY OWN REHABILITATION WAS BROUGHT ABOUT IN THE LONG TERM

I will present this and subsequent practical suggestions in such a way that this chapter is self-contained and hence readers who have turned immediately to it will not be disadvantaged by lack of information from earlier in the text. For the sake of these readers there will be a few instances of repetition but these are very minor.

It was helpful for me to regard myself as having had an *illness*. This made me respectful of the need to maintain and titrate medication. I was eventually able to get by perfectly well on a low dose of haloperidol (2.5 mg *nocte*) and I have stayed on that dosage ever since 1981. I have had no relapses worthy of the term, and the medication has helped me to make more, not less, use of my psychological insight and thus genuinely to gain ground. I have deliberately taken only very few 'drug holidays'. Patients with less insight, and less gain of insight over time I found, generally made less progress.

I was greatly helped by *gradual* re-employment, taking on more part-time work as I became mentally stronger and stronger. If I had had to go straight into full-time employment, say in 1981, even in menial work, I could not have coped. Yet by 1986 I was effectively on a full-time schedule anyway and coping perfectly well.

I eventually married a woman who, when there is conflict between us, makes her own points only by attacking my behaviour not my character. I was brought up in Manchester, at home and at school, by people (my mother included) who tended to have a very spiritually superior, high-minded attitude and who would relentlessly attack my character if 'mistakes' occurred in the way I conducted myself. Behavioural blaming is much less pernicious (Janoff-Bulman 1979; Major *et al.* 1985), as for example in 'that was a rash thing to do' rather than (what I got) 'You bloody swine!'

As psychosis is a lot to do with excessively seeing meanings and signifi-cance in things, even in such trivialities as a man dropping his newspaper in the street, it was very helpful immediately after the episode to mix with people who called a spade a spade and who didn't, in Brunerian fashion, like to go way 'beyond the information given'. This 'sweet converse of innocent minds' (Keats) was deeply healing to me. Indeed, in the first year or so after the crisis, talk about 'the profound significance of things' was extremely counter-therapeutic and mentally loosening. I do not think that many psychodynamically oriented professionals realise this; nor do many other rather intellectual professionals who are eager to explore the neural networks of their patients for interesting data. This kind of intervention, at least to a severe degree, is best left for about eighteen months to two years after a florid episode as the latter leaves the connectivity of one's neural networks damaged. (Because of this, changes tend to be slow and hence staff and family must put patience first.)

Support from other people was absolutely critical. My GP in Fulham, Grant Blair, was particularly helpful by his accessibility, friendliness and genuine interest in my case – and also by *never overreacting* if I had any minor hiccups in the early years of recovery. Non-possessiveness and non-embroiling love from my wife and the respect, warmth, acceptance and affection of my close friends did wonders for my sense of identity and feelings of inner strength.

Knowledge about serious mental illness (and about the medication I myself have been on) has been extremely helpful. However, the anti-psychiatry literature to which I was heavily exposed as an undergraduate was of no preventive value and has been of only subordinate help since. In fact I would say that it was definitely counter-preventive and made me miss tell-tale signs of real approaching illness. The more realistic mainstream knowledge, however (e.g. Claridge 1967, 1985; Eysenck and Eysenck 1976), made me feel less alone, less of an oddball and took a lot of the sinister mystery out of what I experienced. Theoretical work, including my own (Chadwick 1992), which attached my experience to normal motivational processes, cognition and physiology, and which traced the links clearly between mystical and psychotic states, was also therapeutic. I was prepared to accept that what I experienced and thought was extreme (viz: 'illness' – see for example Claridge 1990) but it was not at all therapeutic for me to regard myself either as in some sense categorically different from standard-minded people (e.g. 'he's a genetic schizophrenic') or as 'basically OK really' and merely labelled as ill for political reasons.

As with survivors of child abuse (Egeland 1988), the act of becoming fluent about my experience and the success I had in embedding it in my life experience as a whole was highly therapeutic. Success in seeing it as a progression from my earlier life (Chadwick 1993b) was far more helpful for me, and made me feel less threat-sensitive and 'surprise-wary' than seeing it as a bizarre mental explosion of symptoms coming from some untrodden region of my mind as 'a response to stress'.

Testing out of my rather complex delusions to see which aspects of the system were true (and some literally were) and which were false was very relieving. This I did in the community rather than in the unit (for the latter see P.D.J. Chadwick and Lowe 1990). It is important to note that finding that some of my beliefs were true was actually mentally strengthening not weakening, as it validated my judgemental abilities. Therapists who are continually cynical about their deluded patients' talk (e.g. Berrios 1991) should be mindful of this.

It was exceedingly helpful to have contact with people who were supportive and affectionate to me even when my behaviour was off-putting. (I came to suffer for a time from mild coprolalic Tourette Syndrome – see Chapters 4, 5 and 13). People who strongly showed only very conditional affection reminded me of the past and thus helped me not one iota. Only a fair degree of unconditional positive regard, as Rogers has always maintained, enabled me to develop a trusting and benign rather than paranoid attitude to people, and to see myself as basically good (rather than the 'rotter' and 'poof' that I was brought up to believe I was (see Chadwick 1993b)).

Over the years, insight into how I came to think, feel and believe as I did when I was ill has helped me to understand and forgive myself for behaving in that seemingly absurd way. This has meant work on cognitions, not only work on feelings. However, ventilating the immense anger I had at one time towards the people who shaped my mind, particularly over my first twenty-one years, has been of no therapeutic value whatever. Trying to relive and 'work through' the utter Wildean-level humiliation I suffered in the few years leading up to the time I became ill has also been of no benefit. My subsequent adoption, however, difficult though it was, of a self-accepting positive outlook on life and people has been of immense value and has radically changed the style and content of my existence. The positive orientation has also made me more predictively accurate when dealing with people and actually able to get closer to them. This, of course, is critical in life.

ADDITIONAL HINTS FROM OTHER PATIENTS

The word 'discharge' seems to be pathogenic in itself. It is seen in a way rather like a chuck-out day or an evacuation day. When patients and residents feel that they are soon to be ejected into the community (often seen as hostile), with little or no support or help (and even with no one to go with them to view a flat, for example), they very easily get ill again. This rather dismissive procedure of course was very common in the 1970s and 1980s. Follow-up and continuity of care seem to be vital. Leaving the helping agencies is, like re-employment, better if it is gradual, with no harsh and rigid discontinuities. These latter also are a serious cause of losses to the system.

Going mad is utterly humiliating. Afterwards one is at least temporarily marginalised in society and pejoratively categorised. In this spiritually and physically dishevelled state there are many attitudes and strategies that therapists employ that are experienced by previously psychotic clients as infuriating and counter-productive. Among these are obsession with punctuality, strict adherence to a 50-minute hour, single-theory or one-approach therapists, overuse of the concept of projection, being continually (and wrongly) accused of having 'run away from reality', finding that the therapist childishly rejoices in penetrating and ripping away defences in the service of 'truth', finding that one's psychotic experience in itself is seen as worthless and even demeaning of one's character and integrity, finding that one is not really being listened to and, finally, experiencing the tendency of therapists to hastily force what the client is saying into a pre-existent theory without diligently checking to see whether or not this is fair and appropriate. The recovering psychotic client is really one of the therapist's *employers*; he or she is not an employee, still less a 'love slave', who clocks in and then out to be processed by these absurd procedures.

Bernean pastimes, in which one is basically talking small talk and 'talking about nothing', are found in reasonable measure to be very therapeutic by ex-patients in 'enculturing' the person back into everyday life. (A change of clothes and a new hair-do can have the same effect.) Staff who continually want patients and residents to be doing 'deep insight work' (usually referred to simply as 'work') are in danger of catering for themselves far too much and missing the value of these simple things.

Sending patients back into exactly the same scenario in which they became ill in the first place, whether it be a run-down bedsitter or an emotion-charged family, is a disaster unless the receiving context is itself changed or medication dosage is hazardously high. The same context and the same social 'music' tends to regenerate the same experience.

Too many patients are matched with therapists, befrienders and social workers in a blind-date fashion. Forming relationships is not a science (Storr 1990) although science can help (Argyle 1992). More information at least needs to be made available to patient and professional before otherwise totally incompatible people are thrust together. Blind-date matching is particularly dangerous with people recovering from psychotic experiences, as they may be less able to accommodate and adapt themselves in interpersonal contexts than less distressed people.

GUT FEELINGS ABOUT RECOVERY

People I had known over the years found the positive reconstruction of the psychotic experience I attempted in my thesis work and in *Border-line* (Chadwick 1992) to be refreshing and more fair than the tirade of defamatory inferences about the psychotic mind with which one is often confronted. For example, many of us felt that we were never quite 'there' in reality anyway in the old days – so one cannot 'run away' from a place where one has never been. Psychosis can also open doors within, reveal the deeper potential of consciousness and develop spiritual sensitivity and an outlook on life inaccessible to the person before his or her episode.

Virtually all of us have found that structure to our lives, if not too tightly applied, has been helpful. Empty days and friendless nights only give licence for preoccupation with morbid thoughts – rather like the 'Sunday neuroses' discussed by Fenichel (1946/1982, p. 472). A forlorn meandering life, however, also dangerously motivates the search for 'impossible' experiences and scarlet sensations in a drab existence. This is the route both to illicit drug use and to psychosis.

Getting an overall purpose or sense of mission to one's life, apart from just 'staying out of hospital', gives one a horizon to pilot by. This 'deep steering' is a shift to a health orientation rather than merely an 'avoidance of illness' orientation.

We all felt that more peer-professionals are needed for patients to relate to better (see for example Sutherland 1976, 1992b; Toates 1990; Jamison 1996). Peer-professionals are a valuable linking pin between professionals, paraprofessionals (Orford 1992) and patients. Inside knowledge cannot, after all, be replaced or substituted by the severely neo-classical methods of positivists.

Nobody who becomes seriously mentally ill has high self-esteem. If ex-patients' self-esteem is not strengthened by the peers and professionals they live and work with, they will always remain vulnerable, no matter what medication they take and no matter what case-management or relapse-preventative strategies are assembled.

It is very important that staff do not ostentatiously show the same processing biases and maladaptive interpersonal strategies that patients and, sometimes, their families are found to have. Staff high on expressed emotion, over-talkativeness, guilt induction, coldness, confirmation bias, availability, anchoring and self-serving biases (Kahneman *et al.* 1982; Nisbett and Ross 1980) or decisional over-confidence are not good role models for recovering clients. Yet such staff do exist and can do great damage by their arousing, confusing, overwhelming and 'inner-scream'-inducing behaviour.

Particularly irritating are the occasional anti-psychiatry mental health professionals and paraprofessionals who, although benign in intent, have themselves never slid further than being members of the worried well, and lord it over ex-patients and residents with the claim that, since *they* get by on herbal diets or with psychology and insight work alone and without any medication whatever, so should the patients – who may be seen as 'using a crutch' and 'weak' (see Weller 1984, p. 31). These people may well themselves have suffered, but their tragic masks conceal faces bloated with self-satisfaction. Their eyes may be intense but their words, like their throats, are hollow. They have a two-dimensional view of madness and totally lack empathy with what really serious mental illness is like. We well know that medication may not be necessary for all clients, particularly those returning to low expressed emotion and warm homes. Short-term and long-term side-effects are well documented. Much can be said against medication. But it is dangerous, and perhaps unethical, deliberately to use the 'crutch' argument to deflect the treatment plan of a service user whose life has been stabilised and even revolutionised partly by chemical means.

Most mental health professionals are highly communicative and intelligent, and highly intelligent staff naturally want some intellectually stimulating chats with the patients. When these are not forthcoming for months on end they easily get demotivated or 'single-patient obsessed' if one person provides them with the cerebral nourishment they require. Another strategy is for (basically bored) staff to cluster and knot together in the staff room (say at a day centre) having 'long deep growth-enhancing conversations' with one another. Such (usually small) rooms then have a voiceless atmosphere which is embarrassingly and excludingly thick with private meaning and profundity if one happens blithely to walk in with little notice (say, with a message from the milkman). Service users do notice this and feel the forbiddance. There seems little reason why clients and staff can't 'grow' together.

One of the problems in this field, then, is to keep going when nothing 'interesting' is happening – what I would call 'motivational coasting' as it is not the same, quite, as Keats's 'negative capability' although the two are obviously related. Having expressible interests in things other than mental processes is helpful here – and much appreciated by clients, who often get sick of feeling that their ('sick') minds are forever under a microscope.

The movement from in-patient status to community life has to be gradual and should involve making headway. Rehabilitation is a kinetic concept, but in the end one hopes to be able to say, '*Now* I am well'. One final comment that has to be made is that staff who 'need to be needed' have to know (as do over-protective mothers) when to let go.

To conclude with some comments on schizotypals – and to return in a way to the quote at the head of this chapter – it has to be faced that the actions of many schizotypals are a lyrical mode of behaviour. They are difficult to understand reductively because it is difficult, to put it bluntly, to find physics in poetry. Normalisation of these people in a strict sense would be a meaningless and destructive enterprise, rendering bland that which is potentially colourful. Schizotypal life can be morbid as well as voluptuous but it has a vibrancy that must never be dulled into a bourgeois domesticity by evangelical rationalists lest flowers of genuine beauty be crushed.

Chapter 13

Implications for therapy II
Some specific problems

The rule is perfect: in all matters of opinion our adversaries are insane.
(Mark Twain on psychiatric practice)

Many things a therapist cannot do. He or she cannot pay off a client's debts; or bring back a dead relative or a straying lover. He or she cannot change the government or the past or the company policy of the client's employer. In many ways the therapist is quite powerless. Ideally, to ease psychopathology the world-inclusion-of-person needs to be changed. Alas, the therapist can usually only work with individuals and small groups. This solution is by its very nature far from ideal – as Freud himself recognised – and in some cases, such as those of depressed lower-class women whose difficulties are often largely social in origin (though not entirely so – see Brown 1991), working at the individual intrapsychic level alone can to a greater or lesser degree be actually misguided (Smail 1993).

The therapist or clinician has considerable power, however, in the therapy or treatment process and the danger of this is currently an issue of great concern (Masson 1990; Rutter 1990; Miller 1990; Tudor and Tudor 1994). It is all too easy for clinicians to regard problems as more intra-psychic than they really are in order to enhance their own feelings of competence and self-efficacy in helping the client to solve them. It is also easy for clinicians to devalue both the psychotic experience and the character of the psychosis sufferer in order to protect themselves against feelings of dread and alienation when confronted by someone who has in a sense 'been' to a place where they cannot go and which is beyond their powers of insight and empathy to appreciate. Notwithstanding the potential role of peer-professionals in levelling the status hierarchy it is often considered that the use of paraprofessionals (Orford 1992) may help to eliminate some of the evils of the power imbalance in the therapist–client dyad (see also Chapter 4 here).

In this chapter I will use examples from my own treatment to address these issues and others and hence try to bring them alive in the context of an actual case-management example.

CONFIRMATION BIAS IN MENTAL HEALTH PROFESSIONALS

Psychiatrists, psychiatric nurses and social workers are human beings and not perfect specimens of angelic love, infinite knowledge and immaculate behaviour. They also do not live and work in a social vacuum and are bound to be influenced by prevailing community attitudes and theories no matter how hard they try to counter their effects.

Before discharge from the day hospital in 1979 I attended my final case meeting with the staff at Charing Cross Hospital. I had left hospital as such by then and was planning to move to a hostel for the recovering mentally ill in Shepherd's Bush. One of the residential social workers there, Ruth Carruthers (now Shippey and who, bless her, was always on the patient's side), was present at my final meeting which was chaired by a psychiatrist (neither Hirsch, Oomen nor Weller). I was optimistic about the future, felt good, was *determined* to get fully well again and in quite high spirits. I said that since leaving hospital I had got together a plan to do a Ph.D. on arousal and its links with paranoia and delusional thinking, making use of my own experiences. I was going to approach the Maudsley to see if I could be accepted on a Ph.D. programme with this topic. I was also going to use my experience to enrich my counselling work – which I was determined to continue. The illness was behind me, I felt my insight into it was good and that I no longer needed intense treatment.

Now this was pretty well exactly what I *did* do in the months and years that followed.[1] Alas, the treatment team didn't see the picture I painted like this at all. They thought that the way I was talking showed that I was still rather manic, still ill, full of exaggerated ideas and that my plan to do a Ph.D. at the Maudsley Hospital was utterly laughable and a further and definite symptom of my 'illness'. There was much jollity about all this (in my absence) and it was only when Ruth chipped in with a monologue about my previous qualifications and record that the atmosphere of scornful glee apparently calmed down. When she was later able to say that my application there had been accepted and that Hans Eysenck was interested in the project there was an embarrassed pause. Alas, when I approached Charing Cross Hospital a few years later to see whether I could test patients as part of the experimental work for my doctorate, I was refused access by the head of the ethical committee (although Steven Hirsch privately approved of the plan). I was told that it would be 'highly inappropriate' for me to test patients in the unit where I myself had previously been treated but no reason *why* it would be so 'highly inappropriate' was given (Chadwick 1993a). I think the inference is inescapable, rather paranoid though it may sound, that my plan was turned down because ex-psychiatric patients (former 'nutters') do not, by virtue of their inferior status, command the same *rights* as people who have never been psychiatric patients. We cannot have an ex-patient studying a patient, because only people who are essentially healthy, 'normal' and thus superior to the patient can have the role of researching their condition. (If someone had had surgery in a unit, and later *became* a surgeon, would they be banned from performing surgery in the same unit? I think not.) But to have an ex-psychiatric patient doing psychological research would not be a useful example of patients helping each other; no, it seems it would be seen as an awkward and embarrassing event and an invasion and levelling of the status structure of the hospital. Alas, the head of the ethical committee was the same doctor who thought my application to the Maudsley a sign of mental illness. Perhaps my inferences above will be taken as *further* signs of mental illness.

One might think these anecdotes reflect only isolated and rare opinions and attitudes. This may well not be so. I published my concerns above about access to patients by researchers who had themselves been ill in the March 1993 issue of *The Psychologist*, asking for reactions to and open discussion of this problem (Chadwick 1993a). My letter, which was published as the lead letter in the issue, provoked a deafening silence.

How are we to react to all this? Personally I see the events above as perfectly understandable given the hierarchical nature of the mental health sphere (with patients at the bottom) and given the centuries of discrimination against 'the mad' (Foucault 1965; Scull 1979; Szasz 1971, 1974). One also has to consider the *usual* behaviour of people diagnosed as hypomanic (which means 'less than manic') in case reviews, which often *is* indeed overoptimistic. The doctor above concerned with my own case probably had no detailed knowledge of my academic background, or of the grittiness that I learned (or inherited?) from my mother – and that I learned from years of climbing, field geology, competitive athletics and heavy sports. He was simply making a judgement based on, and confirming, his experience of 'the usual patient of this type'. My case revealed his bias and contradicted his expectations but it could have happened to any psychiatrist – and probably would have done. After all, subclinical levels of hypomania do occur in otherwise normal people and indeed bestow great optimism and drive on their possessor. Not surprisingly, they can be extremely useful in one's career and one's life. So we learn by our mistakes.

The refusal to allow me access to patients does not seem to be a decision made by a lone cynic. It seems instead that the mental health authorities are rather befuddled by this potential scenario (if one agrees that their silence gives licence for such an inference) and that the possibility of a levelling of the status structure in this way by a member of the profession who is also a peer of the patients is felt as singularly uncomfortable (and best left like a sleeping dog) as it presents a direct confrontation between egalitarian and hierarchical attitudes. I leave the readers to assess the fairness or otherwise of my inferences and to draw their own conclusions.

'IT'S A CRY FOR HELP'

Most lay people believe suicide to be often, maybe always, a 'cry for help'. Research suggests that this is not by any means always the case (Durkheim 1897/1951; Mintz 1968; Rosenhan and Seligman 1984/1995, pp. 413–15). Alas, the lay view does percolate through into the minds of some trainee psychiatrists, who thus fail to recognise when it simply doesn't apply. When my suicide attempt under the double-decker bus came up in my case review, I was asked why I gave the driver *any time at all* to stop?

'You must have realised that he *could* have braked and missed you?' said a young male doctor.

'... er ... ' I replied. 'I thought the driver was a member of the Organisation, he'd have to see it was me.'

'But he might have missed you! Surely you thought of that?'

'... er ... well I suppose he might.'

'Yes ... it was a cry for help,' he softly replied, looking downwards and nodding as he said the words (as if speaking the statement softly made it deep and true). There was a gentle murmur of agreement all round.

This experience was thoroughly *exasperating* for me. My utter *despair* at the time of the suicide attempt at having survived was surely enough to show that he was wrong? I felt a strange sense that what I was telling the team was not being taken for what it was but was being as if assimilated into the preconceived schemes and notions in their minds. This is a most unnerving *and pathogenic* experience as this assimilative, confirmation-seeking behaviour of the personnel is exactly the same as one's *own* behaviour, or thought processes, when one was ill! The reader can imagine that seeing or sensing one's treatment team doing this kind of thing (and psychotherapists are renowned for it) is most enraging yet simultaneously mentally *weakening*. One feels one's legs turn to jelly and one's stomach sink when this happens. It is like being on a merry-go-round which leads nowhere. Clearly facing a treatment team with an *advocate* would help to circumvent this kind of problem that emerges in a 'many versus one' situation.

'COLLUSION PHOBIA'

Needless to say, every statement I ever made, in the hospital or in the after-care hostel, about the early evidence for my delusions was reacted to in the same dismissive way (all for my own good). If other patients and residents had not been present to talk to – two of whom also had delusions similar to mine – I would never have been able really to get to grips with the task of reassessing the meaning and significance of this evidence. Again, the value of helping agents other than mental health authorities compels our urgent notice.

On one occasion, for example, when I was leaving the hostel on Wood Lane, Shepherd's Bush, to go to work in a temporary job, two young men were walking towards me on the west side of Wood Lane as I walked north towards White City tube. The one on my left looked at me, as they were both doing, and said to the other: 'Bad, mad or sad?' (I didn't exactly look my best). His companion paused, then replied: 'Sad.' The first young man then said, '*They* say he's bad.'

Now this brief conversation was quite audible and again the lip and head movements perfectly synchronised with what I heard said. Yet it was totally and utterly *impossible* to have a meaningful and useful conversation with *any* hostel staff about this seemingly dreadful event – which all of them totally dismissed as having never happened and having been totally illusory. They were obviously keen not to 'collude' with the patients to the extent that any talk about evidence for delusions *at all* other than to dismiss it was just not in their repertoire. This is well-meaning stupidity of the most infuriating and naïve kind.

After discussion with other residents we came to the reasonable conclusion that gossip (and some actual people) from East London could easily have reached White City estate (which is located further up Wood Lane) so a slender connection between my wild and hectic days in the East and those now in the West of London probably explained this (basically trivial) happening.

In addition a statement (also dismissed) I frequently heard when I was ill, viz.: 'It does look like 'im' was almost certainly referring not to any circulating photographs (see p. 28) but to the slight facial similarity in those days between my ever-present *dog* Penny and me! (The facial similarity between dogs and their owners is of course a common joke in western pet-oriented circles.)

We can see here that mental health workers' refusals to listen to 'deluded talk' out of fear of 'collusion' are utterly *useless* and even pathogenic and mentally weakening therapeutic manoeuvres. The *evidence* for a delusion is not always best dismissed. (No resident is going to say that they see six fingers on their hand when there are only five.) It is the cognitive *interpretation* of that evidence that is mostly valuable as a target for discussion and analysis. Being told by professionals that people (quote) 'couldn't have said that' when they *blatantly did* provokes not peace of mind but an inner *scream* and ends the conversation before it even begins. No useful work can be done. And useful work – we can call it 'cognitive replacement' – certainly *can* be done with deluded patients. Finding an alternative more likely (and usually more *mundane*) interpretation of evidence can genuinely eat away and destroy a psychotic delusion. Telling a person that they're hallucinating all the time gets absolutely nowhere. Professionals *must* learn to *listen* to what their patients tell them, rather than projecting their theories into them. (Needless to say, one of the favourite concepts mental health authorities ironically use in explaining deluded patients' own talk is, as we've seen, projection.)

Alas, an influential theory well known to psychiatrists, that the sensory *evidence* in psychosis is what is faulty, not the thought processes (Maher 1974), is in some cases an almost complete *reversal* of the usual experiences of deluded patients. The thought processes of psychotics are almost always overly *spectacular*, confirmation-seeking, hasty and over-confident, yet their hearing of external stimuli not *necessarily* grossly impaired. It is extremely important that professionals be mindful of these cognitive biases (see Brennan and Hemsley 1984; Huq *et al*. 1988; Kaney and Bentall 1989; P.K. Chadwick 1992; Kinderman 1994) as real change efforts and genuine amelioration of symptoms can indeed be profitably directed at them (Watts *et al*. 1973; Johnson *et al*. 1977; Milton *et al*. 1978; Hole *et al*. 1979; Rudden *et al*. 1982; Hartman and Cashman 1983; P.D.J. Chadwick and Lowe 1990; Lowe and P.D.J. Chadwick 1990; Kingdon and Turkington 1994; Garety *et al*. 1994; Fowler *et al*. 1995; P.D.J. Chadwick *et al*. 1996).

'IT'S PERFECTLY NORMAL'

An intense training in psychiatry and/or abnormal psychology is bound to sensitise a professional to signs of abnormality in others (and of course in themselves). One result of this, however, is overdiagnosis of mental illness (false alarm decisions), as we have seen in the past in the overgeneralisation of the 'schizophrenia' label (Sandifer *et al*. 1968; Cooper *et al*. 1972; Boyle 1990) and in the labelling of sane people as mentally ill (Rosenhan 1973).

Antagonism in recent decades to psychiatry found organised force in the anti-psychiatry movement (Laing 1960, 1967, 1970; Laing and Esterson 1964; Szasz 1971, 1974). Although it is now somewhat subdued, see for example Roth (1973) and Claridge (1990) for severe and moderate reactions respectively to the anti-psychiatrists, it nonetheless lives on in the mental health community. It is well known in the trade, for example, that many residential and day centre social workers are of this inclination (Weller 1984) and may even encourage residents to discontinue medication and go on herbal diets or into psychotherapy as a sole replacement. Another consequence of this theoretical or psychopolitical orientation is the tendency to de-pathologise people's superficially aberrant behaviour. 'It's quite normal and understandable,' say those of this ilk, or 'there's nothing organic to worry about'.

Having been heavily steeped in the theories of Laing, Cooper and Szasz as an undergraduate, I myself tended to operate in this way in the 1970s and can definitely still see their benefits and potential (see Johnstone 1993a, b, 1994, 1996; Newnes and MacLachlan 1996). However, there are problems other than those produced by those who fervently overdiagnose. These 'normalisers', who are understandably strongly against standardisation of thought and behaviour, also, however, produce their *own* crop of victims – people who *are* ill yet are repeatedly told 'There's nothing medically wrong with you'. (My own politically oriented undergraduate training in abnormal psychology, for example, did not prepare me *at all* for what I suffered.) Although the false alarms produced by medical authorities equipped with diagnostic manuals are the subject of much indignation across the board from instances of overdiagnosed childhood disorder to overdiagnosed schizophrenia, the 'misses' of the social workers and anti-psychiatry psychotherapists rarely receive much attention. Most people, after all, are *grateful* not to be diagnosed and labelled and pleased to know how basically normal they really are. Why complain?

This complacency I would suggest is a difficult problem which we need to be alerted to. It is particularly awkward given that many professionals are becoming increasingly enthusiastic (and in many ways rightly so) about greatly enlarging the role of paraprofessionals (volunteers, parents, students) in the care of the mentally disordered (Durlak 1979, 1981; Hattie *et al.* 1984; Cowen 1982). Many residential social workers, it should be emphasised, are also taken from the general community and may have little or no training at the outset in counselling, psychology or psychiatry (Barclay 1982; Weller 1984, 1989). Their job, for some, is the lowest rung of the ladder in the profession. Similarly, most psychotherapists have no background at all in neurology, physiology or biochemistry and their psychological knowledge leans heavily towards various forms of psycho-dynamic and humanistic approaches (Masson 1990; Dryden 1990; Kovel 1991). Their knowledge of chemical interventions and their effects is also usually extremely limited (as of course is that of the patients *on* the medication). This net has so many holes in it that it is surprising that we know so little about the people who have fallen through it. This is such a case.

I suffered, as the reader may recall from Chapter 5, from what was in fact a relatively mild form of Gilles de la Tourette Syndrome from the summer of 1979 to the autumn of 1981, totally oblivious to what was actually wrong with me (though the level of disorder was officially 'mild', the experience was horrendous).

Gilles de la Tourette Syndrome is basically a tic or movement disorder which, strictly speaking, develops before the age of 18 (DSM IV 1994, pp. 101–3). If it develops later, as in my case, at 33, it is usually referred to as a 'Tourette-like Syndrome' (Robertson and Trimble, unpublished). It is named after the man who first systematically catalogued the symptoms, Gilles de la Tourette, in 1885. (A compilation of critical references on this disorder is given in Turpin 1993.) In a certain percentage of cases, higher in the USA than in Great Britain or Japan (Robertson 1989), the movement tics are accompanied by sudden, explosive, offensive or obscene utterances (e.g. 'Fuck!', 'Cunt!', 'Shit!') known as 'coprolalia' ('faeces-talk'). It is only very rarely (and not necessarily) associated with psychosis (see Kerbeshian and Burd 1987; Takeuchi *et al.* 1986) but in me it was. A common attribution of Touretteurs (and of their families) who suffer coprolalia is that they are possessed by demons or the Devil (UK Tourette Syndrome Information pack).

When I was in Charing Cross Hospital, the medication I happened to be on as an in-patient (pimozide and haloperidol) was *precisely* the medication of choice for many people with Tourette Syndrome – not surprisingly, I was almost completely symptom-free when living there. However, soon after discharge, my medication (which was targeted, remember, at *the psychosis*) was changed to chlorpromazine, which is very effective for a schizoaffective disorder but is totally *ineffective* for Tourette Syndrome. By February 1980, then a resident at the aftercare hostel, my 'inner heavings' *reappeared*. (I had decided to take minimal medication anyway.) It is incredible to me now that I did not link their disappearance when I was in hospital with the drugs I was then on. I wrongly assumed that it was the *quantity* of in-hospital medication that had done the trick – and I wasn't going back on *that* dosage for all the tea in China! I was wrong. It was the nature of the medication, not its amount. I also stupidly failed to realise that the inner heavings originally appeared in 1979 just a few days after I gave up tobacco smoking and I did find that a return to smoking helped to allay them a little – but not much.

The staff at the hostel interpreted my inner compulsion to shout out obscenities and insults, particularly since I suppressed the urge to actually *say* them, as due to 'bottled-up anger', which was quite normal. They said they suffered from the same problem themselves at times! A young female psychotherapist at MIND I consulted said the difficulty was 'very common' (the incidence of Tourette Syndrome is about 5 cases per million per year although admittedly many cases are mild and go undiagnosed (Lucas *et al.* 1982; Robertson 1989, p. 148)) and that she had treated five or six people in the last year with 'the same problem'. My solution was to say the words *out loud*! To 'get it all off my chest'. The hostel staff generally concurred. I didn't. After two days of following her advice, the urges were almost uncontainable and, in fact, were close to becoming the more serious form known colloquially as 'through-going Tourette'. I did not keep the next appointment. A friend of mind asked her own psychotherapist, again recommended to her by MIND, about my problem and told her of my concerns that it *was* a medical, perhaps neurological, condition although I knew not what. The psychotherapist (Freudian) said that she had never heard of any such thing and that I was talking complete nonsense. When my friend, slightly upset by this, said in my defence that I was myself 'experienced and qualified in psychology', the therapist puffed herself up and angrily replied, 'I've got more qualifications than he'll *ever* have!' (Interestingly my friend discontinued therapy with this woman, who actually made her a lot worse and who brought on, with her 'treatment', a depression which lasted over five years.) Apart from a total lack of any warmth, she also, at the hardware end, did not even know what a neurotransmitter was, and *despite treating many recovering schizophrenics* reacted to my friend's concerned statement about the well-known dopamine theory of schizophrenia (Randrup and Munkvad 1972; Snyder 1974; Crow *et al.* 1978; Owen *et al.* 1978; Haracz 1982; Deakin 1988; Davis *et al.* 1991) with the haughty retort, 'Dopamine? Never *heard* of it!'

I tried to 'get through' to the hostel staff that this *was* some kind of illness or disease when I told them that the 'heavings' in a physical sense began in my tummy and over the course of a second or two rose up within my body past my chest eventually to my mouth, throat and vocal chords as if I was being 'verbally sick'. I also suggested to them that the impulse might in my case make partial use of the same circuitry as that in the *sneeze* mechanism as the heavings *and even the thoughts accompanying them* were *totally eliminated* when I deliberately held my nose. The ineffectiveness of chlorpromazine also made the 'bottled-up anger' theory highly suspicious as this drug usually *does* calm and control aggressive patients, and indeed prisoners. These latter comments should really have been definitive; anger expression and negative cognitions are hardly inhibited by holding one's nose yet anger expression *is* inhibited by chlorpromazine. What was wrong with me must be essentially something else. All this, alas, made not the slightest difference and was treated as completely irrelevant (and even as evasive and defensive). What I was suffering from, in now smouldering silence, was quite normal, it was a motivational problem (this despite the total *absence* of any coprolalic Freudian slips), and I had only to get my anger out cathartically for the problem to disappear. Eventually, after months of talk and thought of a psychoanalytic nature about this problem, which had not the *slightest* beneficial effect,[2] the hostel staff became bored with it and I decided to keep the whole issue to myself.

Thinking privately that perhaps the problem was due to the almost unbearable frustration of not being able to get down to full-time or near full-time research, I waited until I began my Ph.D. investigations (which had to wait until I could find the money for the fees). But when this *also* had no effect at all, I finally dispensed with psychological theorising and decided to consult my former therapist, the Harley Street psychiatrist Dr Peter Storey via my GP, Grant Blair, who had luckily been trained by Peter at St George's Hospital in South London.

I explained the symptoms in as much detail as I could, basically expanding on the above, and the diagnosis was made immediately.[3] I was returned to a small haloperidol dosage (see Shapiro and Shapiro 1968) (eventually 2.5 mg at night), which is a usual and effective amount for Tourette patients (Golden 1984; Bruun 1984), and the problem, for all practical purposes, was solved. Over two years of wasted time, embarrassment, social phobia, even mild suicidal feelings on occasion, inner anguish, doubt, insult and dismissal, all because people wanted to 'reassure' me that there was 'absolutely nothing medically wrong with me'.

'YOU'RE HEARING THINGS'

It is theoretically interesting that the mysterious rappings I had heard in my side ward (one tap for 'Yes', two taps for 'No') also reappeared about the same time as did my Tourette-style inner heavings. This again was while I was a resident in the mental after-care hostel and their reappearance was in February 1980. The reader can probably easily guess by now that these rappings were immediately 'diagnosed' as auditory hallucinations by staff despite the fact that no standard text in psychopathology, whether it be medical or psychological, has ever cited such a phenomenon as a form of hallucination. (Indeed, this well-meaning interpretation actually made me feel worse.)

When first entering the hostel just before New Year in December 1979, I immediately struck up a relationship with an engaging and pleasing 19-year-old girl called Jeanie Beamish, another resident, who suffered from depression and lack of motivation. Over the following months Jeanie and I became quite close. Our initial bond was a mutual love of dancing.

One evening Jeanie, unexpectedly (and rather uncharacteristically, as she was a sexually shy girl), said to me in the narrow corridor leading from the lounge to the hostel kitchen, 'Peter . . . can I go to bed with you?' As I was not exactly eager to refuse this request, we went to my room on the first floor and lay together on my single bed. But Jeanie was troubled because she had always promised herself since an early age that she would remain a virgin until her wedding night. She was very tense and conflicted and lay there on her back very still. Meanwhile, my own thoughts about this liaison were richochetting around my mind as I felt I had hurt quite enough girls in my life as it was (when I was deluded I had (wrongly) thought two of them were *dead* because of me). I didn't want to add Jeanie to this catalogue of pain.

I was always, in my heart of hearts, very relaxed none the less when I was with Jeanie, and sure enough the surface atmosphere of *doubt* and *uncertainty*, coupled with this feeling of *privacy*, once again generated the rappings. As we lay there in silence, taps and clicks were emanating in profusion from all quarters of my room. Jeanie suddenly raised her head from the pillow and exclaimed: 'God . . . what's all those clicks?' I was quite used to the rappings by then and replied rather lazily, so as not to alarm her: 'They're just my clicks' whereupon she came back with, 'You must be sending out vibrations!'

A few minutes after this Jeanie (surprisingly untroubled by this event) decided that she had to stick by her standards and couldn't go through with our 'night of sin'. She got up and left. We remained good friends although our friendship froze somewhat in the ensuing months as I became more and more absorbed in potential research ideas, intellectual arguments and discussion with Shafiq, another resident, and as Jeanie developed a stronger relationship with another more recent addition to the hostel population. None the less, Jeanie did 'give me my sanity' that night in an unambiguous way. Later my future wife Jill, as we have seen, also confirmed (in terror) that these bizarre acoustic events were not at all hallucinatory (she would always insist that we slept with the light on when they occurred).

It is interesting that, just as Tourette Syndrome may involve a breakdown of inhibition in the limbic system of the brain (Comings and Comings 1987a), so these rappings, whose re-onset was synchronised roughly with that of the Tourette, could well be due to a disinhibition of a limbic-based psychokinetic ability which would otherwise remain latent and dormant.

The rappings, like the awful coprolalia, did none the less seem to be a manifestation of evil at least subjectively. For example, one rapping that followed the spontaneous thought, 'I must not tell anybody about this', was always noticeably louder. Whether these two sets of phenomena *do* involve a spiritual component or whether they could be totally reduced to an explanation in terms of a breakdown of inhibitory synapses, perhaps in the basal ganglia or limbic system, or whether *both* factors are involved in synchrony has always been a quandary for me. What is certain is that a conscious spiritual orientation, where one opens oneself up to loving influences, is effective, particularly in inhibiting the rappings (p. 48) and to a lesser extent the coprolalia. Indeed, I would suggest that this, rather than catharsis, should be the psychological approach of choice to the management of this kind of Tourette problem in those patients where medication is not *completely* successful (as indeed it rarely is). Much to the chagrin of medical authorities no doubt, I, and several other Touretteurs I eventually met at Tourette Association meetings in London, found that tobacco smoking when *combined* with haloperidol also produced a particularly powerful form of chemotherapy for this condition. Mastering of the coprolalia by very positive thoughts or cognitions precisely at the moment of onset of the tic was, I found, a genuinely useful psychological intervention which has been discovered independently and used by many Touretteurs. (Psychological interventions here are also discussed by Grossman *et al.* 1986; Azrin and Peterson 1988; Ostfeld 1988.)

I would not deny that there was a psychological component to my own Tourette disorder; anger suppression was not irrelevant (Shapiro and Shapiro 1968; Prabhakaran 1970) but it was a precipitator not a necessary cause – otherwise Freudian slips of a coprolalic kind would have been common. In fact they were absent. Psychological intervention has therefore been of only supportive value and that of a psychodynamic kind quite useless. As we saw, it even temporarily exacerbated my condition. The fact that my brother George also suffered from acromegaly and compulsive laughing (Chadwick 1993b) suggests a genetic predisposition in us both to obsessive-compulsive disorder (OCD), itself a strong genetic associate of Tourette Syndrome (Comings and Comings 1987b; Robertson 1989, p. 150) and also a genetic predisposition to overactivity in dopamine pathways – as both Tourette (Caine 1985) and growth hormone secretion, and likely oversecretion, as in acromegaly, are dopamine-mediated (Martin 1973; Haracz 1982). Given the dominance of my psychotic conditions by delusions, and the experience I had of the great 'significance' of events around me (the 'meaning feeling'), both of which have long been associated with dopamine pathway overactivity (Snyder 1974), it is inescapable that real hardware malfunctions involving genetic fragility mediate both my own and my brother's clinical pictures – although that of George is complicated by possible brain damage at birth (Chadwick 1993b, p. 240). It is a salutary fact that my own suffering in the 1970s and early 1980s has brought me much closer to my memory of George who, when he was alive, I perceived as really quite weird and very much a distant stranger. It has only been because of my own ordeal that I have come to realise, in my heart, that George, bizarre and deeply ill though he was, was indeed none the less *my brother*.

RAPPINGS FROM HELL?

The ontological status of the disturbing taps and clicks therefore remains, when all is said and done, still mysterious. We have seen that they were certainly not, as professionals thought, hallucinatory as other people could hear them even when not sharing my delusions (*'folie à deux'*) and not prepared or cajoled by argument or persuasion (or by a similar mental state) to expect them. They shocked others as they shocked me. Other psychotic patients have also experienced this phenomenon (see Chadwick 1992, pp. 64 and 158). What seems to be essential for their occurrence is the experiential blurring of the boundary between internal and external, coupled with a sense of doubt and confusion and thus a need for *guidance*. Like hallucinations and delusions, they give a sense of needed certainty – even if their effects are malign. The experience of severe boundary diffusion seems to be sufficient to enable (if not alone cause) this phenomenon. To go more deeply: the inference seems inescapable therefore that mind and matter, at a profound level, are not really different 'stuffs' and that they have or can have characteristics of each other – for example when, as here, sound energy codes mind events for a purpose. This is only possible, it seems to me, if the essential nature of reality is not singularly material but psychophysical. The other side of the materialistic coin is semantics. Both mind and matter have a physical and a representational quality. In this scheme there could well be a deep substrate, a barely thinkable realm of potential, which structures and actualises both these codes (see Appendix I to this book). This remains at present a consideration for future research. However, this research will not be facilitated if professionals insist on denying the reality-status of this, by no means rare, phenomenon.

PERFECTION AND THE SEARCH FOR 'CURE'

In the therapy of schizotypals and in rehabilitation from schizophrenia (Chadwick 1995b), conventional models of mental health (e.g. Thorne 1990, pp. 107–10; Parlett and Page 1990, pp. 178–81; Clarkson and Gilbert 1990, pp. 204–6) should, I suggest, be abandoned. People of these dispositions have their own idiosyncrasies and capacities such that frameworks appropriate for the neurotic or the 'worried well' are not by any means so applicable. The degree of *integration* of such personalities, for example, may never reach a level that would please a Jungian analyst. Similarly, the level of openness to *negative* experience, as well as positive (Thorne 1990, p. 113), may be far more limited in the coping schizotypal or recovering schizophrenic than in clients deemed healthy by Rogerian standards. In such people resilience to negative experience can be more limited or can be permanently damaged at least to some degree. Ventilation of emotion is unlikely to be effective or health-promoting in such clients nor is an assertive, critical, aggressive stance on the part of the therapist – as in rational emotive therapy (Ellis 1962). Splitting aspects of the self into components for each to talk to the other, as in the two chair or empty chair technique (Greenberg 1983), can be *dangerous* for clients vulnerable to very negative and hostile hallucinations or with particularly vicious internal objects. It is also quite wrong to assume that recovering schizophrenic people return after their illness to a schizotypal disposition and thus to treat them accordingly. Many do not; I myself am among this 'deflected' genre. The latter have to be assessed on an *individual* basis as all manner of post-psychotic adjustment styles are possible, some far removed from schizotypy, partly as a function of medication effects but partly also due to reactance (Brehm 1966) to the experienced horrors of the psychotic style of thought and living.

Liberating therapies which decrease living by 'shoulds' and 'ought tos', which are popular for the worried well and for overinhibited guilt-prone individuals, have to be used with care (if indeed they should be used at all) with schizophreniform individuals. Such people have often lived very open-ended free-wheeling lives anyway and benefit more from structure and an emphasis on rehabilitation and *coping*, as has for a long time been the case in community psychiatry (Loeb 1969), rather than on 'cure' and on disinhibiting therapeutic procedures. It is not the job of the clinician anyway to make a West Coast self-actualising, peak-experiencing, optimum-living specimen out of a person prone to schizophrenia. This very proneness carries with it its own heterodox style and conveys capacities that need to be fostered for the person to achieve their own personal mode of intrinsic validity. Psychodynamic and humanistic approaches, including Rogerian methods, have made no inroads into the clinical problems in schizophrenia (Klerman 1984; Mueser and Berenbaum 1990) and this is probably why.

Man-made notions of perfection and normality change with the centuries, even by the decade. They vary across class, sex, age-group, race and country. They even vary across subspecialisms in the human sciences and humanities. What we tend to think of, in our rationalistic neo-classical way, as perfection is still a rather narrowly focused 'algebraic' rendering compared to the total context 'living' perfection of Nature and of God.

In conclusion it has, however, to be said that the degree of coupling to 'reality' of recovering schizophrenic patients and of schizotypals may always be less than that of people of negligible proneness to schizophrenia – and indeed this may be something that they share with high creatives, particularly of the more artistic style (p. 16). Rather than engineering their adaptation to life every step of the way (e.g. Falloon *et al.* 1988), we may well have to accept the relative dominance of such people by their inner life as a genuine dispositional feature of their psychic functioning and work out ways of helping them at least to make the most productive use of it. In this endeavour the arts in their many forms seem likely to offer in the future more space for action and for growth than often is appreciated (e.g. Thomson 1989; Waller and Gilroy 1992; Stanton-Jones 1992). (Recovering patients' artistic work, from patchwork quilts to paintings is also featured regularly in the newsletters of SANE (Schizophrenia a National Emergency). The work is an inspiration and a delight.)

Chapter 14

Conclusions

The strength of a thing can be seen in the resources needed to destroy it.

(Oscar Wilde)

Over the years the identity I have come to choose as a psychologist is that of an 'artist-experimenter'. This book is a product of that identity. But as I have explained in Chapters 3–5 and 13 dealing with my own case: my feet, when the chips are down, are firmly in the territory occupied by the artist even though experimentation is (wrongly in my view) seen as an activity solely to be pursued by scientists. The scientist regards a problem as something external to himself or herself. He or she then seeks to explain a phenomenon and find facts using instruments guided by theories. This is not really my way. The artist, instead, seeks to understand things via what he or she *is* guided by feeling. While the scientist deals in generalities and broad trends and works in the service of *order*, the artist has a feel for detail and individuality and a sense of the momentary and works in the service of *expression*. This latter approach is closer to my own preference for the way psychology should be done. But both the scientist and the artist are enamoured by the search for truth and in this endeavour certainly one must *check*. This is something from which philosophers shy away and has indeed prompted the call for an experimental philosophy (Gregory 1970; Piaget 1972). Rather in this vein this book is a contribution to experimental art.

Reality is not only a set of equations but a story – and energy and meaning are the two sides of what is the case. Psychology in turn is not only a study of the mechanisms of mind but of the natural history of experience (Stout 1901). When we study a person's biography, it is not only the true facts of their life that have shaped them but their selective (and often distorted) view of their past that has done this. A person, then, is a product of veridical memory but also of dream. Their personal truth is just as important in characterising them as is a consensual truth – and on many occasions may predict them better.

Working from within the person's world view, as many psychological professionals now do, is an acknowledgement of the vitality of that personal truth. Even with people such as Deanna (Chapter 8), who lived at the very edges of experience, her ideas have also found mirroring in the activities of some therapists: work is currently being done on past-life regression with transsexuals (Davies 1995).

In this contest of understanding from within, 'madness' and 'insanity' are terrible terms. Indeed, the more we know of the frame of reference of a person's behaviour the less 'crazy' does it seem. It is when behaviour seems not to be contextually embedded in any way that we suspect organic dysfunction (as, for example, in Tourette Syndrome). However, if a man *licks* a page of prose how do we know that the ink does not contain cocaine? If we are told that a woman was known to have *watered the flowers on her curtains* how do we know that she wasn't posing for Magritte? Behavioural and social criteria of 'strangeness' are not always very informative. It is only by listening to and telling the story from within that one can really come to Know – with a capital K. The outside perspective necessarily partakes of norms, standards and categories against which to assess, classify and evaluate people, and the uniqueness and intensity and in a very real sense the true meaning of what they are doing or trying to do with their lives is ignored.

But of course every person does share some characteristics with all humankind and some with many other people. No one is totally unique through and through. Because of this the study of people necessarily has to move between a more art-like domain and one that is more science-like. This I have tried to do in this book – but beginning, I think necessarily, with stories from the inside, as I feel should be the case.

No really intelligent person believes that intelligence can 'solve everything'. The necessity for insight, empathy, care and patience is just as vital to any psychologist as their IQ (interestingly, empathy correlated only –0.041 with verbal intelligence in the London Block study). In the biographical studies I have had to hear Desmond crying without sound or tears, hear Deanna's sinister thunder rumbling at a bass level beneath human audition. Schizotypals are not cognitrons but themselves symphonies, works of art, products of their own craftsmanship. The empathy of both these people was also something that came to their aid as we negotiated their accounts. Indeed the 'pathology' of the highly empathic revealed in Chapter 11 is perhaps not surprising: the sense of self is bound to be weak in the very impressionable as they take on roles indented on them by others and lose their *own* feelings in the inferred feelings of those around them. But if their empathy did not come to their aid in convergent and divergent thinking tasks, it showed itself interpersonally – or those chapters could never have been written (as an aside here: which is more important, the genes of Nobel Prizewinners or the genes of people like Desmond who have a genius for companionship and for making friends? Learning disabled people also often have this latter capacity). If we cannot join with the people with whom we work and empathically indwell in their world, of what use are our generalities? We relapse into professionals talking one language while clients and participants talk theirs: what Robert Lebel would call 'onanism for two' (in Short 1994).

To move away now from the idiosyncratic origins of this work: it is also true that this text has grown very much from work in British psychology and psychological medicine. It builds on early research (Claridge 1967; Eysenck and Eysenck 1976) which has led eventually to the belief in a continuum existing between normality, schizotypy and schizophrenia rather than to a perception of schizotypy as a distinct form of disorder. It is also in sympathy with psychoanalysis, which has always regarded the boundaries between normality, neurosis and psychosis as graded. The evidence at present (Tyrer and Stein 1993; Raine *et al.* 1995; Vollema and van den Bosch 1995; Bergman *et al.* 1996) seems to give licence for multi-stability in our perceptions of schizotypy but it does appear that this, and schizophrenia, are many-faceted constructs whose connections with other conceptual entities such as 'creativity' are themselves multidimensional (Richards 1981; Poreh *et al.* 1993). The links therefore between 'madness' and other aspects of human behaviour and experience are in no way straightforward and the future certainly does *not* give licence for polarised 'all-or-nothing' thinking in the general domain of how psychotic people are to be evaluated. This has been a style of thinking, as we have seen, which has tended to characterise the field until now. There are many areas of psychic functioning where psychotic and what one might loosely call 'pre-psychotic' and 'pre-schizophrenic' people perform normally and even better than stable controls and the outlook for those who have succumbed to psychotic episodes is by no means pessimistic (see Chapters 2 and 11). But the picture is complex and gives no permission for *either* a 'deficit' *or* a 'credit' attitude pre-emptively to be dominant. Certainly the creativity of schizophreniform individuals has been massively understated in much previous research. Perhaps an attitude of 'realistic optimism' is to be preferred. (See also Storr 1972 on the creativity of schizoid and obsessional thinkers.)[1]

The approach I have taken in this research, which in many ways began even before I was myself ill in 1979, has been to attempt the impossible: to be comprehensive, to create, in the terms of Chapter 2, a 'large blanket' approach which genuinely does cover the diverse aspects of schizophrenia and related conditions. No doubt my sympathies for genetic, biochemical, cognitive and neurocognitive research will alienate social constructionists, psychotherapists and social workers. My openness to reports of spiritual and paranormal experiences in schizophreniform and schizophrenic patients will certainly alienate colleagues dedicated to research at the biological and cognitive-behavioural level. It seemed to me, however, that it was necessary for at least *someone* to take this comprehensive view rather than adopt the 'in-house' perspectives that traditionally dominate this fragmented and warring endeavour.

Over this century, since the seminal publications of Kraepelin (1919) and Bleuler (1924), the medical-biological and the psychological perspectives on schizophrenia have alternated in their relative dominance of the research and therapy arenas. To borrow a phrase of Keats's: the slow progression in this field has been characterised by 'alternate uproar and sad peace'. I have always believed that a cross-disciplinary team approach, despite the many vested interests and conflicting aims of the various professionals involved, is the only way we can ever properly evaluate and manage the credits and deficits of schizophrenia-prone people. Schizophrenic illness has multitudinous dimensions; to beat it requires a war of attrition not a magic bullet solution. This involves professionals, sufferers and community personnel being prepared to negotiate and empathise rather than clash and blame. In this spirit, then, I have given due attention and respect to all the many sides of the multifaceted crystal we have come to call 'the schizophrenias'. And sometimes I think that perhaps *only* a former patient who has actually 'been there' and felt on the inside the pushes and pulls of all the forces involved, be they from one's brain chemistry, one's family and school background or from one's spiritual sensitivities, could have done this. This is why I call, in Chapter 5, for more peer-professional research. It is maybe only the sufferers themselves, whose illness has threaded its way through *all* aspects of our lives, who can truly appreciate that intervention and understanding need to be global and multifaceted and not local and specific.

The methods I have used here: empathic indwelling, introspection, biographical accounts, psychometrics and experimentation are, I think, to be advised, as single-method research is limited by the radius of its procedural effectiveness. What you cannot look for, you cannot find. The models of reality that eventuate from empathic indwelling with the schizophreniform individuals described in Chapters 6 to 8 clearly differ very markedly from the models of reality that guide scientists (and psychoanalysts) working on the spectrum of schizophrenic disorders. These non-professional people's associations are looser; they are less cynical; more trusting in belief; more risky in their inferences; more open, at least than scientists, to their own feelings; more sensitive to what their 'higher Self' has to offer; less steady and reliable; less conforming and perhaps more colourful in style than are traditionally minded analytical investigators. As they are different, 'reality' is to them very different. But the models of reality they have do show a great deal of overlap – and have certainly proved far more effective than the teachings of science in organising their experience and guiding them in their lives.

In any attempt to be comprehensive there are bound to be blind spots. I say little here of the political and financial pressures to preserve the often stigmatising term 'schizophrenia' – and of the way diagnostic categories, diagnosis itself and 'medicalisation' of distress serve professional interests. Some people would have put such arguments at the core of a book such as this but I find that such political thinking can easily soar into an intellectual abstract radicalism that on the ground achieves little and that completely loses sight of the nitty-gritty day-to-day issues which I find are so central to the lives of suffering and vulnerable people. There is little doubt that professional interests *are* served by the concept of 'schizophrenia' but even were the term abandoned and research oriented to a microprocess view (something which for me would be preferable to diagnosis-driven investigation), distress and anguish would still be there. To my mind biological as well as psychological and spiritual approaches have their place in alleviating them. There is no doubt that the tractability of 'schizophrenia' to psychological methods is understated – a truth, as I put it myself (Chadwick 1995a), that is 'buried under a mountain of drug company money'. But the effectiveness of biological research in alleviating anguish, in all fairness, deserves mention and respect (see Lieberman and Fleischhacker 1996). What is also important is that biological interventions make psychological therapy itself easier and more productive.

It is no use trying conceptually to erase the existence of this group of illnesses. Recognising that one has *had* an illness, however one labels it, if one does at all, can even be therapeutically beneficial (Chapter 12). But recognising the benefits of one's proneness to this condition is also of merit (Chapters 2 and 11). Labels are, after all, only hypotheses and can be thrown off with time as one becomes weller and weller. Obviously, for-ever thinking of oneself as a 'genetic schizophrenic' is hardly conducive to recovery in the very long term. The best strategy is to accept the illness label in the short term and face and accept one's (often temporary) fragility and vulnerability and then dispense with it as one gains strength.

Knowledge is necessary to help schizophrenic people transcend 'victim consciousness'. This book has perhaps centrally been about confidence – raising and about the empowerment of people prone to schizophrenia and of those trying to recover from it. This to me has been research both from the profession and from the community, from both the inside and the out-side, from art and science. It is vital that schizophrenic people learn more about their own condition and plight (see also MacPherson *et al.* 1996 on this) and adopt a more 'healthgenic' orientation rather than the negative 'staying-out-of-hospital' orientation that pervades the thinking of so many recovering psychiatric patients (and their families). We are living in the 1990s; it is a crass shallow age in which the essentials of what it is to be a human being are rapidly being forgotten. But it is also worth remembering that the only nonsense in the world is man-made. Schizophreniform people tend to be men and women of the Underground; often they talk little and are easily misunderstood. But now there is a chance and here an incentive for those underground people to come above ground and start talking and to gain strength from this work in their own intrinsic validity. The fact of the matter is that the schizophrenic credit really can only be hinted at in case studies, biographies, graphs and tables. In the last instance it lies *within the individual*. The search, even battle, for dignity is in actuality one to be fought by every individual schizotypal, paranoid or schizophrenic person. The *real* evidence, and the answer, in all truth, is *within*. Community involvement in the understanding and acceptance of schizophrenic people is also vital because community paranoia will ease as people gain more knowledge of people who are 'different'. Ignorance, after all, is the fuel of fear.

Will, trust, faith and meaning are the foundations of both art and science, and indeed the foundations of social life. These are the bedrock pillars of all the things we do together. Ironically, direct knowledge of this can be accessed by psychotics in the early stages of spiritual overwhelm. It may be that many insights had at the outer limits of sanity, shining like a sun to the receptive mind, will yet transform our world and save the minds of others who still live without hope.

Appendix I
Half man, half boat, the mind of the Borderline Normal

This book has repeatedly dealt in a more positive way than traditionally is the case with the issue of the paranormal. I have argued that certain states of mind facilitate it (pp. 68, 69, 164) and that my mental state in 1979 was very strongly permissive of paranormal events – particularly psychokinesis (p. 164). It may even be that the dovetailing of events in the world coincidental with my ongoing thoughts during the summer of 1979 (Chadwick 1992, Chapter 4, and 1993b) was at least at times an earlier manifestation of the paranormal, given the subsequent development of the possibly psychokinetic rappings in hospital – where again events detectable by others were synchronised with thought.

In *Borderline* (Chadwick 1992) I presented fragments of the theorising that tried to capture the mental state which was instantiated when these uncanny events occurred. This appendix presents the fullest description of which I am capable of this mental state. It will be clear that the experiences involved in 1979 were far removed from everyday consciousness and it may well be that this partial dislocation from 'ordinary sanity' is what made this strange and terrifying realm accessible to me.

The, admittedly dangerous, conclusion I have drawn from this cluster of experiences and events is that the 'deep ground' of nature is psychophysical rather than material (p. 165). Needless to say, this perspective has not been well received by reductionists. My theorising on this issue was regarded as 'eccentric and speculative' by a psychodynamic therapist (Oswald 1992) and the previous attempt to capture the experience verbally was accused of being an attempt to describe the indescribable (Anonymous review in *Contemporary Psychology Reviews* 1993).

This therefore is my second attempt to 'describe the indescribable' by attempting to reconstruct the basic Borderline manuscript 'Half man, half boat, the mind of the Borderline Normal' (Chadwick 1979b), the original of which was lost (the final remaining copy I shredded the night before the New Kings Road suicide attempt, believing it to be 'Devil inspired'(!)). This appendix is therefore a recreation from my ideas notebooks of the day – which were also used in the writing of the original paper.

The basic argument underpinning this very esoteric document is that the mental condition I had 'accessed' was facilitative of such phenomena as synchronicity and psychokinesis because a realm of existence which partially transcended the distinction between mind and matter had been 'entered'. Jung himself, in his *Collected Works*, referred to this as 'The Psychoid'. (I admit it may require a state of awareness on the very edges of insanity to fully appreciate this territory.) However, Jung makes very scanty, unclear and unsatisfying references to the Psychoid and to the deeper level 'The Continuum'. It was indeed his belief that thought was impossible in the Psychoid realm, so what I have done here is inevitably going to be somewhat obscure. Please note also that the state of mind produced by *reading* it is in no way comparable to the state of mind that obtained in order to *write* it in the first instance (!). If Jung's independently conceived Psychoid realm has any ontological validity, this however is at least one person's attempt at describing it.

In the blazing hot midsummer of 1979, sitting at a small writing table in a bedsitter in East London, the blue wall plaster cracked, the nearest bath a hundred yards away, I was fighting against my real and imagined persecutors for the very right to *be* – as if I had, like a spirit, to *acquire this rather than assume it*. Unemployed, penniless, stones underweight, mind fevered by tobacco and hunger, the route I chose to *being* was the only route I knew, through *theory*. If only I could get *back* of my many roles; if only I could capture some focal point, some viewing point, the transcendental Self, or the Self-as-process in words and theory, the core sense of I-ness surely would return and I would *exist*!

Early intuitions about the nature of my quest were very general and focused my attention on *process* rather than content. Since, as I wrote, 'Peter forever avoids being anything in particular', this was not really surprising. Quoting from my journal of these times:

> My mistake is in assuming – with Karen Horney – that there is some Real true Self hiding away inside. There is some *rhythm* or *beat* – something at the level of summary, at the level of key or mode which is *in there*, waiting for some substance to start beating, waiting for some food to bring it to life – and as it is brought to life, I will be brought to life.

I was convinced that our traditional western ways of thinking about person were, to a degree, arbitrary. The focus on integration of parts and singularity of Self, on content, I was sure was only a social convenience, falsely legitimated as 'healthy' and 'normal' by psychodynamic theorists. Our thinking about Self was perhaps biased, even totally wrong. The being who rejected this was not insane, they were a new form of normality: what I now called a 'Borderline Normal'.

My early research efforts had focused on *shared* biases and illusions of perception and thought (e.g. Chadwick 1976, 1978a). Perhaps even the need for an ego or for a central core Self was an illusion, something that we are merely socialised into in the West for the convenience of social life. If it was, then it was a construction, not a representation of an essential reality (for related and later views on the validity of a concept of Self comprising subpersonalities and a multiplicity of roles see Assagioli 1965; Ornstein 1986; and Rowan 1990). The Borderline Normal therefore reflected the critical truth about the Self.

In my midsummer efforts, I was not, however, trying to describe the 'whatness' of myself. I was like a traveller, shouting to the world from a moving train, about *the 'thatness' of movement*. This was no easy job, as we shall see. I wrote (to the extent that it was possible to write about this at all):

> The Borderliner is process integrated or process useful, process practised. The integration is *that* the machinery is working well and ticking over. The integration is the tuning of the parts to do the job. The Borderliner's personality is well tuned, the integration is not *in* the job that the parts do, it is not in the whatness of the parts. . . . Hence the integration of the Borderline person is analogous to the process play of science in action over time.

INTO THE STRATOSPHERE

Unlike a normal person, whom I thought of as best characterised by nouns, the Borderliner was most accurately perceived with infinitives, adverbs and verbs, 'hence the Normal's bewilderment – his apparatus just cannot handle the job,' I (rather smugly) wrote. Indeed, the state I was reaching to was slippery and hardly *thinkable*. Handholds were becoming hard to find.

There was also the sense, not only of 'not belonging to language' and hence to categories but of not even belonging to any one place or time:

> The Borderliner is both behind the lens and in the scene he is taking.

> Too early, too late mean nothing too. The Borderliner is both out of date and premature, out of time and in it. Seen *as* failing/succeeding, 'chequered in career'.

> Triumph and Disaster – do not characterise the Borderliner's life from the inside. The Borderliner has nowhere to fall and nowhere to go 'up in the world' to. There is no room beneath a Borderliner, and the room above is empty.

As the reader may guess by now, this is, all told, a pretty dangerous state of mind. The Borderliner was the height of ambiguity. Both masculine and

feminine, strong and weak, active and passive, choosing and determined.
The Borderliner lived between the opposites *and* transcended them:

> The Borderliner both happens to be and chooses to be ... is subject
> and object ... finds out and is found out ... is a coherent pattern of
> eventuated opposites ... is the basic generalised person.

> The Borderline thinker sees the reality which the contrasts we usually
> deal with are merely differentiates of. Hence the Borderliner is the fluid
> reality between the concrete dogmatic reality of appearances.

In these obscure journal writings I was probing in order to characterise
a state, which I felt to be extant, of being outside time and space, beyond
language, beyond social conventions, beyond all arbitrary rules. I was
seeking 'the ground' out of which these are merely differentiates or
exudates. Where 'I' therefore existed, in existing in the world at all, was
not even inside my own head; it was in a realm or point between the zone
of *potential* and the zone of *actuality*. This I called 'the point of potential
to kinetic conversion': 'the sparking point, the contact point, between the
inertia of the ground and the blinkered unreflective state of figure'. 'The
Borderliner *tends to* the world ... is a potential ... is the personification of
ratio, analogy and fantasy/reality coalescence'.

It will be apparent here, to those of eastern mystical persuasion, that this
Borderline state was rather like one of access to the ground of all being,
the Tao, if not exactly that. The feelings of immanence through the world,
and of transcendence, of not belonging, even to language, were the result
of opening up Aldous Huxley's 'cerebral reducing filter' to the total array,
both internal and external. Cognizance of the middle ground had given way
to cognizance of 'The All'.

In this psychic condition I felt as if I was hovering conceptually away
from the usual modes of mental life. If it was, as it is, functional to think in
terms of Subject and Object both characterised in terms of the positive and
the negative, i.e.

$$S \overset{+}{} O$$
$$_{-}$$

then this basic 'mind code' was actually retreating from me. I saw it not as
'the true way' to think and be but as a shared bias. Where *I* was lay back
of this, in an, at times, terrifying, undifferentiated realm. I was conceptually
and experientially drifting away from life, away from the mode in which
even space and time themselves are meaningful. I was moving experientially into 'the elsewhere'.

Jung's 'psychoid' state was my 'point of potential to kinetic conversion'.
His 'continuum' was my 'ground' (see Progoff 1973). As I continued to

theorise in my tiny room, my own mental state was starting to be in resonance with 'the fount' or 'source' of mystical thinkers, the realm back of actuality. Now finding words even harder to come by, it was hardly surprising that I feared, as I did, that I would disappear or diffuse away.

A GLIMPSE OF GOD

It was also not surprising that at this fount I eventually came to feel in touch with 'a presence', an awe-inspiring force, which existed, now, as if behind a thin membrane. Any sense of ego or identity was gone, I was a vehicle, a *channel*, my existence was 'vehicular'. Psychosis this was not, at least not yet. For example, there was no Messiah delusion: 'A Christ could be said to *accompany* the world, but not a Borderliner,' I penned. But there was none the less a sense of unearthly knowledge and of joy that pervaded me at this time – objectivity and ecstasy were now fused. My religiosity, such as it was, was magnified a thousandfold. The Lord's Prayer resonated and thundered through my mind. I felt I had been given a spiritual mission of the utmost importance. I could 'see to infinity', I had reached a zone where 'the life system' was strangely making contact, through me, with 'the not-of-this-life system' – as indeed maybe it was.

Had I been less aroused and agitated, if I had, in everyday language 'kept my cool', I would have realised that I had discovered a level of cognitive engineering that characterises not only the mystic but also *the actor*. There was no doubt that (like my grandfather and my mother, from whom I had probably inherited the capacity) I was an actor but on the community stage. I had been using the hardware of the neural networks of my brain to create something beyond myself. I was creating fictions and in creating fictions I was myself, even though the products were constructions. Where *I* lay was in the construction process between potentiality and actuality, between the organic ground and the communal social figure. Indeed the actor is *real* in the process of creation of his or her image. The actor's identity is in the *process*, not the product. Through our masks we are our most true. But somehow I could not see this. It was there for the taking, a genuinely original insight – that the mystic and the actor are psychologically related – but I let it slip through my fingers.

Instead my attributions, in my dilapidated state, had to be more spectacular than this, more self-inflatory. I was surely an agent of God, misunderstood, tormented, crucified yet redeemed and blissfully happy. My energy level rose, I hardly needed to eat and could walk for miles at high speed. At night I was 'at one' with the star-spangled sky; the universe and I were a unity. The beauty that is the cosmos was my beauty, in turn my beauty belonged to the world.

Now my inner vacuity, my sense of being 'nothing', became a positive advantage. Through this inner vacancy left by my 'murdered soul' came the spiritual, came God. Battered by the gossip of the world, betrayed by all, slandered, rejected, existing as 'a hole in space–time' or 'a wound in mind space' as I termed it, I was now 'a cylinder open at both ends', a tunnel or channel for the spiritual realm to enter and indeed to transform the world. From 'nothing and nobody' I became everything and everybody. A euphoric love pervaded me for the world and for the whole of humanity. I felt I had healing and forgiveness powers, that I sensed everyone's thoughts, that the unconscious of the world was known to me. My destiny was with God and in God. Everything that could possibly happen *had* now surely happened; *this* was my terminus, my terminus was Nirvana . . .

It is well known that the early stages of psychosis are often characterised by euphoria and by an enhancement of mental functioning (Breggin 1991). Psychotic states also can develop from religious or mystical states (Lenz 1979, 1983) and desperate (pre-psychotic) attempts at higher 'meaning seeking' can occur consequent on terrible emotional and social stress (Roberts 1991). Clearly all of these phenomena are involved in the narrative above, which was indeed soon followed by outright psychosis. It may be that the Borderline mystical state, such as I have described it, is exceedingly difficult both to think and dwell within and very easily collapses into madness. It is perhaps the other side of madness. It is clearly impossible, however, adequately to reduce the above to biological language or to interpret it in terms of 'regression' (see also Deikman 1977 on this). The experience is too rich and complex and makes reference to ontological states of affairs which deserve explaining rather than explaining away. However, it is fairly easy to see how people could come to see themselves as profoundly significant and spiritual if they were to access this state unreflectively – a state which, after all, if it could happen to me, could happen to anyone.

The significance of the mystical Borderline experience is the licence it gives us then to *wonder*. Have great religious figures of the past been here – but been able to *hold* the state? Does being able to maintain the state *require* colossal spiritual development? Are many people touched by this, but do few *survive* (Greenberg et al. 1992)? It could indeed be that the practitioners of the endeavours of spirituality and of psychophysics have much to say to each other. If the deepest level of reality is a semantic realm which orchestrates (at the observable level) both physical and mental events to fulfil an ever-unfolding purpose, then if one somehow approaches that 'ground', physical and mental events would indeed dovetail together, permitting psychokinesis and telepathy and the events could understandably be felt to be 'pregnant with meaning'. We have the possibility before us of accounting for a wide range of previously esoteric phenomena if we take such experiences as the above seriously.

The alternative conception to this is a neurological account in terms of aberrant brain functioning consequent on low food intake – possibly instantiated by my almost anorexic physical state. This of course arbitrarily dispenses with the reference of my account and essentially claims that 'all' that is involved is a particular patterning of brain activity which is unusual and interesting in itself but of no other substantial significance. This of course is the typical reductionist's fallacy of confusing aetiology with value (Sacks 1986). A particularly unusual mode of neural network functioning may indeed *permit* perception of what are perhaps best described as 'dimensions' of reality not accessible in easily consensually validated states of consciousness.

The critical issue which needs to be faced in order to defend the latter perspective is: can access to this realm prove to be theoretically and empirically *productive*? It has been fashionable among twentieth-century intellectuals to decry mystical states as theoretically useless. However, the work on the transduction of these states to delusional states (Chadwick 1992, pp. 92–4; 1996b) does put the experience to work in solving ongoing problems. Also my concern with the potential-to-actual conversion is in parallel with similar concerns about this issue in quantum physics (Laurikainen 1988). The experience is also consistent with pantheistic beliefs in which God is instantiated in all things but that near-access to the zone of potential via a certain *brain* state does give direct experience of this Presence. The mistake is to attribute the experience to being 'chosen' when really the state is one of 'access'. Clearly the profound effects of experiences such as these (see Donaldson 1993) suggest that they should be encouraged and discussion of them raised in educational contexts. This would surely be preferable to having them subjected to *pre-emptive* interpretation in terms of electrochemical activity alone. As a final comment, however, it is evident that in this realm of experience *words* are poor guides and given, as I stated at the very outset of this book, that body and mind have *limits*, we should be prepared to face the possibility that this 'access' is to territory beyond the capacity of any human to comprehend. On matters such as these, Thomas Hobbes was prudent:

> Words are wise men's counters, they do but reckon with them: but they are the money of fools.

> (*Leviathan* I)

Appendix II
3–4 test of associative thinking and hypothesis testing, with answers

This test, which is referred to in Chapters 10 and 11, is a rather more open-ended, and slightly longer, version of Mednick's (1962, 1967) Remote Associates Test (RAT). In it three everyday words are provided, e.g. 'Bell, Film, Bottle', and the participant has to find a fourth word which is in some way 'connected' to the previous three. In this case 'Blue' would be an appropriate answer. The task requires people to generate possible connected words and then serially test them against the remaining two. Clearly the search for possible answers requires activation spread through an associative semantic network. The task therefore tests both hypothesis-testing strategies (Perkins 1988) and remote associative thinking (Mednick 1967). It is generally found that the remoteness of the connecting solution words is greater in recovering psychotics than in non-psychotic people (Chadwick 1988, 1992) the former therefore seem to have a more risky criterion for the appropriateness of verbal connections. The protocols of recovering psychotics (and probably those of patients acutely psychotic) are different almost at a glance from those of non-psychotic people, suggesting that both the looseness of associations, the data-acceptance criterion and the hypothesis-testing strategies of psychotics are all markedly biased compared to those of neurotic or stable individuals.

The full instructions for the test, the items and the scorable answers are provided below.

This is a test which assesses people's ability to think up appropriate words. It is quite difficult so do not be disheartened if you find that you can only do a moderate or a small percentage of the questions. The form of the test is as follows: three separate words are presented and your task is to find a fourth word which is in some way associated with or related to all of the previous three. The test is somewhat open-ended as there often is more than one word which could be related to a particular triad. You, however, have only to find one word.

Here are some examples with possible answers provided:

Atomic	Sex	Shell:	Bomb
Record	Theatre	Doodle:	Play
Coffee	Drinking	Championship:	Cup
Laser	Ray	Girder:	Beam
Illegal	Row	Tennis:	Racket
Trick	Trot	Beast:	Fox
Monkey	Lion	Giraffe:	Animal
Extract	Snake	Teeth:	Milk
Drugs	Vehicles	Lights:	Traffic
Bell	Film	Bottle:	Blue
Sill	Frame	Glass:	Window

As you can see, the answers can be related in many different ways, in different questions, to the items provided. This means that a number of different aspects of verbal thinking are tapped by this test. It also means that you should not only look for one type of solution word. Try a number of different approaches in your attempts at solutions.

The test itself
(Scorable answers)

1 Good Thin Art: Fine(2); Form(2)
2 Ship Pole Stone: Flag(2); Cat(1)
3 Easy Arm Deck: Chair(2)
4 Finishing Red Ticker: Tape(2)
5 Table Face Dish: Cloth(2); Round(2)
6 Ice Fresh Face: Cream(2); Pack(2)
7 Two Old Egg: Timer(2); Men(1)
8 Judge Jury Law: Justice (Abstract, 2); Court (Concrete, 1); Judiciary(2); Trial(1); Condemn(1)
9 Wall Gate Door: Barrier (Abstract, 2); House (Concrete, 1); Window (Concrete,1); Garden(1); Access (Abstract, 2); Divide(2); Side(1); Front(1); Back(1)
10 Dirty Drab Dishevelled: Scruffiness (Abstract, 2); Unkempt(2); Appearance(2); Tramp (Concrete, 1); Clothes(1); Decaying(1)
11 Jug Pan Kettle: Receptacle (Abstract, 2); Handle (Concrete, 1); Kitchen (Concrete 1) Pot(1); Utensil(2); Vessel(2); Container(2); Cooking(1); Water(1)
12 Angry Double Fire: Cross(2)
13 Umbrella Coat Hat: Protection (Abstract, 2); Gentleman (Concrete, 1); Stand(1); Covering(2); Rain(1)
14 Miscalculation Misprint Blunder: Error(2); Mistake(2)

15 Valid Correct Right: True(2); Sound(2); Affirmative(2); Proper(1);
        Answer(1)

16 Newspaper Memo Letter: Communication (Abstract, 2);
        Medium(2); Document(2); Message(2);
        Office(1); Writing(1); Type(1); Note(1);
        Words(1); Report(2)

17 Typewriter Telephone Calculator: Device (Abstract, 2); Office
        (Concrete 1); Gadget(2)

18 Pen Kitchen Bread: Knife(2); Provisions List(1)

19 Net Madam Flutter: Butterfly(2)

20 Asleep Track Barrier: Sound(2); Fast(1)

21 Land Hopper Roots: Grass(2)

22 View Stand Position: Opinion (Abstract, 2); Football Match
        (Concrete, 1); Place(1); Stance(2); Site(1);
        Aspect(1); Point(2)

23 After Second Abstract: Thought(2); Time(1); Hindsight(1)

24 Sherry Humour Atmosphere: Dry(2); Warm(1); Party(2)

25 Car Landing Course: Crash(2); Test(1); Race(1)

26 Edge Insult Mouth: Lip(2); Sharp(1)

27 Healthy Shaft Water: Well(2)

28 Fall Under Hill: Down(2); Drop(2); Over(1)

29 House Weight Year: Light(2); Fly(2)

30 High Sun Torch: Light(2)

31 Line Stream Land: Main(2); Up(1)

32 Railway Fashion Washing: Line(2)

33 Bask Star Tan: Sun(2)

34 High Line Diver: Sky(2); Water(1); Life(1)

35 Killer Nagging Unbearable: Pain(2)

36 Fire Socialism Anger: Red(2); Raging(1)

37 Punish Cover Pile: Carpet(2)

38 Surprise Dress Line: Party(2); Yarn(2)

39 Water Fire Shock: Proof(2); Earth(1); Disaster(1); Injury(1)

40 Fall Bow Storm: Rain(2); Out(2)

41 Mad Nuclear Game: Power(2); War(2)

42 Cold Pan End: Dead(2)

43 Ash Can Beer: Can(2); Tin(1); Pub(2)

44 Wedding Dream Shift: Day(2); Night(2); Gown(2)

45 Dancing Drinking Eating: Enjoyment (Abstract, 2); Party
        (Concrete, 1); Hedonism(2); Action(2);
        Socialise(1); Merrymaking(2);
        Pastimes(2)

46 Compliance Eagerness Helpfulness: Willingness(2); Cooperation(2);
        Traits(1); Library Assistant(1);
        Positive(1); Benevolence(1)

47 Enthusiasm Fanaticism Fervour: Zeal(2); Keen(1); Drive(1); Wild(1); Passion(2); Dedication(1)

48 Altruist Samaritan Saint: Philanthropist(2); Charity(1); Selflessness(2); Christian(1); Good(1); Humanitarian(2); Benefactor(2)

49 Bitterness Envy Spite: Malevolence(2); Sin(1); Malice(2); Hate(1); Evil(2)

50 Overt Brazen Shameless: Undisguised(2); Manifest(2); Flagrant(2); Wanton(1); Brash(1)

51 Barge Boat Ship: Transport (Abstract, 2); Vessel (Abstract, 2); Water (Concrete, 1); Craft(2); Floating(1); Sailing(1)

52 Bruise Scratch Lesion: Wound(2); Injury(2); Abrasion(2); Pain(2); Hurt(1); Tumour(1)

53 Corner Fisted Fit: Tight(2); Boxing(2); Boxer(2); Fight(2)

Clearly the test given above is flexible and may have potential. It allows testing of associative thinking; synonym creation; concrete and abstract thinking and hypothesis testing. Even the *scoring* of this test by poets and by scientists could be researched. As a point of special interest: males do significantly and reliably better than females (on the original pilot pool of 177 triads) where the required answer is a prefix to *some* words in the triad but a suffix to *others* (as opposed to the manifestly easier task when the solution word is a prefix or a suffix to all three) (Chadwick 1980, unpublished). It is feasible that this might reflect an unconscious or tacit *spatial* process operating in the solution of such triads but a spatial process taking place without imagery. I would argue that the possibilities of this test could profitably be explored.

Notes

2 THE SCHIZOPHRENIC CREDIT SO FAR

1 In my own case, for example, four different diagnoses: schizophrenic episode; atypical hypomania; schizoaffective disorder and mild chronic hypomania were bandied around between September and October 1979, demonstrating in itself the tremendous difficulty even highly experienced professionals can have in distinguishing between schizophrenia and mood disorder.
2 I am grateful to Nellie Price for drawing my attention to this work by Rogo.
3 My thanks to Dr Julian Candy FRCP, FRCPsych., DPM for communicating Lee's research to me.
4 With reference to Frith's critical work on metarepresentation difficulties in schizophrenia (Frith 1992) it is necessary to point out that to have high or low self-esteem (patients usually have the latter) one clearly has to *have a Self* – and be able to reflect on the quality of that Self and take defensive manoeuvres if necessary. This in itself requires metarepresentational processes. These may be in some respects dysfunctional but in positive symptoms patients they certainly are *there*.

3 A JOURNEY BEYOND THE SELF

1 The transformation from white man to black man was performed in the wash room of a local Burton's tailors – whose co-operation was appreciated. Students, located on the opposite side of the street, estimated the distance Glaswegians kept from me in both roles while I repeatedly strolled along a section of a main street in the centre of the city. No significant differences, however, were found.
2 When I was 13 my brother prevented me from tearing a three-foot-square cardboard photograph of my mother to shreds.
3 The sixth form was unbelievably childish. I was thought to be homosexual (or 'latent homosexual') because I styled my hair in those days after Cliff Richard – and because I had body-building magazines in my desk. The persecution was excruciating, particularly because, although I had no homosexual feelings, I sensed in those days that I was a 'latent transvestite' and the psychoanalytic treatises of that time (mid-1960s) (see Kinsey *et al.* 1953/1966) wrongly interpreted transvestism as due to homosexual desires that dare not become overt – i.e. 'latent homosexuality', exactly what I was 'accused' of.
   It is also only fair to state that, although I say that the school produced no poets, there was one boy whom I knew at both school and university and whose soul was subject to the same murder attempts by the First XV rugby team and

First XI soccer team, as was mine, who did have great poetic sensibilities at least in his later youth. Unfortunately, he died in 1982, at 36, possibly by suicide, in a car smash.

4 The development of these delusions was gradual and incremental so that it is difficult to decide when I ceased to be accurate and rational and became irrational and disturbed. Delusions as implausible probability judgements can emerge *gradually* from plausible probabilities (Kahneman *et al.* 1982; Kingdon and Turkington 1994). For this reason longitudinal microprocess study is essential.

4 HOSPITAL LIFE WHILE PSYCHOTIC

1 When my disturbed state was recognised and I was asked formally on admission to Orthopaedics: 'Do you know where you are?' I replied, 'In Charing Cross Hospital'. When the doctor involved then said, 'Do you know where that is?' I came back with, 'I suppose near Charing Cross Station'. This misapprehension was met by silence and was *not* corrected – hence my subsequent delusional elaborations.

2 For a similar state to this see the writings of John Bunyan (Bunyan 1666/1984, e.g. pp. 33–4). Bunyan seems to have suffered from a disorder, on the borderline between a compulsion and a tic, almost identical to mine, at the same time as being overwhelmed by a severe spiritual crisis.

3 Despite this removal of my delusions I was troubled for many years that the two women I had had the longest affairs with, Gwen and Denise, were dead because of me. Eventually only reality testing by checking records of deaths in Saint Catherine's House put my mind at rest. If one cannot receive love, one cannot give it. Just as my mother's love for me was tainted with overpossessiveness, over-involvement, abuse and hateful cynicism, so I thought my love for the critical women in my life was itself tainted and contaminated – and in a hypomanic state so much so that it had the 'infectious' power to kill. I even felt that their giving of love to me itself would harm these women – as my mother had herself been stressed and harmed by mothering me.

5 HOSPITAL LIFE WHEN SANE

1 I am very grateful to Steven Hirsch for full access to my case notes from this period.

2 Now Bishop of Oxford but then vicar at All Saints' Church in Fulham.

3 Iron deficiency may exacerbate akathisia but the evidence is conflicting and the effect, if present, may be small (Sachdev 1995).

4 This exceedingly well-judged decision was made by Malcolm Weller despite the opposition of the whole ward nursing staff. In fact, at the time suicide attempts were well behind me and my financial problems were far more pressing than my neutralised delusional beliefs of old. This decision had a tremendously beneficial effect on making me feel understood and also made me feel that my wishes could be trusted as realistic and that I was *not* a 'fragile bird' to be totally protected and watched over night and day but a man who really was getting better and recovering his common sense and everyday worldliness.

6 DESMOND

1 This chapter has been based on several sources of information. First I have known Des socially for eleven years. In addition, his own account of his life and

personal psychology was collected by three tape-recorded interviews occupying some four to five hours of tape. Des has also, over the years, many times taken personality questionnaires, particularly the STQ (Claridge and Broks 1984; Jackson and Claridge 1991) and the EPQ (Eysenck and Eysenck 1975), the results of which have been discussed with him. Also Desmond read this chapter in very early and again in penultimate drafts and agreed that this draft was the best and was a fair and accurate representation of him. Finally, the drafts were also read by other friends of Desmond – particularly Ivo Wiesner and Geoff Garfield, who offered their criticisms of the earlier efforts and helped this particular piece to come into being. This kind of 'triangulation' of methods is recommended in qualitative research by Banister *et al.* (1994).

7 IVO

1 This chapter is based on three tape-recorded sessions of about two hours each and on the knowledge I have gained of Ivo in knowing him socially for four years. It was read by both Ivo and Desmond, who agreed that it is a fair and accurate representation of the man at the time of writing. Psychometrically Ivo is only a moderate STA scorer on the STQ (Jackson and Claridge 1991). He is included here because his experiences, though not schizotypal, schizoid or paranoid, could be regarded as good examples of psychotic *phenomena* as opposed to psychotic *symptoms* (Jackson and Fulford 1996) imbricated into a perfectly effective and functional lifestyle.

8 DEANNA

1 This chapter is the product literally of hundreds of hours of conversation with Deanna in both her male and female roles. No tape recordings have been made. Other than the psychometric test results reported in this chapter no other triangulation method was possible and my wife Jill, who also met her many times, does not know Deanna well enough to assess the fairness and adequacy of this chapter. Because of the nature of her private life, it is clear that vast amounts of information also have had to be withheld from this piece, which must therefore unavoidably remain the least validated and most vague of the biographies presented. However, I felt it necessary to feature Deanna to demonstrate the purchase of empathic indwelling in the schizotypal person's perspective and the need to establish joint reference with them. Adhering to a mechanistic belief system and neglecting the *meaning* of transvestism and transsexualism may be a major source of disharmony between clients and professionals in these areas.

2 Kinsey *et al.* (1953/1966) point out that transvestism has been recorded in various 'pre-literate' societies, for example: the Novajo; Kwakiutl; Crow; Eskimo (North America); Tanala; Lango; Mbundu (African); Uripev; Dyak (Oceania); Chukchee, Yakut, Yukaghir (Siberia); Lushais (India). In many instances the transvestites are respected and thought to possess magical powers; in other instances they are merely tolerated (Kinsey *et al.* 1953/1966, p. 679).

3 Research so far seeking hormonal, chromosomal or brain-structure differences between male-to-female transsexuals and control males has been mixed (Emory *et al.* 1991 report negative findings). However, brain damage has been linked with transsexualism by Hoenig and Kenna (1979) and a very recent post-mortem study by The Netherlands Institute for Brain Research showed differences in the stria terminalis between men on the one hand and women and male-to-female transsexuals on the other.

9 REFLECTIONS ON THE BORDERLINERS' BIOGRAPHIES

1 All the biographees rejected traditional masculine values. This was particularly due to our revulsion at the Second World War and the licence it gave for brutality and for hatred of all things meek and pliable.

10 EXPERIMENTAL STUDIES: THE RATIONALE

1 A paranoia scale is not likely to produce truthful responses if it is given as a special paranoia questionnaire. Hence I distributed the items which I took to be relevant to paranoia across the EPQ and my own psychoticism scale (P^C). The paranoia scale was thus covert. I would recommend this procedure to other workers. The scale was seventeen items long (Table 10.2).
2 The P^C scale consisted of items based on current theories and descriptive schemes of schizophrenic aetiology and symptomatology (e.g. 'Do you often feel that there is too much happening around you for you to concentrate?' and 'Do you often feel that your personality is false or a put-on?' related to filter (McGhie and Chapman 1961) or cognitive inhibition (Williams 1995) and false-self collapse (Laing 1967) theories of schizophrenia. This scale was thirty-six items long (Table 10.1).
3 I felt that the P^C and P^A scales were necessary supplements to the EPQ as the Eysenckian psychoticism scale (P^E) fails to discriminate psychotics from criminals (Eysenck and Eysenck 1975, table 8, p. 27) and questions have been raised as to its validity as a measure of psychoticism (Bishop 1977; Block 1977). These latter concerns are still current (Chapman *et al.* 1995). It may be that the P scale taps *negative* schizophrenic symptomatology more than positive (Rust *et al.* 1989) or that it is more a measure of tough-mindedness. Hence it may not be revealing a schizophrenia–creativity linkage but a link with coldness and dominance.

11 EXPERIMENTAL STUDIES: RESULTS AND ANALYSES

1 I am extremely grateful to Janie Brod of the Department of Experimental Psychology at Oxford University for analysing the Cambridge Block data.
2 The SPSS package at Royal Holloway College in 1988 only accepted data from 33 out of the 59 participants for computing correlations. The ANOVA analyses, however, were performed for all 59 subjects and the *r phi* correlations computed when validating the creativity tests against criterion also used the data from all subjects.
3 The three upper correlations for verbal confirmation bias with creativity in Table 11.5 (Chadwick 1992, p. 125) regrettably are in error; the positive signs should be negative.

13 IMPLICATIONS FOR THERAPY II

1 I was accepted at the Maudsley to do the research on paranoia but eventually decided to pursue it at the (then) nearer Bedford College (now Royal Holloway College) with John Wilding because John was already working on the links between arousal and higher cognitive function.
2 The role of psychotherapy in the management of Tourette Syndrome is critically discussed by Matesevac (1991).

3 In all fairness to Peter Storey, the diagnosis he gave of Gilles de la Tourette's Syndrome was the *nearest* diagnosis probably available at the time to encapsulate the symptoms I described. An alternative could be 'complex vocal tic disorder' (DSM IIIR 1987, p. 69).

14 CONCLUSIONS

1 The creativity of paranoids is almost certainly underestimated by their performance on tests of ideational fluency and flexibility. Such tests tend to predict arts choice rather than science choice (Hudson 1966; Rump 1982 and replications therein) and it may be that the paranoids have a more convergent style of creativity better suited to subjects such as logic and physics.

Bibliography

Alexandrian, S. (1991) *Surrealist Art*, London: Thames & Hudson.

Allport, D. A. (1983) 'Patterns and actions: cognitive mechanisms are content specific', in G. Claxton (ed.) *Cognitive Psychology: New Directions*, International Library of Psychology, London: Routledge & Kegan Paul, Chapter 2, pp. 26–64.

Anderson, B. G., Reker, D. and Cooper, T. B. (1981) 'Prolonged adverse effects of haloperidol in normal subjects', *New England Journal of Medicine*, 305: 643–4.

—— (1996) 'Drug-induced dysphoria', *British Journal of Psychiatry* (Letters), 168(4: April): 520.

Andreasen, N. C. (1987) 'Creativity and mental illness: prevalence rates in writers and their first degree relatives', *American Journal of Psychiatry*, 144: 1288–96.

Andreasen, N. C. and Powers, P. S. (1975) 'Creativity and psychosis: an examination of conceptual style', *Archives of General Psychiatry*, 32: 70–3.

Anonymous (1993) 'Review of *Borderline* by P. K. Chadwick', *Contemporary Psychology Reviews*, 38(3): 324–5.

Argyle, M. (1992) *The Social Psychology of Everyday Life*, London: Routledge.

—— (1993) *The Psychology of Happiness*, London and New York: Routledge.

Assagioli, R. (1965) *Psychosynthesis*, New York: Dorman & Co.

Atkinson, J. M., Coia, D. A., Harper Gilmore, W. and Harper, J. P. (1996) 'The impact of education groups for people with schizophrenia on social functioning and quality of life', *British Journal of Psychiatry*, 168: 199–204.

Azrin, N. H. and Peterson, A. L. (1988) 'Behaviour therapy for Tourette's Syndrome and tic disorders', in D. J. Cohen, R. D. Bruun and J. F. Leckman (eds) *Tourette Syndrome and Tic Disorders: Clinical Understanding and Treatment*, New York: Wiley.

Baker, H. (1994) 'Creative madness', *The Observer: Life* (30 January): 30.

Baltaxe, C. A. M. and Simmons, J. Q. (1995) 'Speech and language disorders in children and adolescents with schizophrenia', *Schizophrenia Bulletin*, 21(4): 677–92.

Bandura, A. (1962) 'Social learning through imitation', in M. R. Jones (ed.) *Nebraska Symposium on Motivation*, Lincoln: University of Nebraska Press, 211–74.

Bandura, A., Ross, D. and Ross, S. A. (1963a) 'Imitation of film-mediated aggressive models', *Journal of Abnormal and Social Psychology*, 66: 3–11.

—— (1963b) 'Vicarious reinforcement and imitative learning', *Journal of Abnormal and Social Psychology*, 67: 601–7.

Bandura, A. and Walters, R. H. (1963) *Social Learning and Personality Development*, New York: Holt, Rinehart & Winston.

Banister, P., Burman, E., Parker, I., Taylor, M. and Tindall, C. (1994) *Qualitative*

Methods in Psychology: A Research Guide, Buckingham and Philadelphia: Open University Press.

Bannister, D. and Fransella, F. (1971) *Inquiring Man: The Theory of Personal Constructs*, London: Penguin.

Barclay, P. M. (1982) *Committee Report: Social Workers, Their Role and Task*, London: Bedford Square Press.

Barham, P. and Hayward, R. (1990) 'Schizophrenia as a life process', in R. P. Bentall (ed.) *Reconstructing Schizophrenia*, London and New York: Routledge, Chapter 3, pp. 61–85.

Barron, F. (1962) 'The psychology of imagination', in S. J. Parnes and H. F. Harding (eds) *Source Book for Creative Thinking*, New York: Charles Scribner, Selection 19: 227–37.

—— (1972) 'The creative personality. Akin to madness', *Psychology Today*, 6(2; July): 42–4 and 84–5.

Baruch, G. and Treacher, A. (1978) *Psychiatry Observed*, London, Henley and Boston: Routledge & Kegan Paul.

Baruch, I., Hemsley, D. R. and Gray, J. A. (1988) 'Differential performance of acute and chronic schizophrenics in a latent inhibition task', *Journal of Nervous and Mental Disease*, 176: 598–606.

Bateson, G., Jackson, D. D., Haley, J. and Weakland, J. (1956) 'Toward a theory of schizophrenia', *Behavioural Science*, 1: 251–64.

Beatrice, J. (1985) 'A psychological comparison of heterosexuals, transvestites, preoperative transsexuals and postoperative transsexuals', *Journal of Nervous and Mental Disease*, 173(6): 358–65.

Bebbington, P. E. and Kuipers, L. (1994) 'The predictive utility of expressed emotion in schizophrenia: an aggregate analysis', *Psychological Medicine*, 24: 707–18.

Beck, A. T. and Beck, R. W. (1972) 'Screening for depressed patients in family practice', *Postgraduate Medicine* (December): 81–5.

Beech, A. R., Baylis, G. C., Smithson, P. and Claridge, G. S. (1989) 'Individual differences in schizotypy as reflected in cognitive measures of inhibition', *British Journal of Clinical Psychology*, 28: 117–29.

Beech, A. R. and Claridge, G. S. (1987) 'Individual differences in negative priming: relations with schizotypal personality traits', *British Journal of Psychology*, 78: 349–56.

Beech, A. R., McManus, D., Baylis, G., Tipper, S. and Agar, K. (1991) 'Individual differences in cognitive process: toward an explanation of schizophrenic symptomatology', *British Journal of Psychology*, 82: 417–26.

Beech, A., Powell, T., McWilliam, J. and Claridge, G. S. (1989) 'Evidence of reduced "cognitive inhibition" in schizophrenia', *British Journal of Clinical Psychology*, 28: 109–16.

Bell, M. D., Lysaker, P. H. and Milstein, R. M. (1996) 'Clinical benefits of paid work activity in schizophrenia', *Schizophrenia Bulletin*, 22(1): 51–67.

Belmaker, R. H. and Wald, D. (1977) 'Haloperidol in normals', *British Journal of Psychiatry* 131: 222–3.

Benassi, V. A., Sweeney, P. D. and Dreuno, G. E. (1979) 'Mind over matter: perceived success at psychokinesis', *Journal of Personality and Social Psychology*, 37: 1377–86.

Bender, M. (1976) *Community Psychology*, London: Methuen.

Benor, D. J. (1990) 'Survey of spiritual healing research', *Complementary Medicine Research*, 4(3): 9–33.

—— (1993) *Healing Research: Holistic Energy Medicine and Spirituality, Volume 1: Research in Healing*, Deddington, Oxon: Helix Editions Ltd.

Bentall, R. P. (ed.) (1990a) *Reconstructing Schizophrenia*, London and New York: Routledge.

—— (1990b) 'The syndromes and symptoms of psychosis, or why you can't play "twenty questions" with the concept of schizophrenia and hope to win', in R. P. Bentall (ed.) *Reconstructing Schizophrenia*, London and New York: Routledge, Chapter 2, pp. 23–60.

—— (1992) 'Review of *Borderline* by P. K. Chadwick', *British Journal of Medical Psychology*, 65(4; December): 399.

—— (1994) 'Cognitive biases and abnormal beliefs: towards a model of persecutory delusions', in A. S. David and J. C. Cutting (eds) *The Neuropsychology of Schizophrenia*, Hove, Hillsdale: Lawrence Erlbaum Associates, Chapter 19, pp. 337–60.

Bentall, R. P., Jackson, H. F. and Pilgrim, D. (1988) 'Abandoning the concept of "schizophrenia": some implications of validity arguments for psychological research into psychotic phenomena', *British Journal of Clinical Psychology*, 27: 303–24.

Bentall, R. P. and Young, H. F. (1996) 'Sensible hypothesis testing in deluded, depressed and normal subjects', *British Journal of Psychiatry*, 168 (March): 372–5.

Berger, J. (1980) *The Success and Failure of Picasso*, London: Writers and Readers Publishing Cooperative.

Bergman, A. J., Harvey, P. D., Mitropoulou, V., Aronson, A., Marder, D., Silverman, J., Trestman, R. and Siever, L. J. (1996) 'The factor structure of schizotypal symptoms in a clinical population', *Schizophrenia Bulletin*, 22(3): 501–9.

Berrios, G. (1991) 'Delusions as "wrong beliefs": a conceptual history', *British Journal of Psychiatry*, 159: 6–13.

Bett, W. R. (1952) *The Infirmities of Genius*, London: Johnson.

Bilu, Y. and Witztum, E. (1994) 'Culturally sensitive therapy with ultra-orthodox patients: the strategic employment of religious idioms of distress', *Israel Journal of Psychiatry*, 31(3): 170–82.

Bishop, D. V. M. (1977) 'The P scale and psychosis', *Journal of Abnormal Psychology*, 86: 127–34.

Blackmore, S. J. (1982) *Beyond the Body*, London: Heinemann.

—— (1987) 'Where am I? Perspectives in imagery and the out-of-body experience', *Journal of Mental Imagery*, 11: 53–66.

Blaska, B. (1995) 'The 13 commandments for the mental health professional', *Clinical Psychology Forum*, 82 (August): 2–3.

Bleuler, E. (1911/1955) *Dementia Praecox or the Group of Schizophrenias*, New York: International Universities Press.

—— (1924) *Textbook of Psychiatry*, New York: Macmillan.

Bleuler, M. (1978) *The Schizophrenic Disorders: Long Term Patient and Family Studies*, New Haven: Yale University Press.

Block, J. (1977) 'P scale and psychosis: continued concerns', *Journal of Abnormal Psychology*, 86: 431–4.

Bohr, N. (1958) *Atomic Theory and Human Knowledge*, New York: Wiley.

Boyle, M. (1990) *Schizophrenia: A Scientific Delusion?*, London and New York: Routledge.

—— (1992) 'Form and content, function and meaning in "schizophrenic" behaviour', *Clinical Psychology Forum*, 47: 10–15.

—— (1994) 'Schizophrenia and the art of the soluble', *The Psychologist*, 7: 399–404.

—— (1996) 'Schizophrenia: the fallacy of diagnosis', *Changes*, 14(1; March): 5–13.

Brand, J., Davis, G. and Wood, R. (1979) 'Experiments with Matthew Manning', *Journal of the Society for Psychical Research*, 15(782): 199–223.

Braun, C., Bernier, S., Proulx, R. and Cohen, H. (1991) 'A deficit of primary affective facial expression independent of bucco-facial dyspraxia in chronic schizophrenics', *Cognition and Emotion*, 5(2): 147–59.

Breggin, P. (1991) *Toxic Psychiatry: Drugs and ECT, the Truth and Better Alternatives*, London: Fontana.

Brehm, J. W. (1966) *A Theory of Psychological Reactance*, New York: Academic Press.

Brennan, J. H. and Hemsley, D. R. (1984) 'Illusory correlations in paranoid and non-paranoid schizophrenia', *British Journal of Clinical Psychology*, 23: 225–6.

Brewin, C. R. (1988) 'Editorial: Developments in an attributional approach to clinical psychology', *British Journal of Clinical Psychology*, 27: 1–3.

Broadbent, D. E. (1971) *Decision and Stress*, London: Academic Press.

Brown, G. W. (1991) 'A psychosocial view of depression', in D. H. Bennett and N. L. Freeman (eds) *Community Psychiatry*, Edinburgh and London: Churchill Livingstone, Chapter 3, pp. 71–114.

Brown, G. W. and Harris, T. O. (1978) *Social Origins of Depression: A Study of Psychiatric Disorder in Women*, London: Tavistock Publications.

Bruner, J. S. and Potter, M. C. (1966) 'Interference in visual recognition', *Science*, 144: 424–5.

Bruun, R. D. (1984) 'Gille de la Tourette's Syndrome: an overview of clinical experience', *Journal of the American Academy of Child Psychiatry*, 23: 126–33.

Buchanan, A. (1996) *Compliance with Treatment in Schizophrenia*, Maudsley Monograph, London: The Psychology Press.

Buckley, P. (1981) 'Mystical experience and schizophrenia', *Schizophrenia Bulletin*, 7(3): 516–21.

Buckley, P. and Galanter, M. (1979) 'Mystical experience, spiritual knowledge and a contemporary ecstatic religion', *British Journal of Medical Psychology*, 52: 281–9.

Bunyan, J. (1666/1984) *'Grace Abounding' and 'The Life and Death of Mr Badman'*, London and Melbourne: Dent.

Caine, E. D. (1985) 'Gilles de la Tourette's Syndrome: a review of clinical and research studies and consideration of future directions for investigation', *Archives of Neurology*, 42: 393–7.

Canter, S. (1973) 'Some aspects of cognitive function in twins', in G. Claridge, S. Canter and W. I. Hume (eds) *Personality Differences and Biological Variation: A Study of Twins*, Oxford: Pergamon Press.

Chadwick, P. D. J., Birchwood, M. and Trower, P. (1996) *Cognitive Therapy for Delusions, Voices and Paranoia*, Chichester: Wiley.

Chadwick, P. D. J. and Lowe, C. F. (1990) 'Measurement and modification of delusional beliefs', *Journal of Consulting and Clinical Psychology*, 58(2): 225–32.

Chadwick, P. K. (1975a) 'A psychological analysis of observation in geology', *Nature*, 256(5518; 14 August): 570–3.

—— (1975b) 'The psychology of geological observations', *New Scientist*, 68 (18–25 December): 728–32.

—— (1976) 'Visual illusions in geology', *Nature*, 260 (1 April): 397–401.

—— (1977) 'Scientists can have illusions too', *New Scientist*, 73 (31 March): 768–71.

—— (1978a) 'Some aspects of the development of geological thinking', *Geology Teaching* 3(4 December): 142–8.

—— (1978b) 'The perception and interpretation of continuity and discontinuity', *Catastrophist Geologist*, 1(3): 35–48.

—— (1979a) 'Understanding transvestism', *The World of Transvestism*, 1(8): 33–5; 1(9): 47–8.

—— (1979b) 'Half man, half boat, the mind of the Borderline Normal', unpublished manuscript, London.

—— (1981) 'Optical illusions: fooling the eye', *Insight*, 5(66): 1813–17.

—— (1982) '"Earth-boundedness" in geological observation', *Geology Teaching*, 7(3; March): 16–22.

—— (1986) 'Transvestism: the fantasy vehicle', *The World of Transvestism*, 6(10): 7–15; 6(11): 7–14.

—— (1988) 'A psychological study of paranoia and delusional thinking', Doctoral dissertation, University of London.

—— (1992) *Borderline: A Psychological Study of Paranoia and Delusional Thinking*, London and New York: Routledge.

—— (1993a) 'Ex-patients as researchers', *The Psychologist* (Letters), 6(3; March): 115.

—— (1993b) 'The stepladder to the impossible: a first hand phenomenological account of a schizoaffective psychotic crisis', *Journal of Mental Health*, 2: 239–50.

—— (1995a) *Understanding Paranoia: What Causes It, How It Feels and What to do about It*, London: Thorsons.

—— (1995b) 'Learning from patients', *Clinical Psychology Forum*, 82: 30–4.

—— (1996a) 'In search of "deep music": artistic approaches to the study of mind', *Clinical Psychology Forum*, 89 (March): 8–11.

—— (1996b) 'A meeting place for science, art and spirituality: the perception of reality in insane and "supersane" states', *Network: The Scientific and Medical Network Review*, 60 (April): 3–8.

Chadwick, P. K. and Hughes, E. M. (1981) 'Which way-up is upside down?', *Geology Teaching*, 5(3; September): 87–9.

Chapman, J. P., Chapman, L. J. and Kwapil, T. R. (1995) 'Scales for the measurement of schizotypy', in A. Raine, T. Lencz and S. A. Mednick (eds) *Schizotypal Personality*, Cambridge: Cambridge University Press, Chapter 5, pp. 79–106.

Chapman, L. J. and Chapman, J. P. (1959) 'Atmosphere effect re-examined', *Journal of Experimental Psychology*, 58: 220–6.

Christensen, P. R., Guildford, J. P., Merrifield, P. and Wilson, R. (1960) *Alternate Uses*, Beverly Hills, CA: Sheridan Psychological Service.

Ciompi, L. and Muller, C. (1976) *Lebensweg und Alter der Schizophrenen*, Berlin: Springer.

Claridge, G. S. (1967) *Personality and Arousal*, Oxford: Pergamon.

—— (1985) *Origins of Mental Illness*, Oxford: Basil Blackwell.

—— (1988) 'Schizotypy and schizophrenia', in P. McGuffin and P. Bebbington (eds) *Schizophrenia: The Major Issues*, London: Heinemann, Chapter 14, pp. 187–200.

—— (1990) 'Can a disease model of schizophrenia survive?' in R. P. Bentall (ed.) *Reconstructing Schizophrenia*, London and New York: Routledge, Chapter 6, pp. 157–83.

—— (1993) 'What is schizophrenia? Common theories and divergent views', *Journal of Mental Health*, 2(3): 251–3.

Claridge, G. S. and Beech, T. (1995) 'Fully and quasi-dimensional constructions of schizotypy', in A. Raine, T. Lencz and S. A. Mednick (eds) *Schizotypal Personality*, Cambridge: Cambridge University Press, Chapter 9, pp. 192–216.

Claridge, G. S. and Broks, P. (1984) 'Schizotypy and hemisphere function, 1. Theoretical considerations and the measurement of schizotypy', *Personality and Individual Differences*, 5: 633–48.

Claridge, G. S., Pryor, R. and Watkins, G. (1990) *Sounds from the Bell Jar: Ten Psychotic Authors*, London: Macmillan.

Clarkson, P. and Gilbert, M. (1990) 'Transactional analysis', in W. Dryden (ed.) *Individual Therapy: A Handbook*, Chapter 10, pp. 199–225.

Collins, G. R. (1988) *Christian Counselling: A Comprehensive Guide*, Dallas, Texas: Word Inc.

Comings, D. E. and Comings, B. G. (1987a) 'A controlled study of Tourette Syndrome, I–VII', *American Journal of Human Genetics*, 41: 701–866.

—— (1987b) 'Hereditary agoraphobia and obsessive-compulsive behaviour in relatives of patients with Gilles de la Tourette's Syndrome', *British Journal of Psychiatry*, 151: 195–9.

Conrad, K. (1968) *Commencing Schizophrenia: An Attempt at a Gestalt Analysis of Delusion*, Stuttgart: Thieme.

Cooper, A. E., Garside, R. F. and Kay, D. W. (1976) 'A comparison of deaf and non-deaf patients with paranoid and affective psychoses', *British Journal of Psychiatry*, 129: 532–8.

Cooper, J. E., Kendell, R. E., Gurland, B. J., Sharp, L., Copeland, J. R. M. and Simon, R. (1972) *Psychiatric Diagnosis in New York and London*, London: Oxford University Press.

Coursey, R. D., Keller, A. B. and Farrell, E. W. (1995) 'Individual psychotherapy with persons with serious mental illness: the clients' perspective', *Schizophrenia Bulletin*, 21(2): 283–301.

Cowen, E. (1982) 'Help is where you find it', *American Psychologist*, 37: 385–95.

Cox, D. and Cowling, P. (1989) *Are You Normal?*, London: Tower Press.

Cranston, M. (1965) 'The new science and metaphysics', in J. Huxley, G. Barry, J. Bronowski and J. Fisher (eds) *Growth of Ideas: The Evolution of Thought and Knowledge*, London: Macdonald, 142–61.

Crow, T. J. (1980) 'Molecular pathology of schizophrenia: more than one disease process?', *British Medical Journal*, 280: 66–8.

—— (1988) 'Aetiology of psychosis: the way ahead', in P. Bebbington and P. McGuffin (eds) *Schizophrenia: The Major Issues*, Oxford and London: Heinemann, Chapter 10, pp. 127–34.

Crow, T. J., Johnstone, E. C., Longden, A. J. and Owen, F. (1978) 'Dopaminergic mechanisms in schizophrenia: the antipsychotic effect and the disease process', *Life Sciences*, 23: 563–8.

Cutting, J. and Murphy, D. (1988) 'Schizophrenic thought disorder: a psychological and organic interpretation', *British Journal of Psychiatry*, 152: 310–19.

Davies, B. (1995) *Past Life Regression with Transsexuals*, Presentation at the Psychotherapy and Spiritual Healing International Conference, Regents College, 10–11 April.

Davis, K. L., Kahn, R. S., Ko, G. and Davidson, M. (1991) 'Dopamine and schizophrenia: a review and reconceptualisation', *American Journal of Psychiatry*, 148: 1474–86.

Davison, G. C. and Neale, J. M. (1994) *Abnormal Psychology*, New York and Chichester: John Wiley & Sons.

Deakin, J. F. W. (1988) 'The neurochemistry of schizophrenia', in P. Bebbington and P. McGuffin (eds) *Schizophrenia: The Major Issues*, London: Heinemann Medical Books, Chapter 6, pp. 56–72.

Deikmann, A. J. (1966) 'Deautomatisation and the mystic experience', *Psychiatry*, vol. 29, reprinted in R. Ornstein (1986) *The Psychology of Consciousness*, New York: Penguin, Chapter 7, pp. 200–20.

—— (1977) 'Comments on the GAP report on mysticism', *Journal of Nervous and Mental Disease*, 165(3): 213–17.

Dick, P., Cameron, L., Cohen, D., Barlow, M. and Ince, A. (1985) 'Day and full-time psychiatric treatment: a controlled comparison', *British Journal of Psychiatry*, 147: 246–50.

Dixon, N. F. (1981) *Preconscious Processing*, Chichester: Wiley.

Donaldson, M. (1993) *Human Minds: An Exploration*, Harmondsworth: Penguin.

Drake, R. A. (1983) 'Towards a synthesis of some behavioural and physiological antecedents of belief perseverance', *Social Behaviour and Personality*, 11(2): 57–60.

Drake, R. A. and Bingham, B. R. (1985) 'Induced lateral orientation and persuasibility', *Brain and Cognition*, 4: 156–64.

Dryden, W. (1990) *Individual Therapy: A Handbook*, Milton Keynes: Open University Press.

DSM III (1980) *Diagnostic and Statistical Manual of Mental Disorders* (3rd edition), Washington, DC: American Psychiatric Association.

DSM IIIR (1987) *Diagnostic and Statistical Manual of Mental Disorders* (3rd edition, Desk Reference), Washington, DC: American Psychiatric Association.

DSM IV (1994) *Diagnostic and Statistical Manual of Mental Disorders* (4th edition), Washington, DC: American Psychiatric Association.

Durkheim, E. (1897/1951) *Suicide*, New York: The Free Press.

Durlak, J. (1979) 'Comparative effectiveness of para-professional and professional helpers', *Psychological Bulletin*, 86: 80–92.

—— (1981) 'Evaluating comparative studies of para-professional and professional helpers: a reply to Nietzel and Fisher', *Psychological Bulletin*, 89: 566–9.

Dykes, M. and McGhie, A. (1976) 'A comparative study of attentional strategies of schizophrenic and highly creative normal subjects', *British Journal of Psychiatry*, 128: 50–6.

Easterbrook, J. A. (1959) 'The effect of emotion on cue utilisation and the organisation of behaviour', *Psychological Review*, 66: 183–201.

Egeland, B. (1988) 'Breaking the cycle of abuse: implications for prediction and intervention', in K. Browne, C. Davies and P. Stratton (eds) *Early Prediction and Prevention of Child Abuse*, Chichester: Wiley.

Ehrenwald, J. (1972) 'A neurophysiological model of psi phenomena', *Journal of Nervous and Mental Disease*, 194(6): 406–18.

Ellenberger, H. F. (1970/1994) *The Discovery of the Unconscious: The History and Evolution of Dynamic Psychiatry*, London: Basic Books.

Ellis, A. (1962) *Reason and Emotion in Psychotherapy*, Secaucus, NJ: Lyle Stuart.

Ellis, H. (1936) *Studies in the Psychology of Sex*, New York: Random House.

Ellmann, R. (1988) *Oscar Wilde*, New York: Alfred A. Knopf.

Emler, N. (1984) 'Differential involvement in delinquency: toward an interpretation in terms of reputation management', in B. Maher (ed.) *Progress in Experimental Personality Research*, vol. 13, New York: Academic Press.

Emory, L. E., Williams, D. H., Cole, C. M., Amparo, E. G. and Meyer, W. J. (1991) 'Anatomic variation of the corpus callosum in persons with gender dysphoria', *Archives of Sexual Behaviour*, 20: 409–17.

Estes, W. K. (1976) 'The cognitive side of probability learning', *Psychological Review*, 83: 37–64.

Eysenck, H. J. (ed.) (1981) *The Biological Basis of Personality*, Berlin, Heidelberg: Springer-Verlag.

—— (1983) 'The roots of creativity: cognitive ability or personality trait?' *Roeper Review* (May): 10–12.

—— (1995) *Genius: The Natural History of Creativity*, Cambridge: Cambridge University Press.

Eysenck, H. J. and Eysenck, S. B. G. (1975) *Manual of the Eysenck Personality (Junior and Adult)*, Sevenoaks, Kent: Hodder & Stoughton.
—— (1976) *Psychoticism as a Dimension of Personality*, London: Hodder & Stoughton.
Eysenck, S. B. G. and McGurk, B. J. (1980) 'Impulsiveness and venturesomeness in a detention centre population', *Psychological Reports*, 47: 1299–306.
Fairweather, G., Sanders, D. H., Cressler, D. L. and Maynard, H. (1969) *Community Life for the Mentally Ill*, Chicago: Alpine.
Falloon, I., Mueser, K., Gingerich, S., Rapport, S., McGill, C. and Hole. V. (1988) *Behavioural Family Therapy: A Workbook*, Buckingham: Buckingham Mental Health Service, UK.
Faris, R. E. L. and Dunham, H. W. (1939) *Mental Disorders in Urban Areas*, Chicago: University of Chicago Press.
Fenichel, O. (1946/1982) *The Psychoanalytic Theory of Neurosis*, London, Melbourne and Henley: Routledge & Kegan Paul.
Fenigstein, A. (1984) 'Self consciousness and the overperception of Self as a target', *Journal of Personality and Social Psychology*, 47(4): 860–70.
Foucault, M. (1965) *Madness and Civilisation*, New York: Pantheon.
Fowler, D., Garety, P. and Kuipers, E. (1995) *Cognitive Behaviour Therapy for Psychosis*, Chichester: Wiley.
Frankl, V. E. (1969) *The Doctor and the Soul*, New York: Bantam Books.
Freeman, N. H., Sinha, C. G. and Stedman, J. A. (1982) 'All the cars – which cars? From word meaning to discourse analysis', in M. Beveridge (ed.) *Children Thinking through Language*, London: Edward Arnold.
French, C. C. (1992) 'Factors underlying belief in the paranormal: do sheep and goats think differently?', *The Psychologist*, 5: 295–9.
Freud, S. (1911) 'Psychoanalytic notes on an autobiographical account of a case of paranoia (dementia paranoides)', Standard Edition vol. 12, London: Hogarth Press, 3–82.
—— (1915) *A Case of Paranoia Running Counter to the Psychoanalytic Theory of the Disease*, London: Hogarth Press.
—— (1979) *New Introductory Lectures on Psychoanalysis*, London: Pelican.
Frith, C. D. (1979) 'Consciousness, information processing and schizophrenia', *British Journal of Psychiatry*, 134: 225–35.
—— (1992) *The Cognitive Neuropsychology of Schizophrenia*, Hove: Lawrence Erlbaum Associates.
Fromm, E. (1947) *Man for Himself*, New York: Rinehart.
GAP (Group for the Advancement of Psychiatry) (1976) *Mysticism: Spiritual Quest or Psychic Disorder?* New York: Brunner/Mozel.
Gardner, H. (1985) *Frames of Mind: The Theory of Multiple Intelligences*, London: Paladin.
Garety, P. A. (1992) 'Making sense of delusions', *Psychiatry*, 55 (August): 282–91.
—— (1993) 'Psychological aspects of psychosis: subjective meaning and longitudinal course', *Current Opinion in Psychiatry*, 6: 847–51.
Garety, P. A. and Hemsley, D. R. (1994) *Delusions: Investigations into the Psychology of Delusional Reasoning*, Maudsley Monographs no. 36, Institute of Psychiatry, Oxford: Oxford University Press.
Garety, P. A., Hemsley, D. and Wessely, S. (1991) 'Reasoning in deluded schizophrenic and paranoid patients', *Journal of Nervous and Mental Disease*, 179: 194–201.
Garety, P. A., Kuipers, L., Fowler, D., Chamberlain, F. and Dunn, G. (1994) 'Cognitive behavioural therapy for drug-resistant psychosis', *British Journal of Medical Psychology*, 67: 259–71.

Gergen, K. J. (1985) 'The social constructionist movement in modern psychology', *American Psychologist*, 40: 266–75.

—— (1990) 'Therapeutic professions and the diffusion of deficit', *Journal of Mind and Behaviour*, 11: 353–67.

Gittings, R. (1978) *Selected Poems and Letters of Keats*, London: Heinemann Educational Books Ltd.

Gleick, J. (1987) *Chaos: Making a New Science*, London: Abacus.

Glucksberg, S. (1962) 'The influence of strength of drive on functional fixedness and perceptual recognition', *Journal of Experimental Psychology*, 63: 36–41.

—— (1964) 'Problem-solving: response competition and the influence of drive', *Psychological Reports*, 15: 939–42.

Goffman, E. (1961/1991) *Asylums: Essays on the Social Situation of Mental Patients and Other Inmates*, Harmondsworth: Penguin.

Goldberg, S. C., Schulz, S. C. and Schulz, P. M. (1986) 'Borderline and schizotypal personality disorders treated with low-dose thiothixene vs placebo', *Archives of General Psychiatry*, 43: 680–6.

Golden, G. S. (1984) 'Psychologic and neuropsychologic aspects of Tourette's Syndrome', *Neurologic Clinics*, 21: 91–102.

Goldman, A. R. (1970) 'On posing as mental patients: reminiscences and recommendations', *Professional Psychology*, 1: 427–34.

Goldman, C. R. and Quinn, F. L. (1988) 'Effects of a patient education programme in the treatment of schizophrenia', *Hospital and Community Psychiatry*, 39: 282–6.

Goodman, J. (1988) *The Oscar Wilde File*, London: W. H. Allen & Co.

Gosselin, C. and Wilson, G. (1980) *Sexual Variations*, London: Faber.

Gottesman, I. I. (1991) *Schizophrenia Genesis: The Origins of Madness*, New York: W. H. Freeman & Co.

Gottesman, I. I. and Shields, J. (1982) *Schizophrenia: The Epigenetic Puzzle*, Cambridge: Cambridge University Press.

Greenberg, D., Witzum, E. and Buchbinder, J. T. (1992) 'Mysticism and psychosis: the fate of Ben Zoma', *British Journal of Medical Psychology* 65: 223–36.

Greenberg, L. S. (1983) 'Towards a task analysis of conflict resolution in Gestalt Therapy', *Psychotherapy: Theory, Research and Practice*, 20: 190–201.

Gregory, R. L. (1970) *The Intelligent Eye*, London: Weidenfeld & Nicolson.

—— (ed.) (1987) *The Oxford Companion to the Mind*, Oxford and New York: Oxford University Press.

Greyson, B. (1977) 'Telepathy in mental illness: deluge or delusion?', *Journal of Nervous and Mental Disease* 165: 184–200.

Grossman, H. Y., Mostofsky, D. I. and Harrison, R. H. (1986) 'Psychological aspects of Gilles de la Tourette's Syndrome', *Journal of Clinical Psychology*, 42: 228–35.

Haddock, G., Bentall, R. P. and Slade, P. D. (1993) 'Psychological treatment of chronic auditory hallucinations: two case studies', *Behavioural and Cognitive Psychotherapy*, 21: 335–46.

Halberstadt-Freud, H. C. (1991) *Freud, Proust, Perversion and Love*, Amsterdam: Swets & Zeitlinger.

Haracz, J. L. (1982) 'The Dopamine Hypothesis: an overview of studies with schizophrenic patients', *Schizophrenia Bulletin*, 8(3): 438–69.

Harding, C. M., Zubin, J. and Strauss, J. (1988) 'Chronicity in schizophrenia: fact, practical fact or artifact?', *Hospital and Community Psychiatry*, 38: 477–86.

Harré, R., Clark, D. and de Carlo, N. (1985) *Motives and Mechanisms: An Introduction to the Psychology of Action*, London: Methuen.

Harris, N. (ed.) (1991) *Romantics: Their Lives, Works and Inspiration*, London: Marshall Cavendish.

Hart-Davis, R. (1989) *Selected Letters of Oscar Wilde*, Oxford: Oxford University Press.

Hartman, L. M. and Cashman, F. E. (1983) 'Cognitive behavioural and psychopharmacological treatment of delusional symptoms: a preliminary report', *Behavioural Psychotherapy*, 11: 50–61.

Hasenfus, N. and Magaro, P. (1976) 'Creativity and schizophrenia: an equality of empirical constructs', *British Journal of Psychiatry*, 129: 346–9.

Hattie, J., Sharpley, C. and Rogers, H. (1984) 'Comparative effectiveness of professional and para-professional helpers', *Psychological Bulletin*, 95: 534–41.

Heansley, P. and Reynolds, C. R. (1989) 'Creativity and intelligence', in J. A. Glover, R. R. Ronning and C. R. Reynolds (eds) *Handbook of Creativity*, New York: Plenum Press, 111–32.

Hebb, D. O. (1949) *The Organisation of Behaviour*, New York: Wiley.

Heston, L. L. and Denney, D. (1968) 'Interaction between early life experience and biological factors in schizophrenia', in D. Rosenthal and S. S. Kety (eds) *The Transmission of Schizophrenia*, New York: Pergamon, 363–76.

Hewitt, J. K. and Claridge, G. S. (1989) 'The factor structure of schizotypy in a normal population', *Personality and Individual Differences*, 10: 323–9.

Hewstone, M. (ed.) (1983) *Attribution Theory: Social and Functional Extensions*, Oxford: Basil Blackwell.

—— (1989) *Causal Attribution: From Cognitive Processes to Collective Beliefs*, Oxford: Basil Blackwell.

Hirsch, S. R., Platt, S., Knights, A. and Weyman, A. (1979) 'Shortening hospital stay for psychiatric care: effect on patients and their families', *British Medical Journal*, 1: 112–16.

Hodges, R. D. and Scofield, A. M. (1995) 'Is spiritual healing a valid and effective therapy?', *Journal of the Royal Society of Medicine*, 88 (April): 203–7.

Hoenig, J. and Kenna, J. C. (1979) 'EEG abnormalities and transsexualism', *British Journal of Psychiatry*, 134: 293–300.

Hole, R. W., Rush, A. J. and Beck, A. T. (1979) 'A cognitive investigation of schizophrenic delusions', *Psychiatry*, 42: 312–19.

Hollingshead, A. B. and Redlich, F. C. (1958) *Social Class and Mental Illness: A Community Study*, New York: Wiley.

Horney, K. (1937) *The Neurotic Personality of Our Time*, New York: W. W. Norton.

—— (1942) *Self-Analysis*, New York: W. W. Norton.

Hudson, L. (1966) *Frames of Mind*, London: Penguin.

Huq, S. F., Garety, P. and Hemsley, D. (1988) 'Probabilistic judgements in deluded and non-deluded subjects', *Quarterly Journal of Experimental Psychology*, 40A: 801–12.

Irwin, H. J. (1986) 'Perceptual perspectives of visual imagery in OBE's, dreams and reminiscence', *Journal of the Society of Psychical Research*, 53: 210–17.

—— (1993) 'Belief in the paranormal: a review of the empirical literature', *Journal of the American Society for Psychical Research*, 87(1; January): 22–31.

Jackson, M. and Claridge, G. (1991) 'Reliability and validity of a psychotic traits questionnaire (STQ)', *British Journal of Clinical Psychology*, 30(4; November): 311–24.

Jackson, M. and Fulford, K. W. M. (1996) *Spiritual Experience and Psychopathology* (in press).

James, W. (1890) *The Principles of Psychology*, New York: Henry Holt.

—— (1892) *Psychology: The Briefer Course*, New York: Harper Torch Books.

Jamison, K. R. (1989) 'Mood disorders and patterns of creativity in British writers and artists', *Psychiatry*, 32: 125–34.

—— (1993) *Touched with Fire: Manic-Depressive Illness and the Artistic Temperament*, New York: The Free Press.

—— (1995) 'Manic-depressive illness and creativity', *Scientific American* (February): 46–51.

—— (1996) *An Unquiet Mind: A Memoir of Moods and Madness*, London: Picador.

Janoff-Bulman, R. (1979) 'Characterological versus behavioural self-blame: inquiries into depression and rape', *Journal of Personality and Social Psychology*, 37: 1798–809.

Jarvik, L. F. and Deckard, B. S. (1977) 'The Odyssean personality: a survival advantage for carriers of genes predisposing to schizophrenia', *Neuropsychobiology*, 3: 179–91.

Jaspers, K. (1963) *General Psychopathology* (transl. J. Hoenig and M. W. Hamilton), Manchester: Manchester University Press.

Jaynes, J. (1976) *The Origins of Consciousness in the Breakdown of the Bicameral Mind*, London: Allen Lane.

Jeans, R. F. I. (1976) 'An independently validated case of multiple personality', *Journal of Abnormal Psychology*, 85: 249–55.

John, C. (1992) 'Review of *Borderline* by P. K. Chadwick', *British Journal of Clinical Psychology*, 31(4): 510.

Johnson, D. A. W. (1988) 'Drug treatment of schizophrenia', in P. Bebbington and P. McGuffin (eds) *Schizophrenia: The Major Issues*, London: Heinemann Medical Books, Chapter 12, pp. 158–71.

Johnson, W. G., Ross, J. M. and Mastria, M. A. (1977) 'Delusional behaviour: an attributional analysis of development and modification', *Journal of Abnormal Psychology*, 86: 421–6.

Johnstone, E. C., Crow, T. J., Frith, C. D. and Owens, D. G. C. (1988) 'The Northwick Park "functional" psychosis study: diagnosis and treatment responses', *Lancet*, ii: 119–25.

Johnstone, L. (1993a) 'Family management in "schizophrenia": its assumptions and contradictions', *Journal of Mental Health*, 2(3; September): 253–69.

—— (1993b) 'Psychiatry: are we allowed to disagree?', *Clinical Psychology Forum*, 56 (June): 30–2.

—— (1994) 'Values in human services', *Care in Place*, 1(1; March): 3–8.

—— (1996) 'The Genain quadruplets', *Changes*, 14(1; March): 43–9.

Jolliffe, T., Lansdown, R. and Robinson, C. (1992) 'Autism: a personal account', *Communication*, 26(3; December): 12–19.

Joseph, R. J. (1964) 'John Ruskin: radical and psychotic genius', *Psychoanalytic Review*, 56: 425–41.

Josephson, B. D. and Ramachandran, V. S. (1980) *Consciousness and the Physical World*, London: Pergamon.

Juda, A. (1949) 'The relationship between highest mental capacity and psychic abnormalities', *American Journal of Psychiatry*, 106: 296–307.

Jung, C. G. (1955/1985) *Synchronicity: An Acausal Connecting Principle*, London: Ark.

—— (1963) *Memories, Dreams, Reflections*, London: Collins.

Jung, C. G. and Pauli, W. (1955) *The Interpretation of Nature and the Psyche*, New York: Pantheon Books.

Kahneman, D., Slovic, P. and Tversky, A. (1982) *Judgement under Uncertainty: Heuristics and Biases*, Cambridge: Cambridge University Press.

Kaney, S. and Bentall, R. P. (1989) 'Persecutory delusions and attributional style', *British Journal of Medical Psychology*, 62: 191–8.

Kaney, S., Wolfenden, M., Dewey, M. E. and Bentall, R. P. (1992) 'Persecutory delusions and recall of threatening propositions', *British Journal of Clinical Psychology*, 31: 85–7.

Karlsson, J. L. (1972) 'An Icelandic family study of schizophrenia', in A. R. Kaplan (ed.) *Genetic Factors in Schizophrenia*, Springfield, IL: Charles C. Thomas, 246–55.

Kavanagh, D. J. (1992) 'Recent developments in expressed emotion and schizophrenia', *British Journal of Psychiatry*, 160: 601–20.

Keefe, J. A. and Magaro, P. A. (1980) 'Creativity and schizophrenia: an equivalence of cognitive processing', *Journal of Abnormal Psychology*, 89(3): 390–8.

Kelly, G. (1955) *The Psychology of Personal Constructs*, New York: W. W. Norton.

Kelly, G. R. and Scott, J. E. (1990) 'Medication compliance and health education among outpatients with chronic mental disorders', *Medical Care*, 28: 1181–97.

Kendell, R. E. and Brockington, I. F. (1980) 'The identification of disease entities and the relationship between schizophrenic and affective psychoses', *British Journal of Psychiatry*, 137: 324–31.

Kendler, K. S. (1976) 'A medical student's experience with akathisia', *American Journal of Psychiatry*, 133: 454–5.

Kennedy, J. L., Giuffra, L. A., Moises, H. W., Cavalli-Sforza, L. L., Pakstis, A. J., Kidd, J. R., Castiglione, C. M., Sjogren, B., Wetterberg, L. and Kidd, K. K. (1988) 'Evidence against linkage of schizophrenia to markers on chromosome 5 in a northern Swedish pedigree', *Nature*, 336 (10 November): 167–70.

Kerbeshian, J. and Burd, L. (1987) 'Are schizophreniform symptoms present in attenuated form in children with Tourette disorder and other developmental disorders?', *Canadian Journal of Psychiatry*, 32: 123–35.

Kernberg, O. (1975) *Borderline Conditions and Pathological Narcissism*, New York: Jason Aronson.

Kessel, N. (1989) 'Genius and mental disorder: a history of ideas concerning their conjunction', in P. Murray, *Genius: The History of an Idea*, Oxford: Basil Blackwell, Chapter 11, pp. 196–212.

Kinderman, P. (1994) 'Attentional bias, persecutory delusions and the self-concept', *British Journal of Medical Psychology*, 67: 53–66.

King, D. J., Burke, M. and Lucas, R. A. (1995) 'Antipsychotic drug-induced dysphoria', *British Journal of Psychiatry*, 167: 480–2.

Kingdon, D. G. and Turkington, D. (1994) *Cognitive-Behavioural Therapy of Schizophrenia*, Hove: Lawrence Erlbaum Associates.

Kinsey, A. C., Pomeroy, W. B., Martin, C. E. and Gebhard, P. H. (1953/1966) *Sexual Behaviour in the Human Female*, New York: Pocket Books; first published August 1953 by W. B. Saunders.

Klerman, G. (1984) 'Ideology and science in the individual psychotherapy of schizophrenia', *Schizophrenia Bulletin*, 10: 608–12.

Kline, P. (1981) *Fact and Fantasy in Freudian Theory*, London and New York: Methuen.

Knight, R., Sherer, M., Putchat, C. and Carter, G. (1978) 'A picture integration task for measuring iconic memory in schizophrenics', *Journal of Abnormal Psychology*, 87: 314–21.

Knights, A., Hirsch, S. R. and Platt, S. D. (1980) 'Clinical change as a function of brief admission to hospital in a controlled study using the present state examination', *British Journal of Psychiatry*, 137: 170–80.

Kogan, N. and Pankove, E. (1974) 'Long term predictive validity of divergent thinking tests: some negative evidence', *Journal of Education Psychology*, 66: 802–10.

Kosslyn, S. M. (1976) 'Can imagery be distinguished from other forms of internal

representation?: evidence from studies of information retrieval time', *Memory and Cognition*, 4: 291–7.
—— (1978) 'Measuring the visual angle of the mind's eye', *Cognitive Psychology*, 10: 356–89.
—— (1980) *Image and Mind*, Cambridge, MA: Harvard University Press.
Kovel, J. (1991) *A Complete Guide to Therapy*, London: Penguin.
Kraepelin, E. (1919) *Dementia Praecox and Paraphrenia*, New York: Robert E. Krieger.
Kubie, L. S. (1958) *Neurotic Distortion of the Creative Process*, Kansas: University of Kansas Press.
Laing, R. D. (1960) *The Divided Self*, London: Tavistock.
—— (1967) *The Politics of Experience*, New York: Pantheon Books.
—— (1970) *Knots*, New York: Pantheon Books.
Laing, R. D. and Esterson, A. (1964) *Sanity, Madness and the Family*, London: Tavistock.
Laplante, L., Everett, J. and Thomas, J. (1992) 'Inhibition through negative priming with Stroop stimuli in schizophrenia', *British Journal of Clinical Psychology*, 31: 307–26.
La Russo, L. (1978) 'Sensitivity of paranoid patients to non-verbal cues', *Journal of Abnormal Psychology*, 87(5; October): 463–71.
Laurikainen, K. V. (1988) *Beyond the Atom: The Philosophical Thought of Wolfgang Pauli*, Berlin: Springer-Verlag.
Lazare, A., Cohen, F., Jacobson, A. M., Williams, M. W., Mignone, R. J. and Zisook, S. (1972) 'The walk-in patient as a "customer". A key dimension in evaluation and treatment', *American Journal of Orthopsychiatry*, 42: 872–83.
Lazare, A., Eisenthal, S. and Wasserman, L. (1975) 'The customer approach to patienthood', *Archives of General Psychiatry*, 32: 553–8.
Lee, A. G. (1991) 'About the investigation technique of some unusual mental phenomena', *Parapsychology in the USSR*, 2: 34–8 (in Russian).
—— (1994) 'Extrasensory phenomena in the psychiatric clinic', *Parapsychology and Psychophysics*, 1: 53–6.
Leff, J. P. (1991) 'Schizophrenia: social influences on onset and relapse', in D. H. Bennett and H. L. Freeman (eds) *Community Psychiatry*, Edinburgh and London: Churchill Livingstone, Chapter 6, pp. 189–214.
—— (1994) 'Commentary on four papers on psychiatry and religion', *Israel Journal of Psychiatry*, 31(3): 192–3.
Leff, J. P. and Vaughn, C. (1981) 'The role of maintenance therapy and relatives' expressed emotion in the relapse of schizophrenia: a two year follow-up', *British Journal of Psychiatry*, 139: 102–4.
Lemert, E. M. (1962) 'Paranoia and dynamics of exclusion', *Sociometry*, 25: 2–20.
Lenz, H. (1979) 'The element of the irrational at the beginning and during the course of delusion', *Confinia Psychiatrica*, 22: 183–90.
—— (1983) 'Belief and delusion: their common origin but different course of development', *Zygon*, 18(2; June): 117–37.
Lenzenwegger, M. F. and Dworkin, R. H. (1996) 'The dimensions of schizophrenia phenomenology. Not one or two, at least three, perhaps four', *British Journal of Psychiatry*, 168(4; April): 432–40.
Lewis, A. J. (1956) Discussion of Gillespie, W. H., 'Experiences suggestive of paranormal cognition in the psychoanalytic situation', in G. E. Wolstenholme and E. C. P. Millar (eds) *Extrasensory Perception: A Ciba Foundation Symposium*, Boston: Little, Brown & Co., 215–16.
Lidz, T. (1964) 'August Strindberg: a study of the relationship between his creativity and schizophrenia', *International Journal of Psychoanalysis*, 45: 399–406.

Lieberman, J. A. and Fleischhacker, W. W. (eds) (1996) 'Current issues in the development of atypical antipsychotic drugs', *British Journal of Psychiatry*, 168, Supplement 29: 1–56.

Loeb, M. B. (1969) 'Community psychiatry: what it is and what it is not', in L. M. Roberts, S. L. Halleck and M. B. Loeb (eds) *Community Psychiatry*, Doubleday Anchor, 235–50.

Lord, J., Schnarr, A. and Hutchinson, P. (1987) 'The voice of the people: qualitative research and the needs of consumers', *Canadian Journal of Community Mental Health*, 6: 25–36.

Lowe, C. F. and Chadwick, P. D. J. (1990) 'Verbal control of delusions', *Behaviour Therapy*, 21: 461–79.

Lucas, A. R., Beard, C. M., Rajput, A. H. *et al.* (1982) 'Tourette Syndrome in Rochester, Minnesota, 1968–1979', in A. J. Friedhoff and T. N. Chase (eds) *Gilles de la Tourette's Syndrome, Advances in Neurology*, vol. 35, New York: Raven Press.

Lukoff, D. (1985) 'The diagnosis of mystical experiences with psychotic features', *Journal of Transpersonal Psychology*, 17(2): 155–81.

McGann, J. J. (1968) *Fiery Dust: Byron's Poetic Development*, Chicago: University of Chicago Press.

McGhie, A. (1966) 'Psychological studies of schizophrenia', *British Journal of Medical Psychology*, 39: 281–8.

McGhie, A. and Chapman, J. (1961) 'Disorders of attention and perception in early schizophrenia', *British Journal of Medical Psychology*, 34: 103–16.

MacKay, C., Cox, T., Burrows, G. and Lazzerini, T. (1978) 'An inventory for the measurement of self-reported stress and arousal', *British Journal of Social and Clinical Psychology*, 17: 283–4.

McNicol, D. (1972) A Primer of Signal Detection Theory, London: Allen & Unwin.

MacPherson, R., Jerrom, B. and Hughes, A. (1996) 'A controlled study of education about drug treatment in schizophrenia', *British Journal of Psychiatry*, 168 (June): 709–17.

Magaro, P. (1981) 'The paranoid and schizophrenic: the case for distinct cognitive styles', *Schizophrenia Bulletin*, 7: 632–61.

Maher, B. A. (1957) 'Personality, problem solving and the Einstellung effect', *Journal of Abnormal and Social Psychology*, 54: 70–4.

—— (1974) 'Delusional thinking and perceptual disorder', *Journal of Individual Psychology*, 30: 98–113.

Major, B., Mueller, P. and Hilderbrandt, K. (1985) 'Attributions, expectations and coping with abortion', *Journal of Personality and Social Psychology*, 48: 585–99.

Mansfield, R. S. and Busse, T. V. (1981) *The Psychology of Creativity and Discovery*, Chicago: Nelson Hall.

Marks, D. and Kamman, R. (1980) *The Psychology of the Psychic*, Buffalo, NY: Prometheus Books.

Marshall, D. (1991) 'Only one truth?' *Friends' House (London) Preparative Meeting Newsletter* (ed. David Firth), Winter (February).

Martin, J. B. (1973) 'Neural regulation of growth hormone secretion: medical progress report', *New England Journal of Medicine*, 288: 1384–93.

Maslow, A. H. (1968) *Toward a Psychology of Being*, Princeton, NJ: Van Nostrand.

—— (1971) *The Farther Reaches of Human Nature*, New York: Viking.

—— (1973) 'Self actualising and beyond', in G. Lindzey, C. S. Hall and M. Manosevitz (eds) *Theories of Personality: Primary Sources and Research*, New York: Wiley.

Masson, J. (1990) *Against Therapy*, London: Fontana.

Matesevac, H. (1991) 'Toward a psychological understanding of Tourette Syndrome', *Psychotherapy*, 28: 643–5.

Mayerhoff, D., Pelta, D., Valentino, C. and Chakos, M. (1991) 'Real-life basis for a patient's paranoia', *American Journal of Psychiatry*, 148: 682–3.

Mead, G. H. (1934) *Mind, Self and Society*, Chicago: University of Chicago Press.

Mednick, S. A. (1962) 'The associative basis of the creative process', *Psychological Review*, 69(3): 220–32.

—— (1967) Remote Associates Test, Boston: Houghton Mifflin.

Meehl, P. E. (1962) 'Schizotaxia, schizotypy, schizophrenia', *American Psychologist*, 17: 827–38.

Meissner, W. W. (1978) *The Paranoid Process*, New York: Aronson.

Meredith, B. (1993) *The Community Care Handbook: The New System Explained*, London: Age Concern, England.

Miller, A. (1990) The Untouched Key, London: Virago Press.

Milton, F., Patwa, V. K. and Hafner, J. R. (1978) 'Confrontation vs belief modification in persistently deluded patients', *British Journal of Medical Psychology*, 51: 127–30.

Mintz, R. S. (1968) 'Psychotherapy of the suicidal patient', in H. L. P. Resnick (ed.) *Suicidal Behaviours*, Boston: Little, Brown.

Molden, H. C. (1964) 'Therapeutic management of paranoid states', *Current Psychiatric Therapies*, 4: 108–12.

Molvaer, J., Hantzi, A. and Popodatos, Y. (1992) 'Psychotic patients' attributions for mental illness', *British Journal of Clinical Psychology*, 31: 210–12.

Morice, R. (1990) 'Cognitive inflexibility and pre-frontal dysfunction in schizophrenia and mania', *British Journal of Psychiatry*, 157: 50–4.

Morice, R. and Delahunty, A. (1996) 'Frontal/executive impairment in schizophrenia', *Schizophrenia Bulletin*, 22(1): 125–37.

Mosher, L. R. and Menn, A. Z. (1978) 'Community residential treatment for schizophrenia: two year follow-up', *Hospital and Community Psychiatry*, 29: 715–23.

Mosher, L. R., Menn, A. and Matthews, S. (1975) 'Soteria: evaluation of a home-based treatment for schizophrenia', *American Journal of Orthopsychiatry*, 45: 455–67.

Mueser, K. T. and Berenbaum, H. (1990) 'Psychodynamic treatment of schizophrenia: is there a future?', *Psychological Medicine*, 20: 253–62.

Murphy, J. M. (1976) 'Psychiatric labeling in cross-cultural perspective', *Science*, 191 (12 March): 1019–28.

Neeleman, J. and King, M. B. (1993) 'Psychiatrists' religious attitudes in relation to their clinical practice', *Acta Psychiatrica Scandinavica*, 88: 420–4.

Neeleman, J. and Persaud, R. (1995) 'Why do psychiatrists neglect religion?', *British Journal of Medical Psychology*, 68: 169–78.

Newnes, C. and MacLachlan, A. (1996) 'The antipsychiatry placement', *Clinical Psychology Forum*, 93: 24–7.

Newton, J. (1988) *Preventing Mental Illness*, London and New York: Routledge.

—— (1992) *Preventing Mental Illness in Practice*, London and New York: Routledge.

Nisbett, R. E. and Ross, L. (1980) *Human Inference: Strategies and Shortcomings of Social Judgement*, Englewood Cliffs, NJ: Prentice-Hall.

Nolen-Hoeksema, S. (1987) 'Sex differences in unipolar depression: evidence and theory', *Psychological Bulletin*, 101(2): 259–82.

Nowlis, V. (1965) 'Research with the mood adjective check list', in S. S. Tomkins and C. E. Izard (eds) *Affect, Cognition and Personality*, New York: Springer.

Nunn, K. P. (1996) 'Personal hopefulness: a conceptual review of the relevance of the perceived future to psychiatry', *British Journal of Medical Psychology*, 69(3; September): 227–45.

Ollerenshaw, D. P. (1973) 'The classification of the functional psychoses', *British Journal of Psychiatry*, 122: 517–30.

Onyett, S. (1992) 'Review of *Borderline* by P. K. Chadwick', *Clinical Psychology Forum*, November: 42.

Orford, J. (1987) *Coping with Disorder in the Family*, London: Croom Helm.

—— (1992) *Community Psychology: Theory and Practice*, Chichester: Wiley.

Ornstein, R. (1986) *Multimind: A New Way of Looking at Human Behaviour*, London: Macmillan.

Ostfeld, B. (1988) 'Psychological interventions in Gilles de la Tourette's Syndrome', *Psychiatric Annals*, 18: 417–20.

Oswald, I. (1992) 'Review of *Borderline* by P. K. Chadwick', *British Journal of Psychiatry*, 161 (December): 878.

Owen, F., Cross, A. J., Crow, T. J., Longden, A., Poulter, M. and Riley, G. J. (1978) 'Increased dopamine receptor sensitivity in schizophrenia', *Lancet*, ii: 223–6.

Palmer, J. (1971) 'Scoring in ESP tests as a function of belief in ESP. Part 1: The sheep–goat effect', *Journal of the American Society for Psychical Research*, 65(4; October): 373–407.

Parlett, M. and Page, F. (1990) 'Gestalt therapy', in W. Dryden (ed.) *Individual Therapy: A Handbook*, Chapter 9, pp. 175–98.

Paykel, E. S. and Marshall, D. L. (1991) 'Depression: social approaches to treatment', in D. H. Bennett and H. L. Freeman (eds) *Community Psychiatry*, Edinburgh and London: Churchill Livingstone, Chapter 8, pp. 239–67.

Peck, M. Scott (1988) *People of the Lie*, London: Rider.

Penn, D. L., Guynan, K., Daily, T., Spaulding, W. D., Garbin, C. P. and Sullivan, M. (1994) 'Dispelling the stigma of schizophrenia: what sort of information is best?', *Schizophrenia Bulletin*, 20(3): 567–74.

Perkins, D. N. (1988) 'Creativity and the quest for mechanism', in R. J. Sternberg and E. E. Smith, *The Psychology of Human Thought*, Cambridge: Cambridge University Press, Chapter 11, pp. 309–36.

Persons, J. B. (1986) 'The advantages of studying psychological phenomena rather than psychiatric diagnoses', *American Psychologist*, 41: 1252–60.

Piaget, J. (1958) *The Child's Construction of Reality*, London: Routledge & Kegan Paul.

—— (1972) *The Insights and Illusions of Philosophy*, London: Routledge & Kegan Paul.

Pilgrim, D. and Treacher, A. (1992) *Clinical Psychology Observed*, London: Routledge.

Pilling, S. (1995) 'Rehabilitation and its influence on clinical psychology', *Clinical Psychology Forum*, 82 (August): 40–1.

Plumber, N. (1974) *The Crow Tribe of Indians*, New York and London: Garland Publishing.

Popper, K. R. (1959) *The Logic of Scientific Discovery*, London: Hutchinson.

Poreh, A. M., Whitman, D. R. and Ross, T. P. (1993) 'Creative thinking abilities and hemispheric asymmetry in schizotypal college students', *Current Psychology* 12(4): 344–52.

Posey, T. B. and Losch, M. E. (1983) 'Auditory hallucinations of hearing voices in 375 normal subjects', *Imagination, Cognition and Personality*, 2: 99–113.

Post, F. (1994) 'Creativity and psychopathology: a study of 291 world-famous men', *British Journal of Psychiatry*, 165: 22–34.

—— (1996) 'Verbal creativity, depression and alcoholism: an investigation of one hundred American and British writers', *British Journal of Psychiatry*, 168 (May): 545–55.

Powell, B. J., Othmer, E. and Sinkhorn, C. (1977) 'Pharmacological aftercare for homogeneous groups of patients', *Hospital and Community Psychiatry*, 28: 125–7.

Prabhakaran, N. (1970) 'A case of Gilles de la Tourette's Syndrome with some observations on aetiology and treatment', *British Journal of Psychiatry*, 116: 539–41.

Prentky, R. A. (1980) *Creativity and Psychopathology: A Neurocognitive Perspective*, New York: Praeger.

Progoff, I. (1973) *Jung, Synchronicity and Human Destiny: Noncausal Dimensions of Human Experience*, New York: The Julian Press.

Radford, J. (1993) 'The permanence of "confident dogmatisms"', *The Psychologist* (Letter), 6(8): 343.

Rado, S. (1953) 'Dynamics and classification of disordered behaviour', *American Journal of Psychiatry*, 110: 406–14.

Raine, A., Lencz, T. and Mednick, S. A. (1995) *Schizotypal Personality*, Cambridge: Cambridge University Press.

Randrup, A. and Munkvad, I. (1972) 'Evidence indicating an association between schizophrenia and dopaminergic hyperactivity in the brain', *Orthomolecular Psychiatry*, 1: 2–7.

Raven, J. C. (1976) *Extended Guide to Using the Mill Hill Vocabulary Scale*, London: H. K. Lewis.

Raven, J. C., Court, J. H. and Raven, J. (1994) *Mill Hill Vocabulary Scale, Section 5A*, Oxford: Oxford Psychologists Press.

Rawlings, D. and Borge, A. (1987) 'Personality and hemispheric function: two experiments using dichotic shadowing techniques', *Personality and Individual Differences*, 8(4): 483–8.

Reynolds, D. K. and Farberow, N. L. (1976) *Suicide Inside and Out*, Berkeley: University of California Press.

Richards, R. L. (1981) 'Relationships between creativity and psychopathology: an evaluation and interpretation of the evidence', *Genetic Psychology Monographs*, 103: 261–324.

Rief, W. (1991) 'Visual perceptual organisation in schizophrenic patients', *British Journal of Clinical Psychology*, 30: 359–66.

Roberts, D. and Claridge, G. S. (1991) 'A genetic model compatible with a dimensional view of schizophrenia', *British Journal of Psychiatry*, 158: 451–6.

Roberts, G. (1991) 'Delusional belief systems and meaning in life: a preferred reality?', *British Journal of Psychiatry*, 159 (suppl. 14): 19–28.

Robertson, M. M. (1989) 'The Gilles de la Tourette Syndrome: the current status', *British Journal of Psychiatry*, 154: 147–69.

Rogers, A., Pilgrim, D. and Lacey, R. (1993) *Experiencing Psychiatry: Users' Views of Services*, London: Macmillan in association with Mind Publications.

Rogo, D. S. (1990) *Beyond Reality: The Role Unseen Dimensions Play in Our Lives*, Wellingborough, Northants: The Acquarian Press.

Romme, M. and Escher, S. (1993) *Accepting Voices*, London: Mind Publications.

Rosenhan, D. L. (1973) 'On being sane in insane places', *Science*, 179: 250–8.

Rosenhan, D. L. and Seligman, M. E. P. (1984/1995) *Abnormal Psychology*, London and New York: W. W. Norton.

Ross, C. A. (1989) *Multiple Personality Disorder: Diagnosis, Clinical Features, and Treatment*, New York: Wiley.

Roth, M. (1973) 'Psychiatry and its critics', *British Journal of Psychiatry*, 122: 374.

Rothenberg, A. (1973a) 'Word association and creativity', *Psychological Reports*, 33: 3–12.
—— (1973b) 'Opposite responding as a measure of creativity', *Psychological Reports*, 33: 15–18.
—— (1983) 'Psychopathology and creative cognition', *Archives of General Psychiatry*, 40 (September): 937–42.
—— (1990) *Creativity and Madness: New Findings and Old Stereotypes*, Baltimore and London: Johns Hopkins University Press.
Rowan, J. (1990) *Subpersonalities*, London: Routledge.
Rowan, J. and Dryden, W. (1988) *Innovative Therapy in Britain*, Buckingham: Open University Press.
Rudden, M., Gilmore, M. and Frances, A. (1982) 'Delusions: when to confront the facts of life', *American Journal of Psychiatry*, 139(7; July): 929–32.
Rump, E. E. (1982) 'Relationships between creativity, arts-orientation, and esthetic preference variables', *Journal of Psychology*, 110: 11–20.
Russell, R. (1994) 'Do you have a spiritual disorder?', *The Psychologist*, 7(8; August): 384.
Rust, J., Golombok, S. and Abram, M. (1989) 'Creativity and schizotypal thinking', *Journal of Genetic Psychology*, 150(2): 225–7.
Rutter, P. (1990) *Sex in the Forbidden Zone*, London: Unwin.
Ryan, W. (1971) *Blaming the Victim*, New York: Random House.
Sachdev, P. (1995) 'The epidemiology of drug-induced akathisia (Part I: Acute akathisia; Part II: Chronic, tardive and withdrawal akathisias)', *Schizophrenia Bulletin*, 21(3): 431–61.
Sackeim, H. A. (1983) 'Self-deception, self-esteem, and depression: the adaptive value of lying to oneself', in J. Masling (ed.) *Empirical Studies of Psychoanalytical Theories*, Hillsdale, NJ: Lawrence Erlbaum Associates, Chapter 4, pp. 101–57.
Sacks, O. (1986) *The Man Who Mistook His Wife for a Hat*, London: Picador.
Sagan, C. (1977) *The Dragons of Eden: Speculations on the Evolution of Human Intelligence*, Sevenoaks: Hodder & Stoughton.
Sandifer, M. G., Hordern, A., Timbury, G. C. and Green, L. M. (1968) 'Psychiatric diagnosis: a comparative study in North Carolina, London and Glasgow', *British Journal of Psychology*, 114: 1–9.
Saugstad, L. F. (1989) 'Social class, marriage and fertility in schizophrenia', *Schizophrenia Bulletin*, 15: 9–43.
Saykin, A. J., Gur, R. C., Gur, R. E., Mozley, D., Mozley, L. H., Resnick, S. M., Kester, B. and Stafiniak, P. (1991) 'Neuropsychological function in schizophrenia: selective impairment in memory and learning', *Archives of General Psychiatry*, 48: 618–24.
Schmeidler, G. R. and McConnell, R. A. (1958) *ESP and Personality Patterns*, New Haven: Yale University Press.
Schneider, K. (1959) *Clinical Psychopathology*, New York: Grune & Stratton.
Schreiber, F. R. (1975) *Sybil: The True Story of a Woman Possessed by Sixteen Separate Personalities*, Harmondsworth: Penguin.
Schuldberg, D. (1990) 'Schizotypal and hypomanic traits, creativity and psychological health', *Creativity Research Journal*, 3: 218–30.
Schuldberg, D., French, C., Stone, B. L. and Haberle, J. (1988) 'Creativity and schizotypal traits: creativity test scores, perceptual aberration, magical ideation, and impulsive nonconformity', *Journal of Nervous and Mental Disease*, 176: 648–57.
Schumacher, E. F. (1977) *A Guide for the Perplexed*, London: Cape.
Scull, A. (1979) *Museums of Madness*, London: Allen Lane.
Sekuler, R. and Blake, R. (1985) *Perception*, New York: Knopf.

Serban, G. and Siegel, S. (1984) 'Response of borderline and schizotypal patients to small doses of thiothixene and haloperidol', *American Journal of Psychiatry*, 141: 1455–8.

Sergent, J. (1982) 'The critical and methodological consequences of variation in exposure duration in visual laterality studies', *Perception and Psychophysics*, 31: 451–61.

—— (1983) 'The role of input in the visual hemispheric asymmetry', *Psychological Bulletin*, 93: 481–512.

Shallis, M. (1983) *On Time*, London: Pelican.

Shams, M. and Jackson, P. R. (1993) 'Religiosity as a predictor of well-being and moderator of the psychological impact of unemployment', *British Journal of Medical Psychology*, 66: 341–52.

Shapiro, A. K. and Shapiro, E. (1968) 'Treatment of Gilles de la Tourette's Syndrome with haloperidol', *British Journal of Psychiatry*, 114: 345–50.

Shepherd, G. (1995) 'A personal history of rehabilitation (or knowing me, knowing you – Aha?)', *Clinical Psychology Forum*, 82 (August): 4–8.

Sherrington, R., Brynjolfsson, J., Petursson, H., Potter, M., Dudleston, K., Barraclough, B., Wasmuth, J., Dobbs, M. and Gurling, H. (1988) 'Localization of a susceptibility locus for schizophrenia on chromosome 5', *Nature*, 336 (10 November): 164–6.

Short, R. (1994) *Dada and Surrealism*, London: Laurence King Publishing.

Sidgewick, H. A. (1894) 'Report of the census of hallucinations', *Proceedings of the Society for Psychical Research*, 26: 259–394.

Silverman, J. (1980) 'When schizophrenia helps', *Psychology Today*, September.

Silverstone, P. H. (1991) 'Low self-esteem in different psychiatric conditions', *British Journal of Clinical Psychology*, 30: 185–8.

Smail, D. (1993) *The Origins of Unhappiness: A New Understanding of Personal Distress*, London: HarperCollins.

Smith, D. L. (1990) 'Psychodynamic therapy: the Freudian approach', in W. Dryden (ed.) *Individual Therapy: A Handbook*, Milton Keynes: Open University Press, Chapter 2, pp. 18–38.

Snell, B. (1953) *The Discovery of the Mind: The Greek Origins of European Thought*, New York and Evanston: Harper & Row.

Snyder, S. H. (1974) Madness and the Brain, New York: McGraw-Hill.

Soloff, P. H., George, A., Nathan, R. S. *et al.* (1986) 'Progress in pharmacotherapy of borderline disorders: a double-blind study of amitriptyline, haloperidol and placebo', *Archives of General Psychiatry*, 43: 691–7.

Spence, D. P. (1987) *The Freudian Metaphor: Toward Paradigm Change in Psychoanalysis*, London and New York: W. W. Norton.

Stahl, S. M. and Wets, K. M. (1988) 'Clinical pharmacology of schizophrenia', in P. Bebbington and P. McGuffin (eds) *Schizophrenia: The Major Issues*, London: Heinemann Medical Books, Chapter 11, pp. 135–57.

Stanton, J. M. (1995) 'Weight gain associated with neuroleptic medication', *Schizophrenia Bulletin*, 21(3): 463–72.

Stanton-Jones, K. (1992) *An Introduction to Dance Movement Therapy in Psychiatry*, London and New York: Tavistock/ Routledge.

Steinem, G. (1993) *Revolution from Within: A Book of Self Esteem*, London: Corgi.

Stephenson, G. M. (1988) 'Applied social psychology', in M. Hewstone, W. Stroebe, J. P. Codol and G. M. Stephenson (eds) *Introduction to Social Psychology: A European Perspective*, Oxford: Basil Blackwell, Chapter 17, pp. 413–44.

Stoller, R. J. (1969) 'Parental influences in male transsexualism', in R. Green and J. Money (eds) *Transsexualism and Sex Reassignment*, Baltimore: Johns Hopkins University Press.

Stoller, R.J. (1975) *Perversion: The Erotic Form of Hatred*, New York: Dell Publishing Co. Inc.

Storr, A. (1972) *The Dynamics of Creation*, London: Secker & Warburg.

—— (1987) 'Foreword to D. Wigoder'(1987) *Images of Destruction*, London and New York: Routledge & Kegan Paul, ix–xi.

—— (1990) 'The sanity of true genius', in A. Storr, *Churchill's Black Dog and Other Phenomena of the Human Mind*, Glasgow: Fontana, Chapter 12, pp. 249–68.

Stout, G. F. (1901) *A Manual of Psychology*, London: University Tutorial Press, W. B. Clive.

Strauss, J. S. (1988) 'Delusional processes: an interactive developmental perspective', in T. F. Oltmanns and B. A. Maher (eds) *Delusional Beliefs*, New York: Wiley, Chapter 16, pp. 327–32.

Stroop, J. R. (1935) 'Studies of interference in serial verbal reactions', *Journal of Experimental Psychology*, 18(6): 643–62.

Sutherland, S. (1976) *Breakdown: A Personal Crisis and a Medical Dilemma*, London: Weidenfeld & Nicolson.

—— (1992a) *Irrationality: The Enemy Within*, London: Constable.

—— (1992b) 'What goes wrong in the care and treatment of the mentally ill?' in W. Dryden and C. Feltham (eds) *Psychotherapy and Its Discontents*, Buckingham, Philadelphia: Open University Press, 169–86.

Suzuki, D. and Knudtson, P. (1990) *Genethics: The Clash between the New Genetics and Human Life*, Cambridge, MA: Harvard University Press.

Szasz, T. (1971) *The Manufacture of Madness*, London: Routledge & Kegan Paul.

—— (ed.) (1974) *The Age of Madness: The History of Involuntary Mental Hospitalisation*, New York: Jason Aronson.

—— (1976) *Schizophrenia*, Oxford: Oxford University Press.

Takeuchi, K., Yamashita, M., Morikiyo, M. *et al.* (1986) 'Gilles de la Tourette's Syndrome and schizophrenia', *Journal of Nervous and Mental Disease*, 174: 247–8.

Tarrier, N. (1990) 'The family management of schizophrenia', in R. P. Bentall (ed.) *Reconstructing Schizophrenia*, London and New York: Routledge, Chapter 10, pp. 254–82.

Thalbourne, M. A. (1994) 'Belief in the paranormal and its relationship to schizophrenia – relevant measures: a confirmatory study', *British Journal of Clinical Psychology*, 33(1; February): 78–80.

Thigpen, C. H. and Cleckley, H. A. (1954) 'A case of multiple personality', *Journal of Abnormal and Social Psychology*, 49: 135–51.

—— (1957) *The Three Faces of Eve*, London: Secker & Warburg.

Thomson, M. (1989) *On Art and Therapy*, London: Virago Press.

Thorne, B. (1990) 'Person-centred therapy', in W. Dryden (ed.) *Individual Therapy: A Handbook*, Chapter 6, pp. 104–26.

Thorpe, C. D. (1926) *The Mind of John Keats*, New York.

Toates, F. (1990) *Obsessive-Compulsive Disorder: What It Is, How to Deal with It*, London: Thorsons.

Torrance, E. P., de Young, K. N., Ghei, S. N. and Michie, H. W. (1958) *Explorations in Creative Thinking in Mental Hygiene: II Some Characteristics of the More Creative Individuals*, Minneapolis: Bureau of Educational Research, University of Minnesota.

Tudor, L. E. and Tudor, K. (1994) 'The personal and the political: power, authority and influence in psychotherapy', in P. Clarkson and M. Pokorny (eds) *The Handbook of Psychotherapy*, London and New York: Routledge, Chapter 22, pp. 384–402.

Turner, R. J. and Wagenfeld, M. O. (1967) 'Occupational mobility and schizophrenia', *American Sociological Review* 32: 104–13.

Turpin, G. (1993) 'The management of tics and movement disorders (reference library on Clinical Practice)', *British Journal of Clinical Psychology*, 32: 257–9.

Tversky, A. and Kahneman, D. (1974) 'Judgement under uncertainty: heuristics and biases', *Science*, 185: 1124–31.

Tweney, R. D., Doherty, M. E. and Mynatt, C. R. (1981) *On Scientific Thinking*, New York: Columbia University Press.

Tyrer, P. and Stein, G. (1993) *Personality Disorder Reviewed*, London: Gaskell.

Ullman, M. (1973) 'Psi and psychiatry: the need for restructuring basic concepts', in W. G. Roll, R. L. Morris and J. D. Morris (eds), *Research in Parapsychology*, Metuchen, NJ: Scarecrow Press.

Valone, K., Goldstein, M. J. and Norton, J. P. (1984) 'Parental expressed emotion and psychophysiological reactivity in an adolescent sample at risk for schizophrenia spectrum disorders', *Journal of Abnormal Psychology*, 93: 448–57.

Vaughan, W. (1994) *Romanticism and Art*, London: Thames & Hudson.

Vaughn, A. (1979) *Incredible Coincidences*, New York: Lippincott.

Venables, P. H. (1963) 'Selectivity of attention, withdrawal and cortical activation', *AMA Archives of General Psychiatry*, 9: 74–8.

Vollema, M. G. and van den Bosch, R. J. (1995) 'The multidimensionality of schizotypy', *Schizophrenia Bulletin*, 21(1): 19–31.

Wada, Y., Takizawa, Y. and Yamaguchi, N. (1995) 'Abnormal photic driving responses in never-medicated schizophrenia patients', *Schizophrenia Bulletin*, 21 (1): 111–15.

Wallach, M. A. and Kogan, N. (1965) *Modes of Thinking in Young Children: A study of the Creativity–Intelligence Distinction*, New York: Holt, Rinehart & Winston.

Waller, D. and Gilroy, A. (eds) (1992) *Art Therapy: A Handbook*, Buckingham and Philadelphia: Open University Press.

Warner, R. (1995) 'Time trends in schizophrenia: changes in obstetric risk factors with industrialisation', *Schizophrenia Bulletin*, 21(3): 483–500.

Wason, P. C. (1960) 'On the failure to eliminate hypotheses in a conceptual task', *Quarterly Journal of Experimental Psychology*, 12: 129–40.

Wason, P. C. and Johnson-Laird, P. N. (1972) *Psychology of Reasoning, Structure and Content*, London: Batsford.

Watson, L. and Beaumont, D. (1989) 'Transvestism: towards the 21st century', *TV Scene*, no. 7 (February): 28–31.

Watts, A. (1978) *This Is IT – and Other Essays on Zen and Spiritual Experience*, London: Rider.

Watts, F. N., Powell, E. G. and Austin, S. V. (1973) 'The modification of abnormal beliefs', *British Journal of Medical Psychology*, 46: 359–63.

Weber, A. L. (1992) *Social Psychology*, New York: HarperCollins.

Weimer, W. B. (1979) *Notes on the Methodology of Scientific Research*, Hillsdale, NJ: Erlbaum.

Weinberger, D. R., Berman, K. F. and Zee, R. F. (1986) 'Physiologic dysfunction of dorsolateral prefrontal cortex in schizophrenia', *Archives of General Psychiatry*, 43: 114–24.

Weitz, W. A. (1972) 'Experiencing the role of a hospitalised psychiatric patient: a professional's view from the other side', *Professional Psychology*, 3: 151–4.

Weller, M. P. I. (1984) 'So-called care in the so-called community', *World Medicine* (November): 29–31.

—— (1989) 'Mental illness – who cares?', *Nature*, 339 (25 May): 249–52.

Werry, J. S., McClellan, J. M., Andrews, L. K. and Ham, M. (1994) 'Clinical features and outcome of child and adolescent schizophrenia', *Schizophrenia Bulletin*, 20(4): 619–30.

West, D. J. (1948) 'A mass observation questionnaire on hallucinations', *Journal of the Society for Psychical Research*, 34: 187–96.

Wigoder, D. (1987) *Images of Destruction*, London and New York: Routledge & Kegan Paul.

Wilber, K. (1980) *The Atman Project*, Quest.

Wilde, O. (1882) 'The English renaissance of art', in J. W. Jackson (ed.) (1991) *The Uncollected Oscar Wilde*, London: Fourth Estate, 3–28.

—— (1887) 'Two biographies of Keats', in J. W. Jackson (ed.) (1991) *The Uncollected Oscar Wilde*, London: Fourth Estate, 100–3.

Wilde, S. (1987) *Affirmations*, Taos, NM: White Dove International.

Williams, D. (1992) *Nobody Nowhere*, Toronto: Doubleday Canada.

Williams, L. M. (1995) 'Further evidence for a multidimensional personality disposition to schizophrenia in terms of cognitive inhibition', *British Journal of Clinical Psychology*, 34(2; May): 193–213.

—— (1996) 'Cognitive inhibition and schizophrenic symptom subgroups', *Schizophrenia Bulletin*, 22(1): 139–51.

Williams, W. L. (1986) *The Spirit and the Flesh: Sexual Diversity in American Indian Culture*, Boston: Beacon Press.

Woody, E. Z. and Claridge, G. S. (1977) 'Psychoticism and thinking', *British Journal of Social and Clinical Psychology*, 16: 241–8.

World Health Organisation (1973) *Report of the International Pilot Study of Schizophrenia*, Geneva: World Health Organisation.

—— (1979) *Schizophrenia: An International Follow-up Study*, Geneva: Wiley.

Zaehner, R. C. (1957) Mysticism: Sacred and Profane, Oxford: Clarendon Press.

Zigler, E. and Glick, M. (1988) 'Is paranoid schizophrenia really camouflaged depression?', *American Psychologist*, 43: 284–90.

Name index

Alexandrian, S. 112
Allport, D.A. 54
Anderson, B.G. 50
Andreasen, N.C. 12, 14
Argyle, M. 89, 150
Assagioli, R. 175
Atkinson, J.M. 19
Austen, Jane 47
Azrin, N.H. 163

Baker, H. 12
Baltaxe, C.A.M. xi
Bandura, A. 29
Banister, P. 186
Bannister, D. 70
Barclay, P.M. 159
Barham, P. 18
Barron, F. 12, 117
Baruch, G. 38
Baruch, I. 11
Bateson, G. 19
Baylis, G.C. 10, 109
Beamish, Jeanie 162–3
Beatrice, J. 95
Beaumont, Deanna 91–5, 103–5, 112,
    168, 186; confirmation bias 125;
    empathy 124; eroticism 111; male
    and female personalities 95–101;
    missions 101–3; stream of the
    uncanny 110; traits and symptoms
    115, 116
Bebbington, P.E. 20
Beech, A.R. 10, 11, 109
Beech, T. 22
Bell, M.D. 60
Belmaker, R.H. 50
Benassi, V.A. 3
Bender, M. 65, 67

Benor, D.J. 88
Bentall, R.P. 9, 11, 16, 18, 31, 55, 158
Berenbaum, H. 89, 166
Berger, J. 25, 28
Bergman, A.J. 169
Berrios, G. 149
Bett, W.R. xiv
Bilu, Y. 89
Bingham, B.R. 141
Bishop, D. V. M. 187
Blackmore, S.J. 70, 88
Blair, Grant 148, 161–2
Blair, Simon xv
Blake, R. 42, 141
Blake, William 5
Blaska, B. 56
Bleuler, E. 21, 170
Bleuler, M. 18
Block, J. 187
Bohr, N. 3
Boyle, M. 9, 21, 43, 158
Braun, C. xi, 11
Breggin, P. 35, 38, 178
Brehm, J.W. 165
Brennan, J.H. 158
Brewin, C.R. 24
Broadbent, D.E. 109
Brod, Janie 187
Broks, P. 22, 121, 186
Brown, G.W. 55, 60, 153
Brown, John 26
Bruun, R.D. 162
Buchanan, A. 19
Buckley, P. 17
Bunyan, John 185
Burd, L. 160
Burghall, Edith 33–4
Busse, T.V. 120

Subject index

3–4 test 118, 127, 128, 141, 180–3
acceptance 72, 148, 149
affirmations 71, 145
akathisia 50, 185
alyha 94
American Indians 93–4
anger 31, 52, 53, 87, 88, 149
ANOVA analyses 134, 141
anti-psychiatry 148, 158–9
arousal 125, 141
art 114–15
artist-experimenter 106–7, 167
Associative Fluency 132
attention 10–11, 52–3
attentional filter problem 10, 71
attitude to distress 23, 72, 171
Autobiography of a Yogi, An
  (Yogananda) 66

Banstead Hospital 45
beauty 27, 36
Beck Depression Inventory 17
behavioural blaming 147
berdache 94, 104
Bernean pastimes 150
biases 11–12, 151
blame, externalisation of 11, 31
blamelessness 19–20
Borderline: Synchronicity 3–5; *see also*
  Negative Borderline; Positive
  Borderline
borderline states 1–2, 36, 174–8
Borderliners xv, 6, 33, 36, 144–5

Cambridge Block 121–2, 128–9; results
  and analysis 129–37
chaplains 41–2, 47

Charing Cross Hospital 39, 46, 49–51,
  154, 185
childhood schizophrenia 87–8
clairvoyants 102, 103, 104
cognitive inhibition 10–11
cognitive replacement 157–8
cognitive-behavioural therapy 18, 145
collusion phobia 156–8
comedian mystics 67–8
complacency 159
confirmation bias 125–7, 137, 141–3;
  mental health professionals 154–6
confirmatory detection 110–11
consciousness 109
Contemporary Psychology Reviews 173
coping 145, 166
coprolalia 160, 163
creative illness 12–16
creativity xii, 12–16, 115–16;
  Cambridge Block analysis 129–37;
  and confirmation bias 125–7, 142–3;
  and empathy 139–41; London Block
  analysis 137–9; risk and inner
  perception 122–4; and schizotypy
  117–22, 129–37; and smoking 125,
  139–40
Crow Indians 94
cure 165–6

day hospital care 49–51
deception 11, 113
deficits 11–12
delusions 34–5, 39–42, 144, 164–5, 185;
  collusion phobia 156–8; genuineness
  19; successful 16, 17
Devil 34–5, 41, 43, 47–8, 160
Devil in Art and Literature, The 34